Caliente to Cliff

S ANGELES

MOUNTAINS

Bear Mtn.

FT. TEJON

CLIFF

BEALVILLE

CALIENTE

Tunnel No.1

ALLARD

Tunnel No.2

Tunnel No.4

Tunnel No.3

BEALVILLE

Tunnel No.6

ALLARD

Tunnel No.2

Tunnel No.1

NTE

Tunnel No.½

ILMON

BENA

Walker Basin Creek

Caliente Creek

SAN JOAQUIN VALLEY

SAND CUT

-SIGNOR-

SUBDIVISION

tain railway in the world

Santa Fe

SIGNOR
83

SOUTHERN PACIFIC-SANTA FE
TEHACHAPI

JOHN R. SIGNOR

Golden West Books

TEHACHAPI

Copyright © 1983 by John R. Signor
All Rights Reserved
Published by Golden West Books
San Marino, California 91118 U.S.A.
Library of Congress Catalog Card No. 83-20490
I.S.B.N. No. 0-87095-088-6

Library of Congress Cataloging-in-Publication Data

Signor, John R. 1948-
    Southern Pacific—Santa Fe—Tehachapi
    Bibliography:p.
    Includes Index.
    1. Railroads—California—Tehachapi Pass.
    2. Southern Pacific Railroad.
    3. Atchison, Topeka and Santa Fe Railway. I. Title. II. Title: Tehachapi.
TF24.C3S53   385'.09794'88   83-20490

First Printing – October 1983
Second Printing – March 1984
Third Printing – February 1986
Fourth Printing – January 1989
Fifth Printing – June 1992
Sixth Printing – March 1999
Seventh Printing – March 2004

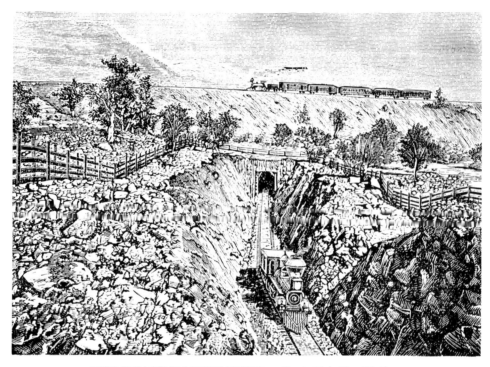

TITLE PAGE ILLUSTRATION — Santa Fe's No. 23, the *Grand Canyon Limited,* overtakes a Southern Pacific freight at Cliff in the Tehachapi on a fine spring morning during the late 1940's. This beautiful painting was created by the author, John R. Signor, especially for this book.

Golden West Books
P.O. Box 80250
San Marino, California • 91118-8250

TO

Henry Herman "Hienie" Bock

Hienie Bock reading the orders on the *Owl* at Mojave, during
October 1956.

Acknowledgments

My interest in the Tehachapi is credited to William H. Schmid who, in a venerable 1953 Mercury woody station wagon, braved a February blizzard to give me my first glimpse of big time railroading that is inherent to the Tehachapi. He also provided me with memories that will last a lifetime.

It is a long way, however, from the wide-eyed wonder of impressionable youth to a completed manuscript. For some time I had entertained the idea of writing a book of Tehachapi Railroading. Yet it was not until I met Henry Herman "Hienie" Bock of Bakersfield — to whom this volume is dedicated — that I was thrust irrevocably down the path to this completed volume. Hienie hired out at River Station, Los Angeles in 1907. Initially he worked as a call boy but was promoted to a Mountain District locomotive fireman in 1909. An advancement to engineer soon followed. Nearly 50 years later, in 1956, Hienie stepped down from the cab of the *Owl* for the last time to begin his retirement. It was my good fortune to meet this affable old gentleman one fine May morning several years ago. To my delight, I found him with a good memory and to be quite a story teller. His experiences, coupled with accounts related by "old-timers" working when he hired out, very nearly span the entire history of the railroad's presence in the Tehachapi Mountains. Many pleasant days were spent on the back porch of his cottage on Baker Street shelling peas or playing dominoes while listening to his fascinating stories. His wife Birdie also added many reminiscences.

Despite Hienie's admonition that Mountain District old-timers wouldn't know much because "their brains is baked", I set about working the Mountain District and talking with all interested parties. Along the way I was fortunate enough to spend time with SP engineers Vincent C. "The Godfather" Cippola (Vince had told me of Hienie), Ralph Townsend, Robert C. Fowler, Don Senior and H.D. "Rock" Padgent. Conductors Neal "Number One" Hallamore, John Peterman, Brian N. Black, Pat Bray, Tommy Day, Carl Billington and brakeman J.B. "Broadway" Brown — all had stories to relate. Telegraphers Mildred Harvey and Herb L. Harshman answered questions as did dispatcher Kenneth "Dad" Gaylan. Santa Fe engineers Phillips C. Kauke, Tommy Johnson and R.O. Stolzenfells provided valuable assistance as did conductors Charlie Bray and J.E. Anderson. I found conversations with retired Road Foreman of Engines Joe Frame to be particularly interesting and valuable.

This book would not be possible without the valuable assistance of a number of people representing the Southern Pacific officially. Among them are George Kraus at Portland; Gordon Adams, R.E. Buike, L.D. Farrar, Malcolm Gaddis, D.K. McNear, W.M. Robertson and Jeff Root at San Francisco; R.C. Hall, Gary McClain and L.A. Squires at Los Angeles; and Galen Hebb, Juan Fierro and Levi J. Franklin (Retired) at Bakersfield. At the Santa Fe in Los Angeles I am indebted to Mike Martin and Tony Anderson. Tony was the key to certain documents involving proposed Santa Fe grades in the mountains. I would also like to thank Ross Sullivan of the railroad's San Francisco office for his help and support.

I am grateful to Migel Abalos of the Los Angeles Department of Water and Power, Carola G. Rupert of the Kern County Museum, Mary Hanel of the Beal Memorial Library in Bakersfield and Jerrie Cowan of the Tehachapi Heritage League for their generous support. Also to Virginia Renner and Alan Jutzie, of the Huntington Library in San Marino, who kindly allowed me the use of their collection and facilities. John Creasor exhaustively combed the map collections of the University of California at Berkeley on my behalf and I am appreciative of his kindness.

The photographs appearing in this volume came from a variety of sources and all are given proper credit in the captions. A few, however, are worthy of special mention. I am deeply indebted to Mrs. Ola Mae Force of Tehachapi for preserving the work of the late Frank Nejedley as I am to Donald Duke for allowing me to rummage at will through his vast archives. Stan Kistler, in addition to his own work, provided many images from his collection as well as undertaking a goodly number of photo restoration projects. I feel fortunate to have examples of the best work of photographers Gary Allen, Ted Benson, Brian Black, Donald Duke, Dick Dorn, Grant Flanders, Robert Hale, Phil Kauke, H.L. Kelso, F.J. Peterson, A.C. Phelps, Donald Sims, Dave Stanley, Richard Steinheimer, Tom Taylor, Will Whittaker and Tim Zukas included in this volume. James H. Harrison, David J. Norris, Gerald M. Best, Guy Dunscomb and A.S. Menke all provided important material as well.

My thanks to L.D. Farrar, J.D. Schmid, Vince Cippola, Gerald Best and Donald Duke, all who helped double check the manuscript for accuracy.

Finally, I am indebted to several long-time friends, SP conductor M.A. "Bo" Golson, Tom and Jamie Schmid, Clifford Prather and SP dispatcher Virgil W. Yeager, who were there on those fondly remembered days from long ago and who share the author's fascination in the continuing struggle between the railroad and the forces of gravity in the remote and wondrous canyon of the Tehachapi.

No. 58, the *Owl,* runs around Santa Fe extra 235 east, the *SCX,* at Cliff during July 1951. — PHILLIPS C. KAUKE

Table of Contents

Introduction

ithout question, one of the seven wonders of the railroad world is California's famed Tehachapi "Loop" where the rails of the Southern Pacific and the Atchison, Topeka & Santa Fe railroads breast Tehachapi Pass between Bakersfield and Mojave.

The rail route over the Tehachapi Range was built during the Southern Pacific's great days of expansion in 1875–76. The celebrated "Loop" made possible the lifting of the grade 2,734 feet from the base of the range to the summit of the pass itself 20 air miles away and 3,969 feet above sea level. The construction of the Tehachapi Pass line involved miles of track laid through abysmal gorges and along narrow shelves in the mountains through many tunnels, climaxed by the "Loop" where long trains pass over themselves as they circle a cone-shaped hill. It is 8.7 additional miles uphill from the "Loop" to Tehachapi Summit. The rails then drop 1,213 feet in 18.3 miles before reaching Mojave at the other end of the pass.

Southern Pacific's engineer William Hood conquered Tehachapi Pass by reversing all the accepted techniques of civil engineering and mountain railroad construction. By surveying his line from the summit downward he was able to achieve his engineering masterpiece, the Tehachapi "Loop," and thus reduce the grade and save several miles of unnecessary construction.

For more than a century the "Loop" and the Tehachapi Pass line have been a wonder and curiosity of tourists, historians, railroaders, and rail enthusiasts. With the advent of fast lenses and faster film following World War II, railroad photographers flocked to Tehachapi Pass to capture on film one of Southern Pacific's cab-in-front articulateds smoking upgrade through a canyon or snaking around a ledge, or make sequence shots of a Santa Fe freight train, powered by three or four locomotives on its head end and cut into the consist at intervals, passing over itself as it emerges from the tunnel that is the "Loop's" distinguishing feature.

I made my first photographic safari to Tehachapi during World War II while still in high school with the late railroad photographer Frank Peterson. The lure of the heavy grade and big steam power helped convince me I should return often. While taking my grandmother out for a Sunday drive, I encouraged my parents to drive and spend the day at the "Loop" picking wildflowers. Since that time I have made periodic safaris to this famous pass to photograph and watch the action and have seen the transition from big steam to giant diesels. While it is not quite as much fun watching diesels tread the same canyons and hole-through the same tunnels, the fascination of big time railroading is still there.

You'll discover in this book an intensely human story of a struggle to move trains over a monumental grade. How the Tehachapi grade was picked over five other choices, construction hardships, the early motive power that worked the hill, proposed line changes, disasters such as flood, earthquake, and wrecks, and about the men that ran the trains.

But let John Signor tell you about a century of railroading on the Tehachapi grade. An authentic Southern Pacific railroader, John has captured the legend and lore that has made this mountain railroad line one of the toughest, yet most colorful in the nation. I recommend both the author and Tehachapi to you.

Donald Duke — Publisher
Golden West Books

San Marino, California
July 1983

Train No. 17, the *Los Angeles Express*, poses atop the Tehachapi Loop several years after this landmark was completed. C. E. WATKINS — JAMES H. HARRISON COLLECTION

10

1

The Early Days
1870-1900

It has been over a century since twin ribbons of steel first surmounted the formidable Tehachapi Range, barrier to trade and travel between northern and southern California. This monumental and pioneering effort was accomplished by the Southern Pacific Railroad Company rushing to complete the first leg of a new southern transcontinental line. The Southern Pacific, which was destined in later years to join with the Central Pacific and others in forming the Southern Pacific system, that we know today, had been incorporated under the laws of California on December 2, 1865. Its charter specified that the company could build a line of railroad from San Francisco south through the counties of Santa Clara, Monterey, San Luis Obispo, Tulare and Los Angeles to San Diego. From there the company could then build east through San Diego County to a junction at the state line with a contemplated road building west from the Mississippi River.

Little headway had been made in the plans of this company, however, until it was reorganized as a portion of a second transcontinental railroad by act of Congress on July 27, 1866. This action auth-

orized the Atlantic & Pacific Railroad Company to build from Springfield, Missouri, by way of Albuquerque and the 35th parallel to the Pacific coast. The Southern Pacific was authorized to build from San Francisco to a connection with the Atlantic & Pacific at the Colorado River. The act provided for a grant of 40 alternate sections in the territories and 20 in the states as well as a 200 foot right-of-way. The act also stipulated that the entire road was to be completed by July 4, 1878.

Provisions of the act were accepted by Southern Pacific Railroad Company officials on November 24, 1866, and on January 3, 1867, they filed a map designating the general route the railroad proposed to take. Starting at San Francisco, the road was to pass through the settlements of San Jose, Gilroy, Tres Pinos — in the Santa Clara and San Benito valleys — then east through Pacheco Pass into the great San Joaquin Valley. Here the road turned south and then crested the Tehachapi Mountains to Mojave, where it headed easterly to the Colorado River. Congress approved this route by a resolution on June 28, 1870 and the original proposal to build to San Diego was in part, temporarily abandoned.

Southern Pacific's first step was to acquire the

line already in operation between San Francisco and San Jose owned by the San Francisco & San Jose Railroad Company. Stock owned by San Francisco County, in this road, was purchased following authorization of the state legislature on March 30, 1868. Three weeks later grading commenced at 4th Street in San Jose on the extension into the Santa Clara Valley. This construction was carried out by the Santa Clara & Pajaro Valley Railroad. Gilroy was reached March 13, 1869, Hollister on July 13, 1871, and Tres Pinos shortly thereafter.

The activities of the budding SP, then controlled by independent capital, were viewed with consid-

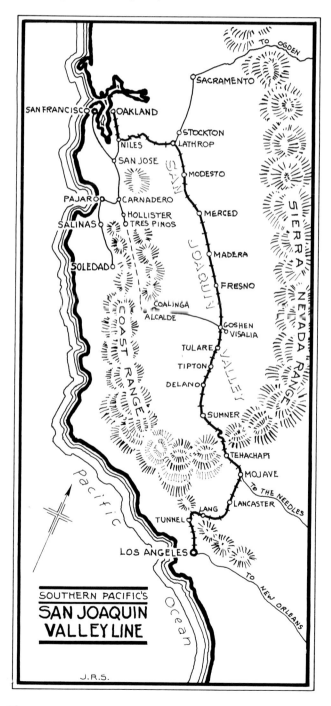

SOUTHERN PACIFIC'S
SAN JOAQUIN VALLEY LINE

J.R.S.

erable apprehension by Governor Stanford and his associates, builders of the pioneer Central Pacific. They realized that when their own railroad was completed, it would bring prosperity to the sparsely settled valleys of California. A return on their huge investments from the eventual passenger and freight traffic was anticipated and they were in no mood to share the rewards. Accordingly, the Central Pacific men moved to gain control and on September 25, 1868, the annual report of the Southern Pacific Railroad Company to the United States Secretary of the Interior gave the first indication of the close relationship developing between the two roads.

This became a matter of official record on October 12, 1870, when the San Francisco & San Jose Railroad Company, The Santa Clara & Pajaro Valley Railroad Company and the California Southern Railroad Company (incorporated January 22, 1870, to build from Gilroy to Salinas), consolidated to form a new Southern Pacific Railroad Company. Among the incorporators were Charles Crocker, Mark Hopkins, Collis P. Huntington and Leland Stanford. From that date forward, ownership and control of the Central Pacific and Southern Pacific properties were in the hands of the same men — the "Big Four" — and their associates. The combined engineering and construction forces were now working interchangeably on the two lines under the supervision of Samuel S. Montague, Chief Engineer of the Central Pacific. Colonel George E. Gray was appointed to the same post at the Southern Pacific.

Several additional explorations and surveys had been made over the proposed route from Gilroy and across the Pacheco Pass into the San Joaquin Valley during 1869 and 1870. Pacheco Pass held preference because it was the lowest crossing in the Central Coast Range. These proposals also included a route over the Tehachapi Range to San Bernardino by way of Cajon Pass, and then southeast across the San Gorgonio Pass into the high desert with an eventual destination at a point near what is today Phoenix, Arizona. The Southern Pacific had no definite route into Los Angeles until March 3, 1871. At this time Congress chartered the Texas & Pacific Railroad company and authorized it to build from Marshall, Texas, by way of El Paso through the New Mexico and Arizona territories, following the 32nd parallel, to a connection with the Southern Pacific at the Colorado River at Fort Yuma. The Southern Pacific was authorized to build from Mojave, by way of Los Angeles, to effect this connection. It should be noted that the Texas & Pacific never built west of Sierra Blanca, Texas, and that due to difficulties in complying with the provisions of the act of 1871, on January 18, 1882, deeded to the "Big Four" controlled companies all of its railroad franchises and property rights in New Mexico, Arizona and southern California for certain concessions east of El Paso.

With the stage set for the penetration of the great San Joaquin Valley, considerable money was spent in locating a suitable line south and east through Pacheco Pass. The anticipated cost of construction and the expense of operation over the mountains were to be substantial. Stanford visited the country personally and found no business there, nor in his opinion any prospect of business. It appeared more practical to reach down into the San Joaquin Valley from a point on the Central Pacific south of the flat Sacramento delta country and with the two companies essentially working as one, there remained no reason to pursue construction in Pacheco Pass. This plan was adopted and the route from Tres Pinos, to a point later known as Alcalde, was forsaken and the land grant eventually forfeited.

Following the joining of the Union Pacific and Central Pacific railroads at Promontory, Utah, in May 1869, men and materials began to converge on Wilson's Station (soon renamed Lathrop), a new town located by Central Pacific's construction company on the mainline between Sacramento and Oakland. It was from this point that the "Big Four" anticipated connecting with the franchised Southern Pacific route in the San Joaquin Valley, a bold step entailing more than 140 miles of railroad construction without the benefits of land grants or government concessions of any kind.

Construction of the line south into the valley commenced December 31, 1869, and about 11 miles were in place extending to the Stanislaus River early in 1870. The level character of the terrain necessitated little excavation and enabled rapid progress. Trains were first operated to Modesto on November 8, 1870; to Merced on January 25, 1872; to Sycamore (Herndon) on April 1, 1872, and to Fresno on May 28th of that year.

Practically all of the larger valley towns of today were just "railroad towns" in the seventies, founded and plotted by the railroad's construction company. Fresno was surveyed and staked out in May 1872 in an area known as the San Joaquin Desert. Water was no nearer than the San Joaquin River, ten miles away. There was no settlement of any kind, not even a shack. William Henry Bishop in 1882 recalled in *Harpers* that the surface of the ground at this spot was "like a graveled school yard." Locals feared taking horses into the area — the network of squirrel burrows making the surface subject to collapse.

The section from Fresno to Goshen was opened to traffic August 1, 1872. Goshen, 146 miles from Lathrop, became the most southerly point of Cen-

William Hood, who as a young civil engineer in the employ of the Southern Pacific Railroad, located the mainline over the formidable Tehachapi barrier in 1875-76. He later rose to the position of chief engineer serving in that capacity for over 40 years. — SOUTHERN PACIFIC COLLECTION

tral Pacific ownership in California. Here the survey for the Southern Pacific between the Santa Clara and San Joaquin valleys, by way of Pacheco Pass, was reached. At this point a roundhouse, machine shop, hotel and depot were put up as the construction company went about its business. The town thrived under the stimulus of the railroad until a fire completely destroyed it several years later and the division point was moved to Tulare.

An SP timetable published in September 1872, announced service three times a week from San Francisco to Tipton where connections were made with stages for the remaining distance of 252 miles to Los Angeles. Assistant Engineer Slade made the final surveys south of Lathrop, as far as Tipton. From this point the line, practically as it remains today, was surveyed all the way to San Antonio, Texas, by William Hood, who later (1883) became Chief Engineer.

Another 20 mile section of line was placed in service to Delano on July 14, 1873. A delay of nearly a year followed in the valley construction while the company's main construction force was moved over the mountains to Los Angeles. The Southern Pacific, having received the favor of Los Angeles voters in the railroad election of November 5, 1872, as being the organization most likely to place Los Angeles on a transcontinental railroad line, was eligible for a badly needed $600,000 sub-

sidy. The company was also entitled to all the stock that the city and county had in the fledgling Los Angeles & San Pedro Railroad Company. As a show of faith, for the next ten months, the "Big Four's" efforts were directed towards extending this line from the station on Alameda Street to Naud Junction where one line was built north to San Fernando, 22 miles, and the other easterly to Spadra, 29 miles. Trains began operating to these points on January 21, 1874. Work was also completed at this time on a branch to Anaheim.

It was not until April 6, 1874, that construction was resumed in the San Joaquin Valley continuing south along the 50 mile tangent that Engineer Hood had located. Visalia was connected to the mainline on August 14, 1874, by a 7.8 mile branch from Goshen built by local citizens in the name of the Visalia Railroad Company. South of Famoso, the railroad took a long curve to the east. In locating the railroad in this area Hood noticed large trunks of trees and other debris scattered over the low country in the vicinity of Bakersfield and presumed them to have been washed there by floods from the Kern River. Bakersfield itself, founded in 1863 by Colonel Thomas Baker and by this time a community of 600, was located on a spot known as Kern Island between the sloughs and outflows of the river. It was to avoid the risk of washouts and to gain the best possible location for a bridge across the river, that the line was kept on an elevation which made it impractical to run directly into Bakersfield. Although, in later years, the railroad's detractors maintained it was Bakersfield's refusal to ante up the customary subsidy that was the over-riding reason for the bypass, Hood's reasons cannot be ignored. Indeed, on February 10, 1893,

The pioneer Keene ranch shown above, located midway up the north slope of the Tehachapi, lay in the path of the railroad. The Southern Pacific was in operation to this point — milepost 338 by May 26, 1876. — HUNTINGTON LIBRARY (RIGHT) A telegraph office — key Bc — siding and watering facilities were established soon after. The photograph was taken prior to the turn of the century. — MRS. BURKHALTER COLLECTION

The Tehachapi Loop, which D. D. Colton in 1876 likened to the Suez Canal as a feat of engineering genius, is without a doubt the crowning achievement of Southern Pacific Engineer William Hood. Calling it just a common sense plan, Hood shrugged off efforts in later years to name the loop in his honor. Legend attributes his inspiration to the meanderings of a mule taking the path of least resistance or to a small child's fanciful designs on a heap of sugar.
—DONALD DUKE COLLECTION

the city of Bakerfield was subject to just such an occurrence as Hood had feared. During the flood that year, water stood several feet deep on Chester Avenue in the downtown area.

The railroad was completed to the north bank of the Kern River and opened for traffic to that point on August 1, 1874. "From the town we can hear the locomotive whistles," reported the *Kern Weekly Courier,* "and for all practical purposes, the railroad has reached Bakersfield." Location for a station was obtained on the higher ground about a mile and a half from Bakersfield. The bridge was ready in a few weeks and trains first ran into the new terminal of Sumner on October 26, 1874.

From Sumner grading gangs had pushed on ahead and by January 2, 1875, the roadbed was ready for more than 20 miles south of town, most of which was on fairly light gradient. A temporary line was laid practically up the stream bed from Pampa (later called Bena) in order to reach Caliente as soon as possible. This was done on the orders of General David D. Colton, then an associate of the "Big Four," who was of the opinion that great profits could be made from a town site on such flat ground as Caliente. It was April 26 before track was laid and trains operated to the site, formerly

known as Allen's Camp. Here the railroad terminus remained for more than a year while the region swarmed with an army of American and Chinese railroad builders. As it turned out, Colton was right. The conquering of the Tehachapi was so universally believed to be impossible that, on an assumption it was destined to remain the eastern terminus of the Southern Pacific, a big land boom took place at Caliente. Lots sold and resold for fantastic prices. The freight traffic received at this point destined for the mines of Havilah, the Cerro Gordo and the Panamint amounted to a considerable business as well. Daily stages, operated by the Telegraph Stage Company, bridged the 98 miles over the mountains to the rail head at San Fernando. By this time, the rail-stage journey between San Francisco and Los Angeles had been shaved to 33 hours. The fare was $20 for the entire trip.

It was from Caliente that the real climb into the Tehachapi Mountains began. Two of the most difficult construction jobs encountered in building the Southern Pacific lay ahead. Rising from the floor of the San Joaquin Valley, Tehachapi Pass was surmounted at an elevation of 4,025 feet by a line of railroad that swerved back and forth up the mountain side through numerous tunnels, clung to the

15

A Ten-Wheeler and crew pose at the north entrance to tunnel No. 10 in the 1870's. — DONALD DUKE COLLECTION (LEFT) The interior of the same bore. Of the 17 tunnels required initially on the north slope of the Tehachapi, 10 were drilled through solid rock. The others, excavated through softer material, required lining of Coast Redwood or Puget Sound Cedar. — HUNTINGTON LIBRARY

side of yawning chasms and at one point looped over itself to climb 2,734 feet in a distance of but 28 miles.

While more than 3,000 men were working the hundreds of horses and dump carts on the Tehachapi grade, a force equally as large was piercing the San Fernando Mountains with a tunnel that was to be the longest in the world for a number of years. Through it, the railroad from the north could link up with Los Angeles.

It had been over 20 years since Tehachapi Pass had been designated as suitable for a line of railroad. Lieutenant R.S. Williamson, in a party of government engineers charged with exploring and surveying the most practical route for a railroad from the Mississippi River to the Pacific Ocean, discovered five more or less available passes through the Tehachapi Mountains of varying degrees of difficulty during the summer of 1853. Beginning with the most easterly, these were as follows: Walker Pass, Tehachapi Pass, Oak Creek Pass, Tejon Pass and San Emidio Pass. Of these, Tehachapi Pass, by reason of gradient and ease of construction, held preference. It was over this pass, called Tah-ee-chay-pah by the Indians, that Colonel John C. Fremont had taken his troops in 1844. The name means to freeze in Southern Paiute, which is only slightly different from the language then spoken in the area.

Preliminary surveys were made over the pass by Southern Pacific engineers as early as 1866. During succeeding years several other additional preliminary rail grades were run in an effort to establish the best possible grade and curvature. William Hood later recalled, in 1924, that during the spring and early summer of 1868, he, acting as leveler, along with J.H. Phelps and C.H. Redington made a preliminary survey from Tehachapi down the north slopes on a 2.2 percent grade holding to the left or west side of the canyon all the way down to Walker Basin Creek about three miles south from present day Bena. From here the line went around the south end of the Sivert Sand Hills from which point a direct line was made to the vicinity of Bakersfield. In the summer of 1872, after locating the railroad as far south as Bakersfield, Hood took his party to Tehachapi and made another survey on a 1.3 percent continuous grade holding to the right or easterly slopes to Bena. After finishing this survey, another was run at a 2.0 percent grade following closely the present position of the railroad to a location just around the hill in the center of the loop. Instead of continuing to curve to the right and tunnel under the track, as the present road does, the survey then curved to the left crossing Tehachapi Creek and continued on the east side of the canyon opposite Woodford. The survey was made to Caliente Creek some distance above Caliente then proceeded to that point and down the canyon as it was eventually constructed. The loop and the grade alignment between it and Caliente, as built, was not selected until the spring of 1875.

Starting from Caliente at an elevation of 1,291 feet, a "U" turn was made and a swerving ascent of the mountains begun. The severity of this curve, long a bone of contention in the eyes of William Hood, was necessary to comply with the wishes of General Colton who in advocating a townsite on flat ground at Caliente had done so at the sacrifice of much needed "distance" in figuring the Tehachapi grade. The idea had been that the stretch laid up from Pampa (Bena) would be relaid within five or six years at a much higher elevation cutting out Caliente Station entirely — something which was never done.

During the mountain construction, 600 kegs of Hercules Powder were used a week. The terrain necessitated the excavation of two tunnels through soft rock, No. 1 (245 feet) and No. 2 (232 feet), before making another "U" turn and heading up grade towards Bealville. Above this station, in order to negotiate Clear Creek Ravine, three more tunnels were required. These were No. 3 (707 feet), No. 4 (257 feet) and No. 5, which was the longest and most difficult to construct on the north slope. This tunnel, 1,156 feet in length, was completed about March 10, 1876, and on April 6, track laying was completed and the first locomotive passed through.

Just above this point tunnel No. 6 (185 feet) was built. Then after a six mile climb from the first horseshoe, the line rounded the head of a canyon from which point the town of Caliente, could be seen, little more than a mile away as the crow flies. Two more tunnels followed, No. 7 (532 feet) and No. 8 (690 feet), as the grade clung tenaciously to the side of a rugged gorge through which meandered Tehachapi Creek far below. The creek, rapidly gaining in elevation as it wound up the ravine, was regained beyond tunnel No. 8 and from that point the railroad pursued more or less the water's course crossing and recrossing the creek several times. The railroad was completed and placed into operation to Keene on May 26, 1876.

Above this station the railroad departed the meanderings of Tehachapi Creek to make the approach to the famous Tehachapi Loop. "It was just a common sense plan," Chief Engineer Hood explained in later years, yet the expedience he used to "make distance" was the talk of the engineering world. Resembling two large circles drawn with a giant compass, the loop tunneled into the side of a ridge, tunnel No. 9 (126 feet), then twisted around the crest of a hill and back over the tunnel gaining an elevation of 77 feet and bringing the line into position for easy gradient to the summit. Down through the years there has been a considerable amount of folklore amassed as to how Hood arrived at the loop idea — none of it substantiated by the facts —but it was from the loop that he had reportedly plotted the road in either direction.

From the first swing of the loop to the station of Girard (later Marcel), a distance of five miles, an elevation of 587 feet was gained. And in the ten miles from the loop to the summit, eight more tunnels were required. These were as follows, No. 10 (306 feet), No. 11 (158 feet), No. 12 (756 feet), No. 13 (513 feet), No. 14 (512 feet), No. 15 (360 feet), No. 16 (262 feet) and No. 17 (260 feet). On the north slope of the Tehachapi, all the tunnels with the exception of Nos. 7, 8, 10 and 11 were excavated through soft rock and required lining throughout their entire length with Coast Redwood or Puget Sound Cedar.

The ruling grade from Sumner to the summit was held to 2.2 percent. Near the summit of the

Reached July 10, 1876, Tehachapi Summit station — later reduced to Tehachapi — was the point in the early days where helpers were cut from trains and turned. The SP telegraph office stands very nearly in the center of this picture taken 10 years after the arrival of the railroad. Although well beyond the heavy climb to the summit, Tehachapi at 3,967 feet was not at the crest of the grade. This occurred two miles farther south at Summit (switch) — elevation 4,028 feet — where by 1885, the Southern Pacific had established facilities for cutting helpers on freight trains. — DONALD DUKE COLLECTION.

pass was located the station of Tehachapi Summit. Trains began operating to this point on July 10, 1876. Residents of the pioneer town of Greenwich, about four miles west, literally picked up their homes and moved them nearer the station alongside the railroad. The settlement was soon deserted except for a few hardy souls and the place became known as "old town."

With the summit reached, construction moved along rapidly across the table land of the Tehachapi Valley then dropped down onto the Mojave Desert utilizing the draw through which Cache Creek flowed. Construction in this section was not too difficult and afforded broad curves although the grade was every bit as steep as on the north slope. Trains were run into Mojave on August 8th and here at the foot of the grade, the railroad laid out a terminal.

From Mojave, the track was laid in practically a straight line across the Antelope Valley towards the mouth of Soledad Canyon. No severe grades were encountered on the floor of the desert, but before entering the canyon, six miles of heavy climbing (2.2 percent) was necessary up to a place called Soledad Summit. From here the construction followed the course of the Santa Clara River descending for 30 miles towards the north end of the San Fernando Tunnel. The canyon itself, about 25 miles in length, and flanked by towering cliffs rising in places from 500 to 2,000 feet above the bed of the stream, had an infamous reputation as a "Robbers Roost." It was the headquarters and home of the notorious desperado Tiburcio Vasquez

and his band of thieves who sought refuge in the area between forays into the surrounding territory. Although Vasquez was hanged March 19, 1875, the brother of this noted thief, against whom there were no accusations, continued to reside at the water stop of Ravena mid-way down the canyon.

Before reaching the station of Lang, two additional tunnels, bored through solid rock, were necessary. These were No. 18 (264 feet) and No. 19 (332 feet).

Meanwhile work had been underway on the huge San Fernando tunnel since March 27, 1875 and it was being pushed night and day by 4,000 men and 300 animals. The softness of part of the material through which the bore was driven and the abundance of water encountered slowed progress. A shaft was sunk and the walls of the mountain attacked from four faces. Designated No. 20, the tunnel was over a mile long measuring 6,966 feet and as such was the longest in the world at the time. The headings met July 14, 1876. Track laying followed closely and soon the rails were extended into the canyon where the line from the north was met September 5, 1876 at the station of Lang.

Los Angeles was now on the mainline of the railroad and driving the last spike at Lang was an event of as great importance to the people of that city and southern California as was the completion of the first transcontinental railroad to the nation seven years before. A special train of five cars, drawn by locomotive No. 25 decorated with flags and streamers, left the station on Commercial and Alameda streets at 9:30 in the morning. More than

18

350 prominent citizens of southern California were the invited guests of the Southern Pacific. Aboard the train, a reporter for the *Los Angeles Evening Express* wrote of the San Fernando tunnel...

"On entering the dark abyss of the long tunnel, a feeling of complete separation from sublunary places seized one and the time dragged heavily during the Cimmerian passage. It took the train just ten and a half minutes to go through... Leaving Newhall (now Saugus), we passed several stretches of fine looking land, well timbered, presenting here and there very handsome groves and soon entered the Soledad region, a wild, weird and seemingly inhospitable section. Reaching the end of track at noon, we were met with one of the most picturesque sights imaginable. Before us formed in a line on either side of the roadbed, was an army of about 3000 Chinamen standing at parade rest with their long-handled shovels."

The Los Angeles contingent was greeted at the end of track by Charles Crocker, Vice President of the Southern Pacific, Colonel George Gray, Chief Engineer and J.H. Strobridge, Superintendent of Construction. A special train from the north hauled by locomotive No. 38 arrived at 1:15 P.M. bringing Governor Stanford, President of the Southern Pacific, General D.D. Colton, Vice President, Mayor A.J. Bryant of San Francisco and 50 other dignitaries from northern California.

When the ceremonies were ready to begin, the canyon was crowded with more than 500 visitors from all over the state in addition to the small army of men comprising the construction crews. There remained about 500 feet of track to be laid before the gap in the railroad would be closed. The roadbed was graded and the ties in place ready for the final rails. A track laying race between the opposing camps from the north and south was staged as a special event for the visitors. J.B. Harris, who was in charge of the track work, dropped his hat as a signal to start. The race was quite close, but the southern crew prevailed to the wild cheers of the contingent from southern California. It had taken eight and one-half minutes to bring the rails together. The honor of driving the golden spike, presented by L.W. Thatcher, a Los Angeles jeweler, was given to Charles Crocker because, as David Colton remarked at the time, "No man living or dead had superintended the construction of as many miles of railroad on the face of the globe." The driving of the last spike was accomplished at 1:58 P.M.

The following day, the *Los Angeles Evening Express* made in part the following editorial comment...

"They (the SP men) have not only lived up to the letter of their promises, but in the face of difficulties that were fairly gigantic, they have reached Los Angeles sooner than the most sanguine of us expected."

This was not the end of railroad building for the Southern Pacific of course. The railhead was along the shores of the Salton Sink bound for Yuma when the spike was being driven at Lang. Over the next few years, the railhead had advanced east from Los Angeles through Arizona, New Mexico and Texas. On January 12, 1883, rails from the east were met on the banks of the Pecos River thus forming the Sunset Route through to New Orleans.

In the two decades following the driving of the Golden Spike at Lang, much additional construction was undertaken along the San Joaquin Valley line to open up the region's vast acreage to settlement. The section from Goshen to Huron was ready for traffic February 1, 1877, then completed to Alcalde in July 1888. That same year, work commenced at Tracy on a southerly line following the west side of the valley. This was opened to Newman on July 1, 1888, and to Los Banos November 1st of the same year. About this time work started on the eastside line in a southerly direction out of Fresno. Porterville was reached July 1, 1888 and the mainline rejoined at Famoso on November 23, 1888, and between there and Fresno July 1, 1892. A line between Bakersfield and Asphalto was completed in 1895. Also in this period, work was begun on the southern link of the Coast Line. Late in 1886 track was laid northwesterly from Saugus towards Santa Barbara reaching that point August 19, 1887.

Southern Pacific also built the railroad from Mojave to The Needles which is now part of the Santa Fe system. This route was over part of the original franchise granted Southern Pacific under the act of 1867 which chartered the Atlantic & Pacific. Although the main thrust of Southern Pacific's effort was to complete the Sunset Route, work was begun on the line to The Needles with the express purpose of preventing the Atlantic & Pacific from entering California. Construction commenced at Mojave in February 1882 and the road was opened for traffic to Amboy on February 12th the following year. The Needles, some 242 miles distant, was reached August 1, 1883. The Atlantic & Pacific reached that point eight days later and through a series of maneuvers managed to acquire the line to Mojave. A contract of lease and purchase was signed August 20, 1884 for certain concessions granted to the Southern Pacific on the west coast of Mexico. The SP retained land grant rights. During the brief period this line was operated by the

A Los Angeles bound passenger train pauses at the isolated station stop of Palmdale about 1895. This area once supported antelope which roamed the area in numbers of 7,000 or better prior to the advent of the railroad. The animals could not cope with progress and piled up against the railroad tracks rather than make the quick jump of a few feet. Their forage exhausted, the antelope starved or became easy prey for coyotes. By 1910 only a few remained. — DONALD DUKE COLLECTION

Ravena, an early day water stop midway down Soledad Canyon, was a shipping point for carloads of *Yucca Draconis,* a carload of which may be seen spotted on the house track in this view taken about 1878. This hardy cactus was used in making a superior grade of bank note paper. Out of sight, in the trees to the right, lay the treacherous Santa Clara River which, in 1886, swept nearly four miles of railroad and the settlement of Ravena toward the sea. That year the railroad was moved to higher ground and the station of Ravenna (note additional *n*) was established about a mile to the west. — HUNTINGTON LIBRARY

Southern Pacific, it was known as the Colorado Division.

The railroad between Lathrop and Los Angeles was initially divided into three operating divisions. A.D. Wilder, with offices at the Oakland Wharf, superintended the Central Pacific's Visalia Divi-

Tailings from the construction of the San Fernando tunnel fan out adjacent to the station of the same name which was situated at the south entrance to the 6,966 foot bore. Today, although the railroad is essentially in the same location, the area is completely obscured by the confluence of Interstate 5 and the Antelope Valley Freeway. — DONALD DUKE COLLECTION

sion between Lathrop and Goshen. Wilder was also superintendent of Southern Pacific's Tulare Division which had jurisdiction over the section from Goshen to Mojave. E.E. Hewitt, superintendent of the Los Angeles Division of the SP at Los Angeles was given jurisdiction over the section between Mojave and River Station (Los Angeles) as well as the branches radiating from this growing city. Principal terminals on the new valley line were located at Lathrop, Tulare, Mojave and Los Angeles.

By 1885, the importance of the Tehachapi Mountain District as a vital "bridge line" was being realized. In October of that year, the Los Angeles Division acquired the railroad from Mojave to Sumner in order to better administer the affairs of the entire district. Sumner was made a terminal and the facilities at Tulare were, for the large part, abandoned. On July 25, 1892, the 168 mile district between Bakersfield (changed from Sumner in 1890) and Los Angeles, as well as the branches being extended from Burbank and Saugus, were incorporated into the Mojave Division. T.J. Urkhart was appointed superintendent with headquarters in the station building at Mojave. His successor, D. Burkhalter, in January 1895, moved the division headquarters to Bakersfield where extensive yards

and shops were being built and from that day forward Bakersfield has been the center of operations for the San Joaquin Division.

At this time the traditional limits of the San Joaquin Division were established encompassing all the tracks from Fresno, which was fast becoming the largest city in the valley, south all the way to Los Angeles. Also included were the branches from Burbank and Saugus as far as Elwood just north of Santa Barbara. It should be noted that the division lost all territory south and west of Saugus to the Los Angeles Division in 1909.

Early operating points on the fledgling Mountain District were Sumner (later Bakersfield), Pampa (later Bena), Caliente, Bealville, Keene (later Woodford), Girard (later Marcel), Tehachapi Summit (later just Tehachapi), Cameron, Mojave, Sand Creek (later Rosamond), Lancaster, Alpine (later Harold), Soledad Summit (later Vincent), Acton, Ravena, Lang, Newhall (later Saugus), Andrews (later Newhall), Tunnel, Fernando and Sepulveda. These locations in many cases had water available. Turntables were installed at Caliente, Tehachapi, Summit, Mojave and Tunnel with the major repair points being located at Tulare and Los Angeles. Modifications to this arrangement were

21

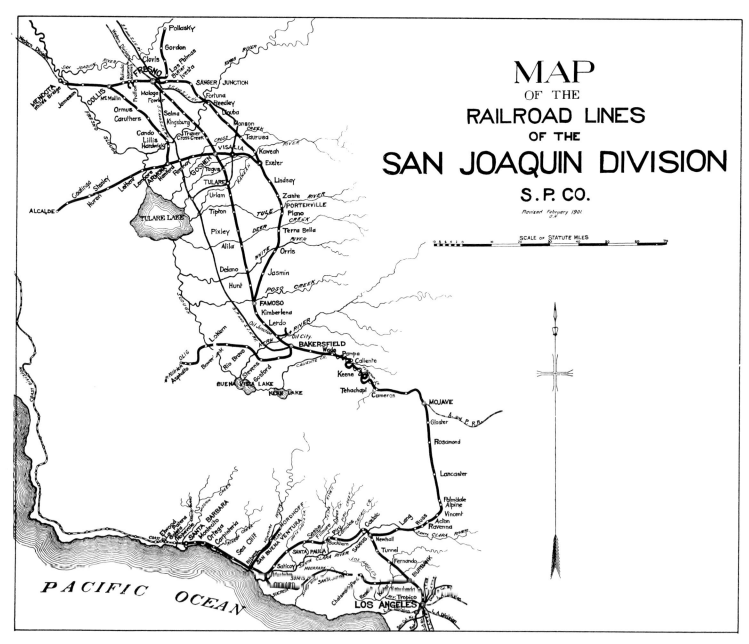

MAP
OF THE
RAILROAD LINES
OF THE
SAN JOAQUIN DIVISION
S. P. CO.

Revised February 1901
O.N.

SCALE OF STATUTE MILES

forthcoming.

Mojave quickly became a point of railway operating significance. Situated at the foot of the southern ascent of the Tehachapi and a convenient place for taking on helper engines, facilities were concentrated there. At the time of construction, a 15-stall engine house, several office buildings, a station, turntable, sand house, coal platform and seven track yard were built at Mojave. Daily stages made the connection to such isolated points as Darwin, Lone Pine, Independence and the Panamint. All passenger trains stopped at Mojave for meals and trains tended to accumulate there. The addition of sidings at Nadeau, five miles north of town, and Gloster, seven miles south to relieve congestion was almost immediate. A siding at Kent, between Lang and Saugus, was installed quite early.

As trains began to run with increasing frequency over the Mountain District, it became

apparent there just wasn't enough capacity on the Tehachapi grade. Accordingly, in 1884-85, sidings were laid at Wade (later known as Edison) and Rowen, three miles below Keene. The six miles of grade approaching Soledad summit from the north was another trouble spot. Palmdale was established at the foot of this grade to facilitate adding pushers in this same period. Also Soledad Summit was expanded into a siding and became Vincent.

The period of 1888-91 brought another rash of siding construction. At this time a new siding was built three miles up the grade from Mojave at Fram and another further up the hill at Warren. The Soledad section also received two new sidings in this period; one at Harold between Palmdale and Vincent, and another between Lang and Saugus called Honby.

Many modifications to the original alignment in the early days were due to washouts. The original line of 1875-76 had been built pretty much down the

22

middle of the canyon in the tempestuous Soledad region and consequently was subjected to the severe storm runoffs that periodically occurred.

The first floods and washouts came in 1884 when all 19 crossings of the Santa Clara River were damaged or destroyed along with extensive damage to the roadbed. These crossings of the Santa Clara were piled trestling of 16-foot spans. When the bridges were rebuilt, 15 were changed to iron trusses and four to 64-foot wooden spans. Portions of the old roadbed were abandoned and the railroad location moved to higher ground. The major changes were near Saugus where 1.6 miles of new track was laid to the north of the original roadbed eliminating the station of Kent. Considerable damage occurred at Lang and Acton as well where about two miles of track was relaid. During this storm, General Colton's "temporary" line between Pampa and Caliente suffered washouts necessitating the relocation of about two miles of line at a higher elevation. It was during this construction that it was found necessary to bore tunnel No. ½.

Upwards of four miles of road were rebuilt in Soledad Canyon following another flood in 1886. This work avoided two river crossings, but necessitated the construction of two new tunnels, Nos. 17½ and 17¾ as well as 23,000 feet of new roadbed. Realignments were made between tunnel No. 18 and No. 19 near the present station of Russ where the new tunnels were located. The new tunnels were daylighted sometime prior to 1905. The station of old Ravena (sic), now in the channel of the river, was moved almost a mile west to higher ground and the new location became Ravenna.

Soledad Canyon was again awash during 1890 and once more some bridges were lost. With only a four year interval between this and the preceding storm, extensive plans were laid for a realignment of the track in the area. The episodes of 1884 and 1886 had apparently taught a lesson that recurring floods could best be handled by locating the track higher above the water. The original line of 1875-76 had been the most economical to build, but it was proving extremely costly to maintain. Appearing as if to make amends for past short comings, a series of line changes totaling over 14 miles were made. The new line included five new tunnels and the track curvature was increased, but there were six fewer crossings of the Santa Clara River. The sidings at Humphreys and Russ were set up during this construction.

Long before all these improvements had been made, the Southern Pacific was running trains over the Mountain District with a vengeance. Indeed, it had only been one day after the Golden Spike at Lang that regular train service had been inaugurated between Los Angeles and San Fran-

cisco. The *Los Angeles Express,* train No. 18, made the run north in 24 hours and 40 minutes and train No. 17 made the run south in 23 hours and 30 minutes. An emigrant train (combination train with freight and passenger cars of spartan utility) made the trip north in 34 hours 55 minutes and south in 44 hours 30 minutes. As time went on, these early schedules were augmented by other trains.

Following the completion of the Sunset Route, on January 15, 1883, service was established between San Francisco and New Orleans by way of the Valley Line. The first through daily trains departed their initial terminals on February 1st, as No. 19, the *Atlantic Express* and No. 20, the *Pacific Express.* These two trains were, at times, known collectively as the *Sunset Express.* Beginning in November 1894, the deluxe extra fare *Sunset Limited,* trains No. 1000 and 1001, were run weekly through April 1895. The following winter the *Sunset Limited* operated again on a bi-weekly schedule. The service was repeated each winter on through the turn-of-the-century.

The need for an exclusive overnight express between Los Angeles and San Francisco was indicated and December 18, 1898, Southern Pacific established the *Owl Limited* between these two cities on a 14 hour 45 minute schedule. Eastbound (to Los Angeles), No. 26 departed San Francisco at 5:00 P.M. and arrived in Los Angeles at 7:45 A.M. the next morning in time for breakfast and connections with morning trains for the interior of southern California. Westbound, No. 25, departed Los Angeles 7:00 P.M. and arrived at the Oakland Wharf at 9:45 A.M. permitting transfer to the *Overland Limited.* These trains were an immediate success and made no stops between Bakersfield and Los Angeles except for water. Further changes were made to the timecard the following December 16th when the *Los Angeles Express,* running as No. 7 and No. 8, were made into local trains with lengthy schedules and many stops en route to accommodate rural traffic.

All of these trains were scheduled over the Mountain District in darkness. Those travelers fortunate enough to catch a late train, or a following section, were rewarded with scenery unparalleled with anything else along the inland route. Travel in the Tehachapi was characterized by a series of remarkable loops and circles that might cause one to think that "the sun do move" unless he was alert to catch the curves and right his mental compass accordingly.

Runaways were a periodic occurrence in the early days. What is generally regarded as the last major passenger train runaway in the United States occurred in the Tehachapi Mountains the

Heavy mountain engines rest in front of the Sumner roundhouse in the 'eighties'. As the Southern Pacific was building down the San Joaquin Valley from the north in 1872, Goshen was designated as the division point closest to the Tehachapi Mountains. Following a drastic fire several years later, the terminal was moved to Tulare. Still 63 miles from the base of the mountains, Tulare saw little of the activity that occurred in the Sumner yards at the very foot of the Tehachapi grade. In 1885, Sumner was made the terminal. Ten years later the place — now called Bakersfield — became the headquarters of the San Joaquin Division. — GUY DUNSCOMB COLLECTION

night of January 20, 1883. Train No. 19, the *Atlantic Express,* had arrived at the summit about 2:00 A.M. As it was the custom to place the helper — added at Caliente— ahead of the first car, it was necessary to cut both engines away from the train to free the helper so it could return down the mountain. While the forward brakeman was engaged in side-tracking the road engine and running the helper onto the turntable, conductor Reed was en route to the depot to confer with the telegrapher. Leaving the train completely unattended, rear brakeman Patton escorted a pretty young woman to the depot to see if he could arrange accommodations for her. As time passed, the air brakes leaked off and, as fate would have it, a stiff north wind was also blowing this night. Shortly the seven cars of No. 19, standing on the brink of the 2.2 percent grade, began to move.

Rolling off down the hill, the train began to gather momentum. Soon it was careening down the mountain at terrific speeds. "To say seventy miles an hour," reported the *Kern Weekly Record,* "was to put it at its lowest estimate." The movement of the runaway cars was so violent that it upset the stoves in both sleeping cars setting them afire even before they left the rails. Three and one-half miles down grade the sleepers and three head-end cars plummeted into the ravine near the sixth crossing of Tehachapi Creek. Seventeen people, including the wife of former Governor Downey of California, two porters, an express agent and two

tramps perished in the wreck and subsequent fire. The remaining coach and smoker — broken free from the rest of the train — continued to speed down grade. Awakened by a small girl, those on board were able to brake the remains of the runaway to a stop near tunnel No. 11. Although the railroad hastened to place the blame on transients, overwhelming public opinion led to the arrest of the train crew on a charge of criminal negligence. Several days later, they were bailed out by the Southern Pacific.

While the air brake systems then being developed left something to be desired, they were a vast improvement over the way things had been done previously. Trains not equipped with air brakes had to be controlled by hand. To avoid overheating wheels to the point of fracture, the brakes were applied systematically by starting at the head end of a train and setting up every other car. To avoid accidents freight trains descending the Tehachapi grade, and Soledad Canyon between Vincent and Lang, were to keep 15 minutes apart at speeds not exceeding 15 miles per hour. Passenger trains were allowed a speed of 20 in the Tehachapi and 22 in Soledad Canyon.

Considerably less dangerous, but difficult none-the-less, was the task of dragging trains up the hill. A Ten-Wheel (4-6-0) type was first used on the Mountain District with 57-inch drivers, 18 x 24-inch cylinders weighing about 98,000 pounds on drivers. Then, in 1882-83, the company purchased

Three husky compound "hogs" move 20 cars of fruit up the 2.2 percent grade about a mile above Keene in the late 1880's. Pulling trains uphill, while difficult, presented no threat to safety. But down the other side was another matter. The brakemen, strung out across the tops of the cars, were charged with regulating a speed of 13 miles-per-hour by means of hand brakes and the possibility of a runaway was a constant threat. — DONALD DUKE COLLECTION

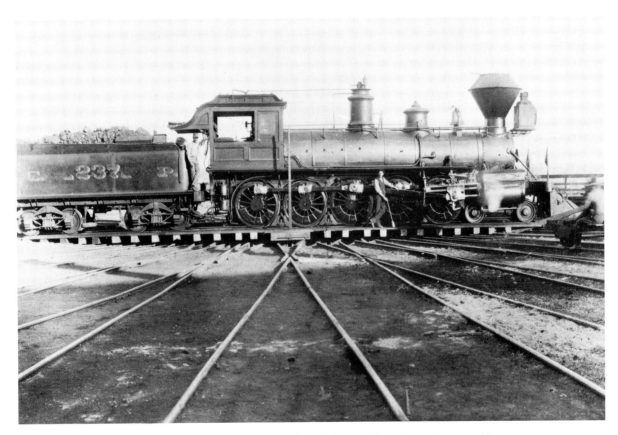

The *El Gobernador* — polite Spanish for "the boss" — sits on the turntable at Mojave ready to do battle with the Tehachapi grade. A one-of-a-kind experiment and considerably larger than other locomotives of its time, the *El Gobernador* spent most of its short working life in Tehachapi helper service. — SOUTHERN PACIFIC COLLECTION

what were commonly called "Cooke Hogs." These were the largest locomotives operated on the Tehachapi grade until 1894, with one exception. Because of their size, these locomotives were limited to 25 miles per hour over the entire district.

The exception was the one-of-a-kind *El Gobernador,* which was especially built in 1883 in the railroad's Sacramento Shops by Superintendent of Motive Power A.J. Stevens. This 4-10-0 had 57-inch drivers, 21 x 36-inch cylinders and a total engine weight of 146,000 pounds. Numbered CP 237, this behemoth was shipped to Sumner inoperable, set up in the local shop, and placed in service between there and Mojave in March 1884. Used primarily as a helper, the "Largest Locomotive in the World" at the time, made daylight trips only and returned to the terminal frequently backwards as there was no turntable big enough to accommodate it on the mountain and it was considered unsafe to wye it at summit. There was considerable apprehension on the part of its hand-picked crew, engineer George Cooper and fireman J.D. Haines, who were frequently seen at the edge of the gangway ready to jump as the engine negotiated the recently strength-ened bridges. Special instructions were issued requiring all trains, passenger included, to take siding when meeting the engine as it was feared too heavy for secondary trackage. To make matters worse, the engine steamed poorly and was always stopping for water because its tank lacked adequate capacity. The *El Gobernador* was the object of much criticism and in 1893 was sent back to Sacramento never to return.

There followed a succession of Twelve-Wheel engine advancements — some cross compounds —bringing SP locomotive technology up to the turn-of-the-century. The largest of these engines was delivered in 1898 by Schenectady as cross compounds with 55-inch drivers, 23 & 35 x 32-inch cylinders, and with an engine weight of 192,000 pounds on drivers. These engines, Nos. 2914-2923 in the 1901 general renumbering, found particular favor in Mountain District service, mostly as helpers, and a few spent their entire lives in service on the San Joaquin Division. These engines were supplemented by Consolidations (2-8-0) and more Ten-Wheelers for passenger service from the Cooke and Schenectady Locomotive Works.

The San Francisco & San Joaquin Valley Railway

Up to this point the Mountain District had been a purely Southern Pacific operation, but a chain of events was already in motion that would soon subvert the SP's exclusive position. It is to the credit of the directors of the SP that they saw fit to build a line of railroad into such an inhospitable region as the great San Joaquin Valley. The prosperity this region enjoys today is in a large part due to the daring of these men. Sadly, it is in this same region that the Southern Pacific garnered a great deal of ugly publicity spawning a whole era of muckraking in the State of California. So bitter was the opposition to the SP in the San Joaquin Valley in the 1880's, that a whole line of rail road was conceived with one purpose in mind — to break the monopoly of the "Big Four."

In the matter of rates, the people of the San Joaquin Valley had particular reason to complain. Following the completion of the SP through the area, a policy of all the traffic would bear was ruthlessly pursued by the road and the list of inequities in this matter filled newspapers and legal briefs of the period. In some cases it cost more to ship goods from valley points to San Francisco than it did to ship the same goods from North Atlantic ports to the Golden Gate by way of Cape Horn.

The granting of certain government lands in California to the railroads as a subsidy instead of direct financial aid was another subject widely contested. This land, previously open to cost-free homesteading, was withdrawn from use then later offered for sale by the railroads. Southern Pacific land grant lands were the location of a dispute in western Tulare County (presently Kings County) which became the battle cry of the railroad reformists in the state.

It began May 11, 1880, on the farm of Henry Brewer about five miles from Hanford. A Southern Pacific land agent, a Federal Marshal and two deputies, who had come to serve eviction papers, were met by a mounted and armed squadron of 40 members of the "Settlers Grand League." Shooting broke out and when the dust settled, seven men lay dead or wounded.

The battle was first described in a rather unemotional account in the *Tulare Weekly Times* of May 15, 1880. Indeed the local press in sober examination later held that the railroad had acted completely within the law and had not deceived anyone. The root of the trouble seemed to revolve around land speculation. The most vocal of the Settler's League were speculators, not farmers, and in the actual shooting no shots were fired at either the SP man or the Marshall — only local men (the two deputies) who had purchased land on which others were squatting.

The San Francisco papers, however, reported the incident in lurid detail implicating the SP machine as the final culprit. While the local press practically ignored the league member's trial which ensued, the San Francisco press gave it front page treatment. Later, about the turn-of-the-century, the incident was adopted by the anti-railroad reformers in California as the "Mussle Slough Tragedy" fully 20 years after the worst of the area's problems had taken place. The time was now ripe for the development of a competing road down the valley.

With local support assured, a traffic association was formed in San Francisco and attempts at organizing and constructing an independent railroad in the San Joaquin Valley were made in the summer of 1893 and the fall of 1894. It was on January 22, 1895, at the meeting of the association that real progress was made, largely due to the energy of one man, Claus Spreckels of San Francisco, the leading sugar refiner on the Pacific Coast. Spreckels was a speaker at the January meeting and when the formal proceedings were over, he came forward with an offer to subscribe $50,000 provided that the amount for incorporation be raised from a previously advertised, but ineffectual $350,000 to $5 million.

The subscription in definite amounts received at the meeting did not exceed $20,000, but on January 24th, Claus Spreckels was elected chairman and soon after larger pledges began to appear. A week later, over $1,200,000 was pledged and with such sums of money and Spreckels connected with the project, people hastened to share in the anticipated success.

Unruffled by the turn in events, SP's Collis P. Huntington smugly remarked in the March issue of the *San Francisco Examiner* that he thought there was room in California for both the Southern Pacific and the new line. It required, he said, only a space of 13 feet from the center of one track to the center of another. And since there was lots of room in the state, the projectors of the new road would have no trouble in finding room.

Local support in the form of rights-of-way, depot grounds, terminal facilities and stock subscriptions was forthcoming from such communities as San Jose, Stockton, Fresno, Madera, Modesto, Hanford, Merced, Visalia, Selma and Bakersfield. In February 1895, articles of incorporation for the San Francisco & San Joaquin Valley Railway Company were filed at Sacramento and construction was begun late that same year at Stockton. "The Peoples Road," as it was widely regarded, was in service some 26.1 miles to the Stanislaus River by December. During 1896, the track reached Fresno and May 27, 1898, Bakersfield was attained. On June 30, 1898, the company reported a total trackage of 278.91 miles including a branch to Visalia.

The effect on Southern Pacific rates was imme-

diate and as was anticipated, all published rates of the newcomer were met or undercut by the SP. In order for the S.F.&S.J.V. to survive, it was recognized that it must ally itself with a larger road. Early on talks had been underway with the directors of the Atchison, Topeka & Santa Fe Railway and these culminated in the Valley Road coming under Santa Fe control through stock ownership in December 1898. With the deal consummated, President E.P. Ripley of the Santa Fe paid a visit to Huntington in New York to tell him of the news. It was a sad day for the old mogul and the Southern Pacific organization. Huntington had longed for the day when "Spreckels would come and beg me to

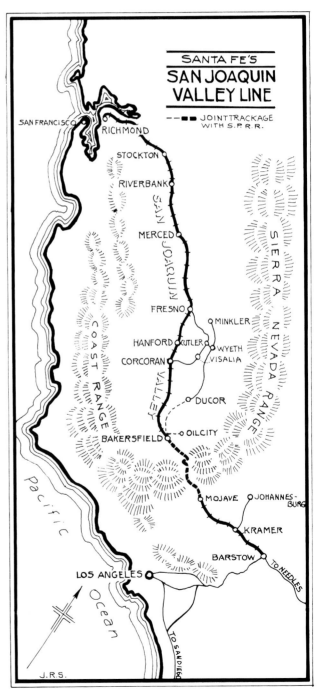

27

take the white elephant off his hands."

The Santa Fe was by now at Mojave having leased the railroad between there and The Needles some years before. The Southern Pacific had built this line in 1882–83 in a calculated attempt to keep the Atlantic & Pacific (Santa Fe) out of California. At that time, President William Barstow Strong of the Santa Fe had met the situation by a counter move of establishing a Pacific Coast connection in old Mexico. The Sonora Railway, as it was called, extended from Benson, Arizona Territory, down the west coast of Mexico to Guaymas. The Santa Fe was determined to get into California anyway and threatened to build a second track from Needles to San Francisco if necessary. Huntington, seeing the futility of these two lines stretching across the barren Mojave, agreed to a lease of what would quickly become a costly white elephant of his own if these threats were carried out. The agreement was signed August 20, 1889. During 1896, Huntington and Ripley of the Santa Fe had come to terms on an exchange of ownerships of the Mojave line for the Sonora lines which were of similar value and of no strategic importance to either of the companies as things stood. An agreement was reached July 15, 1898, on the exchange, but because

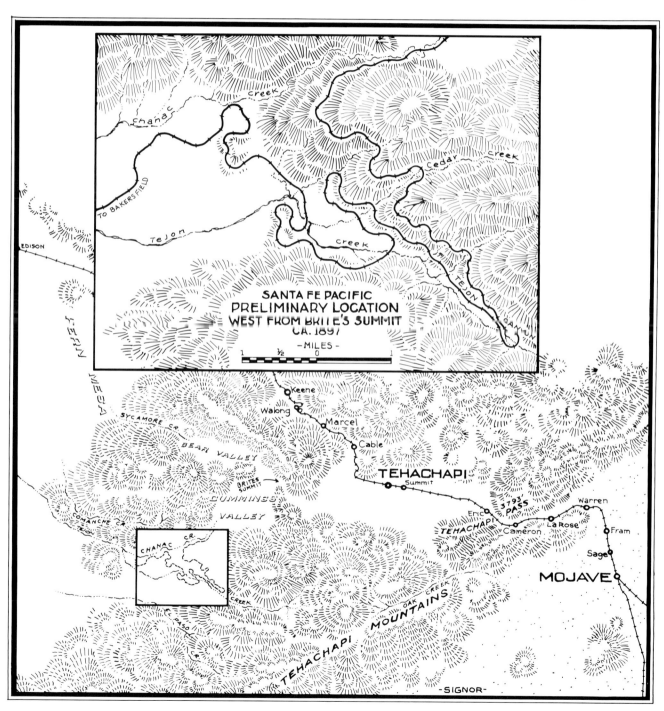

of certain legal considerations, the actual deal was not consummated until December 27, 1911. It is interesting to note that the SP retained the right to run its trains as far as Goffs if necessary.

By December 1898, all that remained for the Santa Fe to have a direct route into the heart of California was the 68 mile gap between Mojave and the Valley Road's yards at Bakersfield. A number of plans had been proposed for making the connection, chief of which was a proposition to build through the Tejon Pass to Rogers. With this in mind, on September 23, 1898, the Bakersfield & Los Angeles Rail Road Company was incorporated in San Francisco with Claus Spreckels as principal of the enterprise. Included in the estimated 5 to 6 million dollar cost of the 82 mile line was a tunnel 8,000 feet long. The Santa Fe proposed a line of its own over the barrier as well. Still in existence today are the preliminary drawings of a remarkable two percent line west from Brite's Summit attributed to the Santa Fe Pacific in 1897. The route was to utilize the Cummings Valley and Tejon Creek Canyon to conquer the Tehachapi. With the Santa Fe all but a reality in Central California, perhaps the directors of the Southern Pacific saw a way to help recover some of the horrendous construction and maintenance costs incurred in the district. At any rate, ultimately, and much to the surprise of industry observers, they allowed the Santa Fe joint use of the Tehachapi grade. With this matter settled, the Bakersfield & Los Angeles Rail Road was disbanded April 28, 1900.

On January 16, 1899, a joint trackage agreement was arrived at between the two roads providing for the equal use of the 67.28 miles of Southern Pacific line between Mojave and the SP yards at Bakersfield. Joint operation was to commence on the first day of July 1899. For this concession, the Santa Fe was to pay $80,000 per annum and one-half of all taxes assessed. All employees engaged in the maintenance, improvement or operation of the joint line were deemed joint employees except for train and engine crews engaged solely in the service of either party.

The joint trackage was to extend from the easterly margin of the yards at Mojave station to Bakersfield yards together with all roundhouses, turntables, sidings, stations, water and telegraph services and other facilities or appurtenances necessary to or used in the operation of the joint line with the stipulation that it would not extend to SP's Bakersfield station or facilities.

The joint line was to be governed under the rules and regulations of the Southern Pacific Railroad which was to handle the dispatching of trains belonging to both roads. Passenger trains were to be given precedence over other trains while the two

railroad's trains were to be given equal dispatch according to their class.

Work was started May 13, 1899, on a connection between the Valley Road's yards and the Southern Pacific in Bakersfield. The rails were extended from their yards along 15th Street nearly to Union Avenue, then northeasterly paralleling Central Avenue (Truxtun) to Baker Street, then onto the Southern Pacific midway between the roundhouse and stock yards. As the date for commencing joint operations neared, skeptics among 25 year veteran mountain men in the Southern Pacific camp voiced concern over the Santa Fe crews ability to operate on heavy grades. Nevertheless, the frogs were in place at Kern Junction Tower on June 13, 1899. The Santa Fe, which now had direct access to the interior of California, lost no time in utilizing it. Operations commenced July 1st right on schedule and the first train from the east arrived in Stockton, California, at noon July 3, 1899. Stockton was the temporary northern terminal as five tunnels in the Contra Costa Hills were still being holed-through.

With the Santa Fe sharing trackage, the number of regularly running trains on the grade doubled overnight. Although Santa Fe trains were running regularly in the Tehachapi, they were run as extras and it was nearly two years before their trains were added to the timetable. Released on March 14, 1901, San Joaquin Division timetable No. 55 listed three Santa Fe schedules each way. Towards San Francisco, No. 103, the *Limited,* No. 107, the *Overland* and a freight, No. 133, were scheduled. In the opposite direction, the numbers 104, 108 and 134 were utilized. Early power on trains in mountain territory consisted of 600 and 700 series Consolidations in freight and helper service and 400 series Ten-Wheelers in passenger service.

Plans to expand the S.F.&S.J.V. terminal between 14th and 16th streets in Bakersfield were laid out and a depot and Harvey House erected between D and E streets. Crews operating on Santa Fe's Arizona Division were trained in the Southern Pacific rules and ran through from Barstow over Tehachapi to Bakersfield. Following the lead of the SP, helper terminals were established at Bakersfield and Mojave. At the latter point, space in the SP's roundhouse was negotiated and separate fuel facilities constructed to accommodate Santa Fe helper engines.

The Santa Fe, having made its entry into the heart of California, was there to stay. In the succeeding decades it was to expand its network of tracks in the San Joaquin Valley and contribute much to the excitement of railroading in the Tehachapi Mountains.

An eastbound Southern Pacific freight encircles the loop in the 1920's. — JAMES H. HARRISON COLLECTION

2

The Glory Years
1900-1929

The first three decades of the twentieth century, a period marked by a dramatic growth in the economy of the far west, witnessed tremendous increases in traffic levels on the Tehachapi grade. Despite the inauguration of through service between San Francisco and Los Angeles by way of Saugus and the Coast Route in March 1901, most rail traffic north and south in California continued to funnel through strategic Tehachapi Pass. For the Southern Pacific, there simply was no more direct way to go than via the San Joaquin Valley Route. The Santa Fe had no other choice. It was during this period that Tehachapi Pass first earned the distinction of possessing one of the busiest single track mountain railroads in the world.

As the new century dawned, Southern Pacific crews were operating trains through from Los Angeles to Bakersfield — a distance of 168 miles. But after the Federal Hours of Service law was imposed in April 1908, adjustments were made to this rather lengthy district. It was found to be extremely difficult for train and engine crews to make the entire distance within the limit of 16 hours imposed by the law so the district was split at

Mojave. Santa Fe Arizona Division crews, running between Barstow and Bakersfield, a distance of 140 miles, were unaffected.

Even with Mojave set up as a turn around point, situations developed in which 16 hours could easily be consumed. Train speeds were slow and there were many stops for water, meets and the setting of retainers. Beyond Mojave, the Santa Fe had a run of 70 miles across a relatively flat and featureless desert. But virtually the entire Mountain District from Bakersfield to Los Angeles was helper territory for the Southern Pacific and the delays attributable to the handling of these engines were numerous.

On the east end on the Mountain District lay the burgeoning city of Los Angeles. Here River Station was the center of SP's freight activity. The River Station yards, known locally as the "Cornfield," stretching along San Fernando Street (now North Spring) dated back to the earliest days of the railroad's presence in the city. River Station itself, nothing more than a store front, had been taken over by the railroad in 1884. All train crews went on and off duty here and engines were dispatched from the roundhouse located across the yards from River Station against the bluffs of Elysian Heights.

These rather cramped quarters sufficed until more space was obtained across the Los Angeles River at Alhambra Avenue and Lamar Street along the SP line to Colton and the East. Here, in 1902, the commodious Alhambra Avenue roundhouse and shops were built.

Southern Pacific passenger service originated in Los Angeles after February 1888, at the elaborate Arcade Station. Patterned after Central Pacific's station at Sacramento, the essentially gothic structure was located on Central off Alameda Street between Fourth and Sixth streets. For 26 years all Southern Pacific passenger trains entering or leaving the city used this depot. On November 30, 1914, however, the more functional Central Station was opened at a cost of $750,000 on an adjoining site and the venerable Arcade Station razed. After 1924, Central Station also served the trains of the Salt Lake Route (Union Pacific). The double track down Alameda Street linking this facility with River Station Yard, the roundhouse and lines to the north and east was very busy indeed.

With the city growing as it was, the yards at River Station soon became inadequate and quite early additional tracks were laid on a fill to the immediate north along the bluffs below Elysian Park. This new yard was soon called the "Bull Ring." In 1914, the Los Angeles River, swollen by heavy rains, went on a rampage destroying virtually every railroad crossing of the river, including SP's double track Dayton Avenue and Alhambra Avenue bridges. The flood that year also took out a sprawling pigeon farm to the west of the tracks above Dayton Avenue and in the rebuilding following the deluge, the SP took over the property the farm had once occupied and began laying out what became the vast Taylor Yard complex. Today, nearly 70 years later, there still is a track at Dayton Avenue Tower known as the "pigeon farm" and pigeons, in great quantities, still inhabit the underpinnings of bridges in the immediate vicinity.

By 1905, Harriman Common Standard Consolidations had been delivered in sufficient numbers to dominate SP Mountain District freight operations. Once free of the confines of Los Angeles terminal, one Consolidation could drag 49 or 50 cars unassisted west towards Bakersfield. Beyond Glendale, the clutter of the city was soon left behind and the rails entered the surrounding San Fernando Valley dotted with peach orchards and alfalfa fields. Traffic was congested as far as Burbank with Coast Division trains. Even on the fastest freight schedule, one and one-half hours were allowed to San Fernando Station—the first point of operating significance. The slow speeds can be attributed to the steady rise of one percent or better all the way from River Station Yard.

At San Fernando, the road engine was watered

and a helper cut in ahead of the caboose on freight trains or added to the point if necessary on passenger runs. Eight or nine 2900 series Twelve-Wheelers were utilized in this service and the helper would stay with the train to Soledad Summit at Vincent. Retainers were set up there to control the descent to Palmdale, while the helper was cut out. Periodically one of these 2900's would stay with the train down to Palmdale and relieve an engine and crew whose previous three or four days had been spent pushing tonnage from this lonely outpost up the hill to Vincent. This was a harsh assignment, and at the time, Palmdale was no more than a wide spot in the road. There was no electricity in the desert and water came from SP wells at Harold. Because of the extremes in temperature, crews sought shelter in holes in the ground—or dugouts—in the center of the wye and counted the days until their relief. No helpers were used across the floor of the desert to Mojave, although the 1.3 percent Ansel hill, beyond Rosamond, could offer some resistance. Rather than use a helper, this short grade was doubled if necessary.

Mojave (pronounced Moharve by the rails) served as the terminus for SP freight crews from both Los Angeles and Bakersfield. Passenger crews continued to run across the entire district. All SP freight trains were yarded here. The crews were put up in the Harvey House, in the depot maintained by the Santa Fe and at local rooming houses or in bungalows provided by the SP to the west of the yards. Mojave yard itself was laid on a one percent grade necessitating stringent rules for the securing of unattended trains.

The town had grown since the time of its construction in the mid-seventies. Considerable development had occurred during the early days of the Randsburg mining boom in the nineties. Mojave was the closest point at which miners, their provisions, and materials could leave the railway. The junction with the Santa Fe at this point in 1899 had brought increased importance to the desert oasis. Mojave also served as a base camp during the construction of the Los Angeles aqueduct.

Since there was no water at Mojave, it was brought in initially by tank car from Southern Pacific Company wells 12 miles up the grade just beyond Cameron. Later a pipeline was laid from this source to supply the town's needs and a huge tank erected west of the west switch for storage. While water was essential to the railroad at Mojave and for certain domestic functions, the local population had other options available to quench their thirst. By 1910, Mojave boasted a sizeable business district along J Street fronting the railroad yards and reportedly every other door led to a saloon. Cat houses and unpaved streets added to the general unseemliness of the place.

Mojave, then as now, by right of its position on the edge of the desert, was subject to nearly continuous winds. "Mojave Zephyrs" occasionally blew with enough velocity to blow off the roof of the roundhouse or remove the tops of standing box cars and fuel oil tank roofs. On one occasion a dome casing was stripped from a standing locomotive. Adding insult to injury, the extreme heat of summer and the harsh winters made conditions so unfavorable at this spot that few volunteered to be assigned here. San Joaquin Division officers frequently complained to the General Offices in San Francisco that it was very difficult to retain competent help at Mojave to service the equipment. Perhaps it was among the dens of inequity along J Street that the population of Mojave took solace in their plight.

In addition to the facilities in Mojave for through trains and crews, both the Santa Fe and Southern Pacific maintained helper crews and engines here—usually three each—for boosting trains westward to the summit of Tehachapi Pass. The two roads shared a modest eight stall frame roundhouse until 1920 when a modern concrete enginehouse was installed. Locomotives used on the Owenyo Branch were also quartered here after 1908.

Unquestionably the most difficult stretch of railroad to operate on SP's San Joaquin Division Mountain District lay in the 68 miles between Mojave and Bakersfield over the Tehachapi. To get a train over the mountains in either direction was a demanding job requiring many engines and skilled men. On account of the heavy curvature and grades on the mountain, as well as the heavy locomotives used, the maximum speed of freight trains was limited to 18 miles per hour. For a time, after the installation of automatic block signals, passenger trains were allowed 30. But, as the story has it, this speed limit was trimmed following an unfortunate incident involving a Southern Pacific official. It seems that one night General Manager Kruttschnitt was rudely thrown from his bed while descending the mountain aboard his private car which was attached to the rear of No. 25. Upon arrival at Bakersfield the engineer, Morris Shean, was called into the office to explain the unfortunate incident. Shean, an engineer with considerable experience, having been promoted in April 1900, protested his innocence of any wrongdoing. A check of the dispatcher's train sheet for the night showed that No. 25 closely followed the schedule and that it would have been impossible for it to have been exceeding the speed. Shean was vindicated but the next day, in a wire from the General Office, speeds for passenger trains in this section were summarily reduced to 25.

Because of physical conditions on the mountain forbidding the construction of side tracks of sufficient length, freight trains were limited to 60 cars. As a further precaution against congestion there was a rule that between 7:00 P.M. and 3:00 A.M., when passenger trains were frequent, westward freights were limited to only 40 cars — the capacity

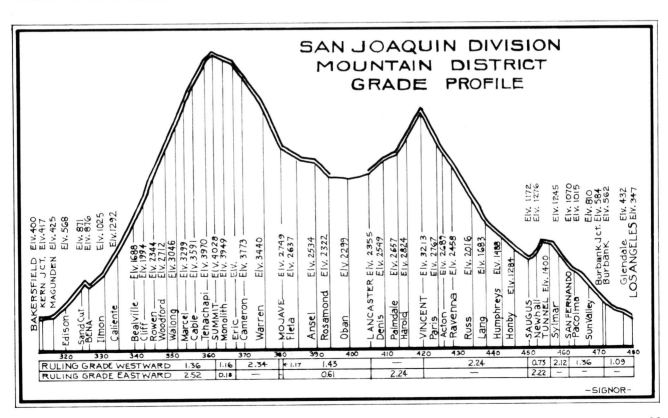

of the most restrictive sidings on the north slope — and spaced from one to two hours apart leaving Mojave. Schedules were arranged so that all trains ascending were superior, from their departure point to the summit. This was done because there would be less likelihood of freight trains having to start up from a dead stop on the grade. It had been proven that in so doing, the danger of damage and delays resulting from break-in-twos would be reduced.

It was the custom of both roads to add helpers at Mojave for the heavy 2.2 percent westward grade. For the SP, these helpers took the form of 2500 or 2600 series Consolidations (rated at 505 tons Mojave to Eric) or 2900 series Twelve-Wheelers. The Santa Fe employed 700 and 800 series Consolidations. One or more of these locomotives would assist westbound tonnage. Many times with no other power or crew available, a Santa Fe engine might be assigned to an SP crew or vice versa and the sight of one road's engines shoving a train of the others up hill out of Mojave was not uncommon.

Water was usually taken on all west (Bakersfield) bound trains at Cameron. From the beginning of operations in the Tehachapi, Mojave helpers had been cut at Summit but their services were only really required up to a point about a mile above Cameron where the grade slackened appreciably. A wye was built in 1899 at this place, the site of water wells supplying Cameron and Mojave, and called Eric (pronounced *ear*-ic by the rails). Thereafter, the operation of cutting helpers from westbound trains was accomplished here. Retainers, an innovative part of the airbrake systems then coming into general use, were also set up at this time. Located near the brake wheel on each car, the retaining valve allowed the train airbrake system to recharge while holding an application — vital to mountain railway operation.

With retainers set, it was a smoky ride down the mountain to Bena, with periodic stops for meets and to cool wheels. The twisting trackage on the north slope, despite certain spectacular incidents previously reported, was generally considered easier to break and runaways were not as much of a problem here as on the desert side. Upon arrival at Bena and knocking down (releasing) the retainers, westbound freights faced the short rise of 1.16 percent up to Sivert on Sandcut hill. This usually presented no problem, but the doubling of Sandcut hill was not unknown.

At the west end of the Mountain District, at the foot of the Tehachapi grade, lay the rough and tumble town of Bakersfield. Southern Pacific operations terminated in their yards on the fringe of town while the Santa Fe diverged at Kern Junction for their own yards in the heart of the fast growing community. Both roads maintained extensive yards and roundhouses at Bakersfield. Reflecting the number of locomotives requred in a normal days operation on the mountain, the roundhouses and shops at Bakersfield were among the largest on their respective systems. The Santa Fe completed their Bakersfield facilities in February 1909.

Fronting the SP yards on Jackson and Sumner streets in (East) Bakersfield were many hotels for the accommodation of railroaders and travelers. Names like the Metropole, the Saint Francis, the Quincy, the Rankin, the Imperial and the Jackson Rooms were typical. Nestled among these boarding houses were the saloons, barber shops and card rooms. The cat houses were right there too. It was this section of town which largely fostered Bakersfield's reputation for harboring bad women and gamblers. Sumner was linked to the city of Bakersfield in 1888 by the Bakersfield & Sumner Street Railway which was electrified in 1901. Sumner (Bakersfield after 1890) was soon enveloped by the fast growing city of Bakersfield and was annexed in 1909.

On the north slope, the custom was for freight trains departing Bakersfield for the mountains, to have at least four Consolidations (rated at 450 tons on the north slope) per train with helpers cut in at specified intervals. Passenger trains, if running heavy with six or more cars, would receive one helper on the point. Water was available at several places on the hill, but Caliente and Woodford were most often used. Two hours could easily be consumed in watering a multi helpered train at these points. This was due to the necessity of cutting engines to spot for water and the required procedure for tying and untying handbrakes on the train as each engine took its fill. Upon arrival at Summit, all helpers were cut from freight trains. Passenger helpers were removed while making the station stop at Tehachapi. These helpers would accumulate in the number one siding across from the depot at Tehachapi awaiting orders. It could take a returning helper eight or more hours to cover the 48 miles from Tehachapi to Bakersfield often drifting downgrade during busy periods in groups of a half dozen engines or more with those of both roads intermixed. Sixteen hours could easily be consumed in nursing a freight over the mountain.

Plans were continually afoot to increase the capacity of the motive power regularly assigned to the Mountain District. Between 1901 and 1910, for the SP, Harriman Common Standard Consolidations held down the heavy freight and helper assignments. The Santa Fe, however, developed a ten-coupled engine, the 2-10-2, and 70 of these were delivered in the 900 series commencing in April 1903. In 1905, 74 more of these 2-10-2's, essentially carbon copies of the earlier versions, were delivered in the 1600 series. These engines, as delivered, were ungainly looking tandem compounds. Dubbed the Santa Fe type, they were found to be particularly suited to drag mountain service and although used system wide, they were common to the Tehachapi throughout their working lives.

So successful were these Santa Fe type engines, that when the railroad's later involvement with Mallet locomotives proved unproductive, even larger 2-10-2's were developed. The Santa Fe had been the first to experiment with Mallets on the Tehachapi grade. Between 1909 and 1911, a total of 83 of these engines were created in the railroad's Topeka shops with wheel arrangements varying from a 4-4-6-2 on up to a 2-10-10-2, but as far as known to this writer, the canyons of the Tehachapi echoed the exhausts of only four classes of Santa Fe Mallets. In June 1910, the 1700 series 2-8-8-2's (two engines, Nos. 1700 and 1701, later Nos. 1798 and 1799) were introduced and saw service on the Tehachapi grade. They were rated at 1,100 tons on the north slope for oil service and 1,050 tons for mixed service. In October 1910, the 1398 series 4-4-6-2's were introduced on oil drags, but proved unsatisfactory in this capacity. There followed a brief stint of mountain passenger schedules before being withdrawn entirely from the district — the primary complaint being excessive slipping of the front engine.

In another experiment in the spring of 1910, seven 900 and 1600 series 2-10-2's were selected to be the rear engines of the new 3000 series 2-10-10-2's with the front engine being delivered from Baldwin. These giants, the largest locomotives in the world at the time, also saw service between Bakersfield and Barstow. Their problems were manifold, however. Being somewhat rigid, operating over the Tehachapi with its 10 degree curves caused serious problems for both track and engine. Poor visibility due to steam leaks was another cause for complaints — especially in cold weather. They were soon banished to less curvatious Cajon Pass.

The most successful Santa Fe Mallets used in the Tehachapi were the four engines in the 3296 series produced in 1911 from 1950 class Consolidations. These engines were regular helpers on the north slope throughout the 1910's. Maintenance was a recurring problem with all of the Santa Fe Mallets, however, and one by one they were returned to the company shops to be divided into two engines once again, the last of this work being accomplished by 1924.

Quite the opposite from these Santa Fe failures, the Southern Pacific embraced Mallet locomotive technology and utilized it in the Tehachapi Mountains for many years. They began assigning Mallets to Bakersfield about 1913. An articulated engine of the MC-4 or MC-6 class, being 2-8-8-2's Nos. 4017-4048, could generate enough power to out pull an old Consolidation more than two to one on the grade between Bakersfield and Summit. Although successful, there were a few things that the engine crews had to get used to when operating these beasts. In order to get full power it was necessary to keep a low water glass, otherwise the engines would work water. There was a fine line between a low water glass and a boiler explosion. On February 24, 1914, at 2:30 P.M., the boiler on the No. 4037 working upgrade at Edison was blown completely away leaving the frame on the rails and killing the entire crew. Despite this occurrence and several other close calls, the Mallets were popular with the men because of the cab's forward location — a real asset in the many tunnels — and earned the moniker "Mudhens." They were widely used in freight and passenger service between Bakersfield and Los Angeles. To accommodate them, an engine shed was built and a 100 foot turntable installed at Bakersfield, and a wye built at Mojave — all in 1913.

By 1917, the Southern Pacific was developing a 2-10-2 of its own design. In the next six years the company was to acquire 164 of this wheel arrangement. The earlier, lighter versions had been experimented with in passenger service, but by 1920 enough of the 2-10-2's had been delivered to make serious tests in mountain freight service. In a spectacular move in the summer of 1922, an order of 20 of these engines was shipped west from the Baldwin Locomotive Works as a solid train. Dubbed the "Prosperity Special," the engines garnered a great deal of publicity for Baldwin and the SP on its travel to Los Angeles via the Sunset Route. Upon arrival at Los Angeles, the special was split into two groups of ten engines, one of which was dispatched north over the Tehachapi the night of July 5, 1922.

The Santa Fe, in 1919, introduced a heavier 2-10-2. More advanced than their predecessors, these engines, Nos. 3800 through 3940, were delivered throughout the 1920's. Largely because of their 63-inch drivers and the terrain they were frequently operated in, the main driving wheel on each engine of this class was blind, having no flange.

The advent of heavy Santa Fe type engines in the mountain service of both roads began to affect operations in the Tehachapi rather significantly. Three 2-10-2's could take 56 cars up the hill where previously four or more Consolidations had been required. This reduced motive power requirements and congestion on the district. The Southern Pacific was pleased enough with the 2-10-2 operation in the Tehachapi to rely on them almost exclusively in the early 1920's, while all of the Mallets were reassigned north and east from Roseville. For several years then, the Mountain District was devoid of the characteristic exhaust of the articulateds.

An outgrowth of this development was the reestablishing of a helper station at Caliente. Helpers had not been assigned there since the early 1890's. This was done a short time prior to July 1, 1925, at the insistence of Stanley Bray, then assistant superintendent of SP's San Joaquin Division. He reasoned that with the 2-10-2 engines it was possible to bring a train up to Caliente unassisted thereby saving yard delays, engine hours and crews. A wye was built on the outside of the Caliente horseshoe, at this time, to facilitate turning helpers. The track layout was altered to allow easy cutting in of these engines. During the peak period of the summer and fall, six helper crews — three each of both roads — were placed here. The motive power was usually Consolidations.

Unfortunately the new helper operation was almost immediately beset with problems. As train speed was excessively slow without the extra engine on the moderate but steady pull up the Kern Mesa to Sandcut, it was not too long before the extra helper was back on the hotter trains departing Bakersfield for the mountains. The crews assigned to Caliente had reason to complain. The rooms in the old Caliente Hotel where the men resided were dilapidated. Six months after the helpers were returned to Caliente, on January 2, 1926, a fire of unknown origin consumed the hotel forcing the men to seek shelter in tents. Later the company provided an old passenger car body for the men, but meals remained a problem. The floods of the early 1930's, necessitating a line change between tunnel No. ½ and Caliente, were the ultimate undoing of the helper station at Caliente. In relocating the line to higher ground, it was necessary to stiffen the grade to a point where it was no longer practical to conserve helpers below Caliente. With the completion of the line change in the summer of 1936, Caliente as a helper terminal was abolished. The wye was removed the following July.

Commencing in 1928, the Southern Pacific began assigning their new AC-4 and AC-5 class 4100 series articulateds to the San Joaquin Division Mountain District. These powerful machines ushered in the modern steam era on the district and soon the SP began to transfer some of its fleet of 2-10-2's elsewhere. The Santa Fe, however, stayed with the 2-10-2 until the end of steam.

Mention should be made of the evolution of mountain passenger locomotives in the same period. The Southern Pacific was an enthusiastic supporter of the Ten-Wheeler, building them in their own shops as late as 1920. One locomotive in particular, the No. 2370, was the largest of its type in the world. These engines in the T class were the basic mountain passenger engine for many years, but as time went on heavier engines were developed. The super-heated 3200 series Mikados, introduced in 1911-1914, were particularly suited to mountain passenger assignments. Experiments followed commencing in 1917 with the lighter versions of the F class 2-10-2. After 1925, the SP class 4-10-2's

SOUTHERN PACIFIC MOUNTAIN POWER
DELIVERED BETWEEN 1900 and 1930

Nos.	Class	Type	Date Delivered	Service
2274-2384	T	4-6-0	1901-1920	Pass
2513-2857	C	2-8-0	1901-1919	Frt
3200-3277	MK	2-8-2	1911-1917	Pass/Frt
3600-3769	F	2-10-2	1917-1925	Pass/Frt
4017-4028	MC	2-8-8-2	1911	Frt
4029-4048	MC	2-8-8-2	1912	Frt
4100-4150	AC	4-8-8-2	1928-1930	Pass/Frt
4200-4211	MM-2	4-6-6-2	1911	Pass/Frt
4300-4349	MT	4-8-2	1923-1927	Pass
5000-5048	SP	4-10-2	1925-1927	Pass/Frt

SANTA FE MOUNTAIN POWER DELIVERED
BETWEEN 1900 and 1930

Nos.	Class	Type	Date Delivered	Service
439-453	408	4-6-0	1901	Pass
498-502	439	4-6-0	1900	Pass
729-864	729,759, 769,789 and 825	2-8-0	1900-1901	Frt
900-985	900	2-10-2	1903-1904	Frt
988-989	988	2-10-0	1902	Frt
1398-1399	1398	4-4-6-2	1909	Frt/Pass
1600-1673	1600	2-10-2	1905-1907	Frt
1674-1705	1674	2-10-2	1912-1913	Frt
1798-1799	1798	2-8-8-2	1909	Frt
3000-3009	3000	2-10-10-2	1911	Frt
3296-3299	3296	2-8-8-0	1911	Frt
3450-3459	3450	4-6-4	1927	Pass
3700-3750	3700	4-8-2	1918-1924	Pass
3800-3940	3800	2-10-2	1919-1927	Frt

were occasionally seen heading up the *Owl* or the *San Joaquin Flyer*. But it was not until the 4300 series MT class Mountains arrived in the mid-1920's that the SP found the modern engine most suited to passenger work in the Tehachapi. Yet, even as the country faced the lean years of the 1930's, the able Ten-Wheelers were still to be seen.

Santa Fe trains were generally quite short and a Ten-Wheeler in the 400 series was usually adequate to handle the road's passenger service. But beginning about 1910, a Pacific type (4-6-2) was run over the mountain on occasion. In 1918, 4-8-2's Nos. 3700 and 3701 were assigned to the Barstow-Bakersfield runs. Other locomotives of their type appeared on the run in succeeding years. These engines represented the ultimate in Santa Fe passenger power used on the mountain run during the period and were familiar sights throughout the 1920's.

The importance of developing mountain passenger locomotives of greater capacity was in direct relation to the alarming increases in passenger service experienced by the San Joaquin Mountain District during the first three decades of this century. In 1901, the SP was operating six schedules daily through the area; No. 25 and 26 — the prestigious *Owl*, Nos. 7 and 8 — the *Los Angeles Express* and Nos. 9 and 10 — the *Sunset Express*. In March of that year, however, the new Coast Line of the Southern Pacific was opened via Saugus (the Chatsworth tunnels were to take three more years to complete) resulting in Nos. 9 and 10 being transferred to the Coast Route on December 6, 1901. That same year, the Santa Fe operated four schedules; Nos. 103 and 104 — the *Limited* and Nos. 107 and 108 — the *Overland*. These schedules remained essentially the same for a time augmented in 1908 by a new Southern Pacific daily train between Fresno and Los Angeles. On the mountain, the eastbound train was known as the *Los Angeles Express* and was numbered No. 108. Westbound the *Fresno Express* ran as No. 107. These two trains became the first to be regularly scheduled in the Tehachapi during daylight hours. Certain train number adjustments were made because of them and the Santa Fe *Overland* trains were accordingly renumbered Nos. 117 and 118. SP's No. 8 became the *New Orleans Passenger* and No. 7 the *California Passenger*.

By 1912, the Santa Fe was becoming more aggressive and sought to compete with Southern Pacific's crack overnight, the *Owl*. On January 20th of that year, a new overnight service between Los Angeles and San Francisco was inaugurated. Westbound the train traveled the Tehachapi as No. 115 and was known as the *Saint*. Eastbound it was known as the *Angel* and ran as No. 116. These two trains boasted of the finest coach and sleeping car equipment available with a through car to San Diego. The extra 111 rail miles encountered operating between Los Angeles and Mojave by way of Barstow, included 26 miles of helper territory between San Bernardino and the summit of Cajon Pass making for some rough competition. On December 31, 1918, the *Saint* and *Angel* were discontinued due to World War I wartime restrictions and were never revived. For nearly seven

years they operated, however, and in April 1912, with the addition of SP's Nos. 49 and 50, the *San Joaquin Flyer*, the Tehachapi line was seeing 14 regularly scheduled passenger trains a day. Train Nos. 49 and 50, early predecessors of the famous *San Joaquin Daylight*, were renumbered Nos. 51 and 52 on March 30, 1927.

From May 27, 1914 to February 28, 1915, the westbound *Sunset Express*, No. 9 and eastbound *Sunset Limited*, No. 102, were run down the Valley Line with their counterparts taking the Coast Line. It was in this period, just prior to World War I, that passenger train operations in the Tehachapi Mountains reached their zenith. The timecard of January 9, 1916, listed 16 schedules divided equally between the two roads. The following season — May 28, 1916 through January 1917 — SP's *Sunset Limited* once again operated via the Valley Line providing the Southern Pacific temporarily with ten first class schedules in the Tehachapi. With the addition of Nos. 59 and 60, in 1920, ten first class trains for the SP became standard. Known at first as the *Sacramento Passenger*, the train northbound became the *Puget Sound Express*. The southbound train was called the *Southern California Express* reflecting an extension of service to Portland, Oregon in November 1924. On June 1, 1927, these trains became the *West Coast*.

Meanwhile, Santa Fe schedules began to decline. The November 14, 1920 timetable listed only three Santa Fe schedules each way and by the end of the decade, this was down to two.

Although the passenger trains carried with them the aura of romance and adventure, it was the freight trains that generally paid the bills. It was the freights, too, which commanded the vast majority of the motive power congregated in the roundhouses at Bakersfield, Mojave and Barstow. This traffic, rising steadily as the west began to develop, jumped dramatically when Kern County erupted in an oil boom. Almost overnight Bakersfield was transformed from a sleepy agricultural community into a thriving city and major rail center. The effect on the density of traffic in the Tehachapi was nothing short of catastrophic. So important to the railroad operation was the development of the oil fields of Kern County that its story bears telling here.

Sections of the great valley of California, including the territory surrounding Bakersfield, had for centuries been holding incredible wealth. The Indians had known of this thick black substance called "Brea" and long used it as a construction material. It remained, however, for the more enterprising Anglos to capitalize upon it.

The first production of oil in the area adjacent to a seepage near Buena Vista Lake, southwest of

Bakersfield, had been dug from shallow pits in the summer of 1864. Production continued on a small scale through the 1870's and 1880's. Although oil was being refined into lubricants and distilled into kerosene and other illuminating oils, its use as a fuel for heavy industry was slight. In the 1880's the railroad industry in California was using coal or wood for locomotive fuel, although tests were being conducted in the use of oil for this purpose. An important factor in pursuing these tests was that coal had to be imported at considerable expense while there were ample deposits of oil on the west coast.

In February 1885, the SP began to convert its ferries on San Francisco Bay from coal to oil. But the real turning point came in October 1894, when a series of tests were conducted by Union Oil. They outfitted a Southern California Railway (Santa Fe) locomotive with the necessary equipment and performed test runs on a stretch of Southern Pacific track near Santa Paula. SP supplied the crew which reported that the engine steamed well and performed adequately on all counts. The experiments showed that fuel oil permitted savings of over 25 percent and the two railroads were now convinced. Soon plans were afoot to convert existing power gradually to burn oil. By July 1900, 70 locomotives on SP's Pacific Lines were so equipped and the ranks were growing. It was this conversion along with similar ones being made by west coast

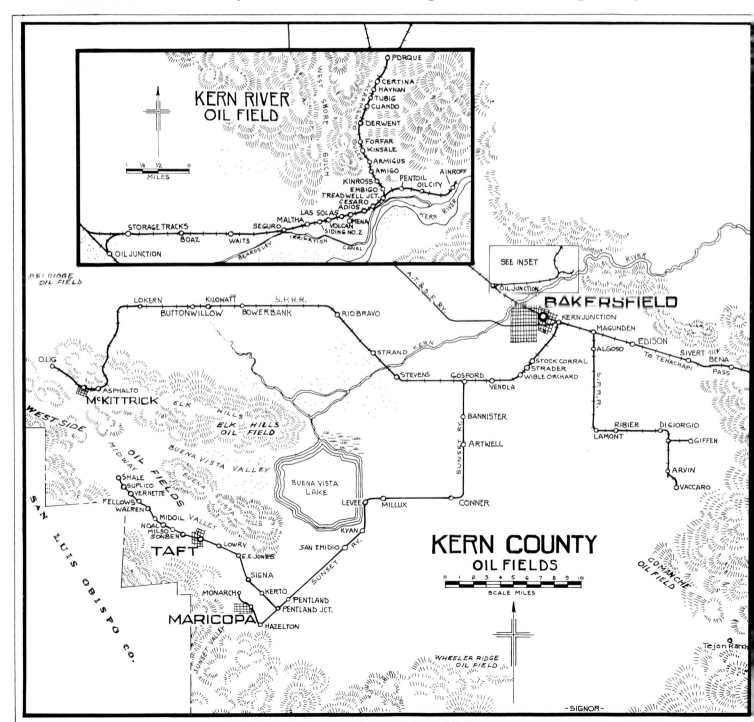

KERN RIVER OIL FIELD

KERN COUNTY
OIL FIELDS

SCALE MILES

- SIGNOR -

heavy industries — the beet sugar refiners, power companies, iron and steel firms and cement companies — which set the stage for one of the most explosive growth periods experienced in Kern County.

The Southern Pacific and Santa Fe, now firmly committed to using oil for fuel, began actively scouting territories in their vast land holdings for deposits. Kern County, possessing a checkerboard of railroad lands and proven deposits, was a prime target. E. L. Doheny, for the Santa Fe, and J. B. Treadwell for the SP, began pioneering valley fields in 1899. The development of the great oil fields of the Sunset, Kern River, McKittrick and Midway transformed formerly docile agricultural Kern County into a major oil producing region. Bakersfield, the county seat and in the center of all the activity, mushroomed as men, money and materials poured into the district. A network of branch lines radiated out from the city to tap this newly developed wealth and the tank train became a familiar sight in the local yards and on the Tehachapi grade as Kern County oil began to be distributed to points in the west and southwest.

The line of railroad from Bakersfield, more or less due west, to Asphalto was opened in 1893 to serve developing asphalt quarries at the terminus of the line. By 1899, the SP was drilling in the nearby McKittrick and Belleridge oil fields. At this time the field contained 17 producing wells. The following August tank cars began to roll off the branch in increasing numbers.

In the Kern River territory, east of Bakersfield, which the Santa Fe had pioneered in 1899, there were by the end of August 1900, 134 wells and production approached 1,000 barrels a day. The SP rapidly pushed a branch line into the area during the summer of 1900 from a connection on the valley mainline a short distance north of Bakersfield at Oil Junction. When completed in November 1900, this spur provided an eagerly awaited signal for a boom in production. In a short time the branch required continuous service day and night by two switch and two road crews. Fifteen stations, all tank car loading spurs, clustered along the 5.7 mile branch. Twelve more were located along the Porque Branch, an extension wyeing off at Treadwell Junction and continuing on up Sacramento Gulch about two more miles.

Production of oil on the Kern River Branch jumped from 960 carloads in December 1900 to 1,700 by July of the following year. In September 1901, production stood at an incredible 2,000 carloads. Of the 2,364 carloads shipped in November, between 800 and 850 were for the SP's consumption and nearly 300 for the Santa Fe. About 4,000 cars of oil per month were shipped out of Kern River

Branch in 1905. The peak of production was reached in 1907, when 16 million barrels of oil were taken from the field. During October of that year, 5,080 cars were loaded making an average of five or six trainloads per day. At this time, as many as 16 crews were working night and day spotting cars for loading. Waits Station on the Kern River spur was acknowledged to be the heaviest revenue producing station on the Southern Pacific system and much of this traffic made its way over Tehachapi Pass.

Even as the oil fields at Kern River were just beginning to realize their potential, additional oil exploration was being carried out on the West Side, some 35 miles southwest of Bakersfield. Here significant deposits were found in what was known as the Sunset fields. A railway was needed to bring in supplies and tools, as well as to carry out the production of the fields. Issac E. Blake, a man with early ties to the Continental Oil Company, took leave of his railroad promotions in the northwest to champion the cause of the Midland Pacific. This railroad was designed to move oil from the developing West Side fields up and over the mountains to the coast at Port Harford near San Luis Obispo. The scheme never materialized.

A more practical idea was forthcoming, however. On March 17, 1900, the Sunset Railroad Company was incorporated with the stated purpose of building just such a line into the West Side from a connection with the SP Mountain District mainline near Bakersfield. The Sunset from the outset was controlled by both the SP and Santa Fe, each of which held 50 percent of the outstanding stock. With considerable oil bearing lands in the West Side within their grasp, it was in their own best interests to build a railroad over which they had direct control. The organization and construction of the Sunset Railroad was under the joint supervision of William Hood, chief engineer of the SP, and R. B. Burns who served in the same capacity for Santa Fe's Coast Lines. Actual location of the initial line to Monarch (Maricopa) was carried out by S. F. Cochran and J. T. Williams, appointed locating engineer and chief engineer respectively.

Construction of the line from Gosford on the Southern Pacific's McKittrick Branch was started in April 1901 and completed and open for operation to Sunset (Hazelton) November 15, 1901. The Santa Fe took over the Sunset for the first five years of operation. The extension to Monarch was completed in 1904. Then SP assumed control in November 1906, and as was the case with the Kern River spur, capitalized on a tremendous boom in its first five years of operation.

The entrance of the railroad into the Kern River and Sunset fields had actually demoralized the industry and created a glut of oil on the market. In November 1901, following the opening of the Kern Field spur, 34 producers were pounding the streets of Bakersfield seeking buyers. It was several years before the railroads, and later pipelines, operating at capacity, were able to absorb the full production. While the new Sunset Railroad was busy, there had been no urgency to fully develop the fields that it served.

The real boom in the West Side came when rumors of impending sweeping governmental controls led to a tremendous surge of men and materials to the area. In the fall of 1909, following the formal announcement by President Taft of a new policy withdrawing oil lands from the public domain, the rush was on. The status of much of Kern County's oil lands were in doubt, but one thing was clear, possession was nine-tenth's of the law. The development of claims, in order to hold them, became the primary concern. There was a sudden glut of traffic on the Sunset road. Two passenger trains ran daily between Bakersfield and Taft. It was standing room only most of the time. Three hundred freight cars were waiting to be unloaded on sidings in the vicinity of Taft, the second largest receiving station in California in 1909.

Despite all of this frenzied activity, it was January 20, 1910, before the first convincing well was drilled. Then Union's Lakeview No. 1, a tremendous gusher, blew and flowed for 545 days producing from 8 to 10 million barrels of marketable oil. The activity in the West Side was responsible for maintaining a high level of oil related traffic over the San Joaquin Mountain District well into the second decade of the twentieth century.

The bulk of freight moving north and south along the Pacific Coast also had to contend with the Tehachapi and as the west had developed, so had this movement of freight. The Santa Fe had no alternate routing. The Southern Pacific did, but at this time was pursuing a policy of diverting northwest traffic away from its Ogden gateway connection to the long-haul Sunset Route. The existence of through shipments to and from the East were reflected in the schedules of the *Sunset Freight Limited* appearing in the timetable from the very beginning down through the 1920's. The rapid growth in the economy of southern California consumed an inordinate amount of lumber and forest products from Oregon and the Pacific Northwest. Many of these commodities could be found entrained on freights departing Bakersfield for the mountains.

Although the bulk of Southern Pacific's share in the San Joaquin Valley perishable crop moved traditionally north to Roseville, then East over the Overland Route, the SP did manage to run a few

solid perishable trains in season over the Tehachapi. The Santa Fe, once established in the valley, pursued an aggressive course in attracting perishable business. Throughout the 1910's, the Santa Fe penetrated the grape and citrus country on the east side of the San Joaquin Valley between Fresno and Porterville. Here they generated a tremendous amount of business, all of which had to go south over the Tehachapi. The two roads went into partnership in the summer of 1923 in order to open up the area southeast of Bakersfield. The Arvin Branch, extending from the Mountain District mainline at Magunden, was completed to DiGiorgio July 14th, and reached Arvin August 7th of that same year. The branch was run on an alternate year operating scheme devised between the two roads. This section, known as the Kern Mesa, was particularly suited to citriculture and the growing of grapes. Bakersfield was a marshalling point for this traffic and both roads maintained extensive icing facilities there. The perishable rush would start up in July with the canteloupes and watermelons, and continue on with grapes in late August. The grapes would peak in November just in time for the citrus rush. As with the returning lumber cars, there was a considerable amount of unprofitable backhaul in the perishable business. Virtually all westward movements of refrigerator cars in the Tehachapi were empties with solid strings of the colorful orange and yellow cars returning to the valley in advance of each season. The exception to this rule were the banana trains.

Unique to the SP, earlier versions of these legendary banana trains ran through from the Port of New Orleans to points on the Pacific Coast, in many sections, as far north as Seattle. A banana loading facility was located in southern California in the early 1920's. When one of the ships belonging to United Fruit Company's "Great White Fleet" arrived at the wharves in San Pedro from Panama, it wasn't too long before a number of banana trains were on the road. Generally limited to approximately 25 cars each, these trains were usually double-headed and allowed passenger train speeds in all but the most steeply graded territory.

Although the perishable trains had preferential treatment, there were no fast freight trains as such. Until the threat of competing highways began to be felt in the late 1920's and early 1930's, the Southern Pacific was content to move their tonnage on non-expedited schedules. The Santa Fe trains, although traditionally lighter and faster, didn't move all that fast either. Eight to ten hours were required to move a train the 68 miles over the mountains to Mojave during the busy season. Freights departing Mojave or Bakersfield (scheduled for the joint track Tehachapi line) were dispatched, as near as practicable, at two hour intervals in order to avoid interfering with passenger trains. As the volume of traffic continued to rise, this scheme became impractical. There were just too many freight trains awaiting clearance before tackling the mountains, and they began to clog the yards at Bakersfield and Mojave.

In 1901, six freight schedules appeared in the timetable for the joint track; Nos. 243 and 244, the *Sunset Freight Limited,* Nos. 241 and 242, a scheduled SP freight, and Nos. 133 and 134, a listed Santa Fe tonnage train. Although the numbers changed from time to time, the quantity of schedules remained the same up until World War I. Only on rare occasions would there be a following section of any of these schedules. All the excess traffic usually ran as an extra movement. During World War I, however, things were quite hectic and with the United States Railroad Administration running the railroads, more schedules were introduced into the timetable and the practice of running sections instigated. It was at this time that Santa Fe freight trains lost their own schedule numbers (for operating purposes) and trains of either road were run on published SP schedules. This practice was to continue for as long as the Tehachapi line was operated under timetable and train order rules.

The Mountain District, as a general rule, was not a major traffic generator in itself. One of the larger shippers was just outside of Bakersfield where in 1909, the Edison Land & Water Company had formed a citrus colony and set about covering the Kern Mesa with orange groves. Packing sheds began to accumulate at Edison. In season, an engine was sent up daily from Bakersfield to perform local switching and bring back the loads for icing. The Washington Navels at Edison were among the first of the season with the picking beginning in November and continuing on through February.

The fertile grasslands and prairies in the mountain valleys of the Tehachapi Range had attracted sheepmen to the region as early as 1872. It was in July of 1899 that the first carloads of sheep were loaded at Tehachapi, and the flocks continued to grow. In 1919, Kern County ranked number one in the state for sheep raising with a count of 239,503 head. The county was also number one that year in cattle as well, maintaining 156,394 head. The handling of stock cars on the mountain was a common occurrence with the loading being accomplished at most points on the line.

There were other less significant operations that required a car or two. At Tamar spur, lime, obtained in nearby Tweeder Canyon, was fired in kilns at trackside, then loaded into gondolas. About a mile above Tamar was the Quarry Spur. Here materials

were obtained for railroad construction and highway subgrade. At Woodford, a carload of cinnabar was obtained from time to time. Cinnabar is mercuric chloride, a heavy bright red material whose principal refined product is mercury. Tehachapi had several fruit sheds. Bartlett pears had been set out in the surrounding valley in 1910 and by 1920 about 125 cars a season were being shipped from this station. The land around Palmdale was also being cultivated for pears. In 1920, several hundred cars of the fruit originated there. The kilns of the Summit Lime Company were located at Tehachapi with the raw material coming from nearby Antelope Canyon. Two miles east of Summit, was Proctor Lake from where quantities of salt were obtained at one time. This material was loaded into cars at Salt Spur. Aside from a few scattered lemon sheds and an olive oil plant located east of the San Fernando Tunnel, this was the extent of the local traffic on the Mountain District. That is except for the traffic generated in the period from 1907 through 1914, by of all things, the city of Los Angeles.

Growing at record rates since the introduction of the railroads in the 1870's, Los Angeles was, by the turn-of-the-century, on the verge of a serious water shortage. There simply was not enough of the vital fluid available locally to provide for its burgeoning population. The city had grown from 11,000 inhabitants in 1880 to 102,000 by 1900 and, incredibly, was expected to triple that figure by 1910. To alleviate the problem, the city's chief engineer, William Mulholland, envisioned a series of canals or aqueducts with pumping plants running over nearly 250 miles of desolate country. The aqueduct would then tap the drainage of the sparsely populated Owen's Valley on the eastern slope of the Sierra Nevada Mountains. The drainage of the Owens River was figured at 124,929 acre feet of water in Inyo and Mono counties. The necessary land was acquired and the hotly contested project funded. The aqueduct took five years to complete (1908-1913) and in the process generated a terrific revenue for the Southern Pacific. So much so as to cause the construction of 118 miles of new railroad northeast out of Mojave.

During the summer of 1907, a huge cement plant was constructed by the city of Los Angeles in the Tehachapi Valley. Its purpose was to supply the needs of the aqueduct project. The plant, located along the SP mainline 2.5 miles east of Summit had a capacity initially of 12,000 barrels daily. The site had been chosen due to its close proximity to suitable deposits of limestone along White Rock Creek immediately north of the mill site. At first, however, due to legal problems, the limestone was obtained from the south quarry about six miles

Los Angeles Aqueduct construction camp at Cantil, circa 1910. — LOS ANGELES DEPARTMENT OF WATER & POWER

Temporary Southern Pacific depot at Cantil, as it looked in 1910. — LOS ANGELES DEPARTMENT OF WATER & POWER

The Red Rock Railroad was built under contract by the Southern Pacific to aid in the construction of the Los Angeles Aqueduct. — LOS ANGELES DEPARTMENT OF WATER & POWER

southwest of the mill which was reached by a 5.25 mile narrow-gauge railroad and 4,700 feet of aerial tramway. In 1912, the Cuddeback Ledge area in Antelope Canyon was opened up, the railroad extended to the new site and the tramway abandoned. Later this operation was abandoned when the White Rock Creek deposits became available and the two-foot gauge railroad to the south was

ripped up. As long as it was in use, the route paralleled the SP to the north from the plant before crossing under the SP near Sullivan's Spur and heading for the mountains to the south.

A complete town was erected at the mill including 21 dwellings, six frame tent houses, seven bunk houses, a school house, a mess hall and kitchen, a hospital and general store. Although named Aqueduct at first, the railroad adopted the name Monolith for its agency which received shipments of over one and a quarter million barrels of cement during the life of the aqueduct project. All of this material had the short rail haul of 17.5 miles to Mojave before it was dispatched to various points along the aqueduct where needed. The city of Los Angeles continued a small scale commercial operation of the plant after the giant project was completed. It was then sold in 1920 to the Monolith Portland Cement Company who expanded the operation considerably and the firm continues to run it today.

Studies were made to determine the best way to transport the necessary construction materials and supplies for the aqueduct over the 130-mile long haul north out of Mojave. Teams of animals were considered, but the area was unoccupied desert in which very little forage or water could be obtained. A railroad was clearly required and overtures were made to both the Santa Fe and Southern Pacific about the construction of one. Even the Western Pacific was approached, but the SP was the only interested party. A contract was signed on April 10, 1908 with the Southern Pacific for the construction of the railroad and for the transportation of local and transcontinental freight connected with the project.

The railroad, a branch line extending north out of Mojave 100 miles by city survey, was increased to 118 miles by SP engineers seeking an easier gradient over the El Paso Mountains near the present station of Searles. Actual construction of the railroad commenced at Mojave in May 1908 and was completed to a connection with SP's Nevada & California Railway subsidiary at Owenyo on October 22, 1910. Although grading was light, the construction of this line was a grueling task because of the arid terrain and harsh temperatures encountered. Water was a very real problem along the branch and only two significant wells were located on the new line. One at Cantil and the other at Haiwee. Due to the requirements of the city, the branch had an abnormal number of "wye" tracks for its length, which were located at Linnie, Searles, Garlock, Mabel and Owenyo. With the detour made by SP engineers over the El Paso Mountains, it was necessary for the city to construct nine miles of railroad from Cantil up Red Rock Canyon to the site of the aqueduct. Exceedingly

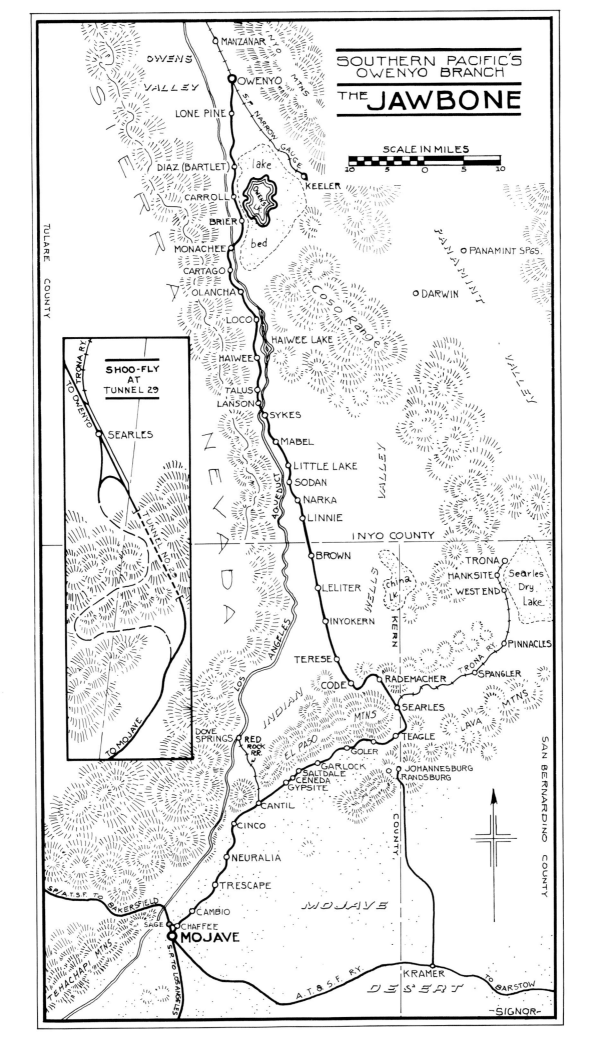

SOUTHERN PACIFIC'S
OWENYO BRANCH

THE **JAWBONE**

SCALE IN MILES
10   5   0   5   10

SHOO-FLY
AT
TUNNEL 29

43

-SIGNOR-

sandy soil in this area made freighting with teams impractical. A contract was entered into with the SP to build a line known as the Red Rock Railroad, in September 1908. The nine miles were completed in January the following year and operated continuously for 22 months prior to its abandonment and dismantling by the SP in September 1910.

It wasn't too long after aqueduct construction was underway that a grading crew unearthed a Sabertooth Tiger's jawbone in a canyon north of Cantil. The place became known as Jawbone Canyon and soon the entire railroad, although officially known as the Owenyo Branch, became known as the "Jawbone."

During the time the aqueduct was abuilding, the branch hummed with activity. A cutoff built from Sage on the mainline out to Chaffee on the branch allowed trains of cement destined for the branch to bypass Mojave. In 1913 the last of the temporary camps erected by the city of Los Angeles were hauled out and things settled down to two diminutive trains a day each way. The mixed trains, Nos. 401 and 402, traveled the line at night in order to effect connections with other trains on either end of the branch. A daily local freight was run as an extra up one day and down the next with an on duty time at Mojave of about 10:30 in the morning. For many years prior to the depression Consolidation No. 2553 was the regular power on the run. Fitted with a special lubricator designed by her crew, the engine was kept up with particular pride and it was always in immaculate condition. The boiler jacket of Russia iron was cleaned regularly with lye and was said to shine like the proverbial Negro's heel.

Departing Mojave with a handful of cars, including two tank cars used exclusively for extra water, the No. 2553 steamed out to Cantil, about 23 miles, where the engine and water cars were filled to capacity. Some switching was done at Saltdale and Searles, then it was on its way up to Brown, the half-way point. A section crew maintained a ranch

house there where the crew would obtain a meal. Children belonging to the workers there, who helped serve the meal, caused the crew members to speculate on the difficulties of raising a family in this remote location — it being so quiet that it was impossible to even raise a disturbance.

On the Jawbone, there were two significant grades of 1.75 percent. It was a tough climb from Saltdale, to the tunnel west of Searles, and from Little Lake up to Haiwee. If tonnage was heavy, such as during winter months when sheep were being loaded at Owenyo, a helper would assist the local as far as Haiwee from Mojave. Haiwee was the last place on the branch to obtain water and once again all tanks were filled to capacity. At Cartago, a five million dollar plant was located on Owens Lake to extract soda and potash. These commodities were then shipped to Japan via San Francisco. The local crew laid over at Owenyo then repeated the trip back to Mojave. During the night an engine watchman siphoned water from the tank cars, to keep the engine in steam, as there was no water available at Owenyo.

The prospects of heavier freight business on the Jawbone was realized in 1914 when the Trona Railway — 36 odd miles of standard gauge line —was built out to Searles Dry Lake from Searles Station. Machinery was hauled in for the American Trona Corporation. By 1916 the firm had the first unit of a plant in operation to tap the borax deposits of the lake bed. It was not until March 1918 that a refinery at San Pedro was equipped to handle the ore. The commodities obtained at Trona — borax, potash, soda ash and salt cake, all play a part in everyday consumer items. As soon as the refinery was in production, the Trona Railway business became so heavy that the SP was forced to put on a Searles Turn to handle the traffic. Because of the weight of the shipments, "Mudhens" (4000 class Mallets) were frequently employed in this service.

Engine No. 1434, a regular locomotive on the "Jawbone" passenger run, with "Pop" Fuller at the throttle, meet disaster at Monachee in 1910. The washout was caused by the collapse and rupture of the aqueduct. "Pop" lost his life in the incident. — LOS ANGELES DEPARTMENT OF WATER AND POWER

The Mojave Green rattlesnake — the most deadly of its breed. — F. A. NEJEDLY — OLA MAE FORCE COLLECTION

Activity at Mojave centered around the depot. The station building housed the ticket office and waiting rooms of the railroad, the telegraph office for the dispatching of trains, as well as, a hotel, lunch room, kitchen, and store rooms operated by the Fred Harvey Company. The two structures south of the depot were the ice house and beer house, so essential to such an outpost in the desert. The freight depot was north of the station and out of view of these two scenes. Mojave served as a terminus for both Santa Fe and Southern Pacific helper crews, and SP freight crews working out of Los Angeles and Bakersfield. Following extensive double-tracking on the hill in 1926, the crews returned to through runs between Bakersfield and Los Angeles on the Southern Pacific. Santa Fe crews continued to run through from Bakersfield to Barstow. (ABOVE) Freight No. 263 is seen pulling into the No. 1 yard track to take on helpers shortly after the changeover. — V. C. CIPPOLA COLLECTION (BELOW) View of the station with the town of Mojave in the background lined with boarding houses, restaurants, and bars. — SOUTHERN PACIFIC COLLECTION

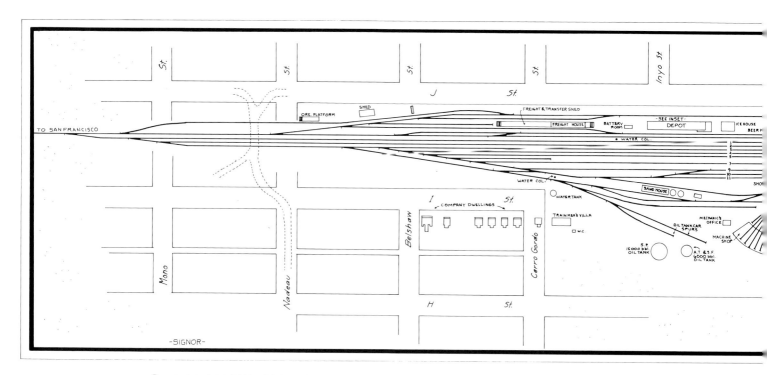

"Mojave Zephyrs" occasionally blew with such velocity as to blow off the roundhouse roof, however, the damage in this 1915 view is attributed to a roof fire. — VERNON SAPPERS COLLECTION

Mallet No. 4034 awaits another call on the mountain at the Mojave engine facility. — HIENIE BOCK COLLECTION

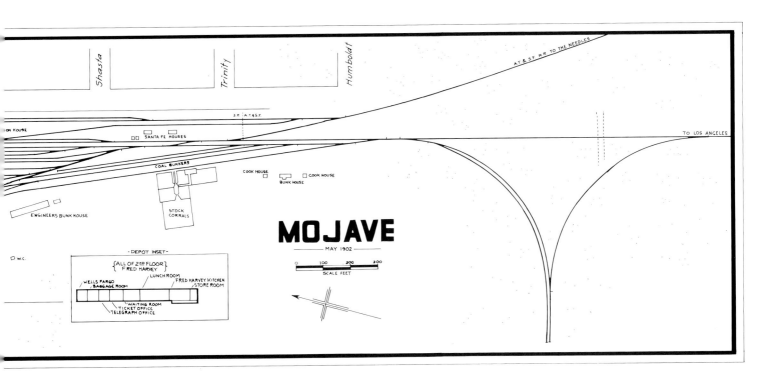

MOJAVE
— MAY 1902 —

Shasta

Trinity

Humbolat

S.P. A.T.S.F.

AT & S F RR TO THE NEEDLES

TO LOS ANGELES

ION HOUSE

SANTA FE HOUSES

COAL BUNKERS

COOK HOUSE

COOK HOUSE

BUNK HOUSE

ENGINEERS BUNK HOUSE

STOCK CORRALS

W.C.

- DEPOT INSET -

{ALL OF 2ND FLOOR} FRED HARVEY

LUNCH ROOM

FRED HARVEY KITCHEN STORE ROOM

WELLS FARGO BAGGAGE ROOM

WAITING ROOM
TICKET OFFICE
TELEGRAPH OFFICE

100   200   300
SCALE FEET

Mojave Engine House   12-14-20

Most of the concrete work had been performed in erecting a new four-stall engine
house at Mojave, when these photographs
were made December 14, 1920. — BOTH
VERNON SAPPERS COLLECTION

Mojave Engine House   12-14-20

mojave, yard

The storms of January 1915 have left a mantle of dusting snow on the depot and yards, at Mojave, the surrounding desert, and the Tehachapi range in the distance. Noted for its blistering summer heat, Mojave could also experience winter extremes. With the "Mojave Zephyrs" ever present, blizzard conditions were common. — BOTH F. A. NEJEDLY — OLA MAE FORCE COLLECTION

Santa Fe's Arizona Division crews who worked the Tehachapi grade had Barstow, 71.4 miles east of Mojave, as their eastern terminus. This overall view of Barstow was taken from the southwest end of town on January 23, 1921, by Santa Fe locomotive engineer R. P. Middlebrook. — STAN KISTLER COLLECTION

Railroader/photographer R. P. Middlebrook was on hand during the mid-1930's to record the expansion and changes that had taken place in the Barstow yard within a ten year period. The Santa Fe's Barstow station and Harvey House hotel/restaurant may be seen at the left just over the viaduct. — STAN KISTLER COLLECTION

Mountain District locomotives radiate from the turntable at the Lamar Street roundhouse in 1902. The facility was located on the east side of the Los Angeles River at the junction of Alhambra Avenue and Lamar Street. — DONALD DUKE COLLECTION

The roundhouse at River Station yard. This was the first engine facility used by the Southern Pacific at Los Angeles. The original River Station may be seen in the background to the right of the roundhouse. — DONALD DUKE COLLECTION

The Lamar Street roundhouse — also known as the Alhambra Avenue roundhouse or the "shops" — as photographed from the air about 1924. Today this area is entirely occupied by the Southern Pacific's Los Angeles intermodal facility. — DONALD DUKE COLLECTION

A variety of interesting rolling stock fills the River Station yard, southern terminus of the San Joaquin Mountain District. The yard, shown above, stretched along San Fernando Road, now North Spring Street. This yard and a combination of two smaller yards served as SP's main freight terminal in Los Angeles until Taylor yard was built in the 1920's. — DONALD DUKE COLLECTION (LEFT) The original River Station was torn down to provide more yard tracks. The second River Station was nothing more than a store front on San Fernando Road. The structure served as SP's Los Angeles passenger station until 1888 when the Arcade Station was built. — VERNON SAPPERS COLLECTION

After 1888, Mountain District passenger schedules originated and terminated at the Arcade Station. The barn-like structure was located off Alameda Street between Fourth and Sixth streets. (RIGHT) The Arcade Station was replaced by Central Station built a bit west on an adjoining site in 1914 as shown in this scene — VERNON SAPPERS COLLECTION (BELOW) Two switchers work the north end of Arcade Station which was a near duplicate of SP's Sacramento Station. — JAMES H. HARRISON COLLECTION

The first section of the *San Joaquin Flyer* has just arrived from Bakersfield at the Central Station on February 8, 1921. — R. P. MIDDLEBROOK — A. S. MENKE COLLECTION

Engine No. 2914, an 1898 Schenectady product, is seen in helper service at San Fernando on July 16, 1917 — the point where extra engines were added for the stiff climb to the San Fernando tunnel and Vincent. — R. P. MIDDLEBROOK — A. S. MENKE COLLECTION

Saugus, for many years the dividing point between the San Joaquin and Los Angeles divisions and a junction of the Mountain District mainline with the Santa Paula Branch, was a point of great activity. — SOUTHERN PACIFIC

Helper crews working out of San Fernando would find themselves based at Palmdale, seen here about 1913, working for three or four days at a time pushing trains from the floor of the Antelope Valley up to Vincent. It was a harsh assignment. The settlement could offer little in the way of creature comfort because of extremes in temperature. To keep cool, crews sought shelter in holes dug in the ground in the center of the wye. The men counted the days for their relief. — SOUTHERN PACIFIC COLLECTION

Lancaster, an important water stop midway across the desert, had a typical Southern Pacific style depot. — SOUTHERN PACIFIC

Rosamond, originally Sand Creek, had a novel depot structure when this photograph was taken in 1913. — SOUTHERN PACIFIC

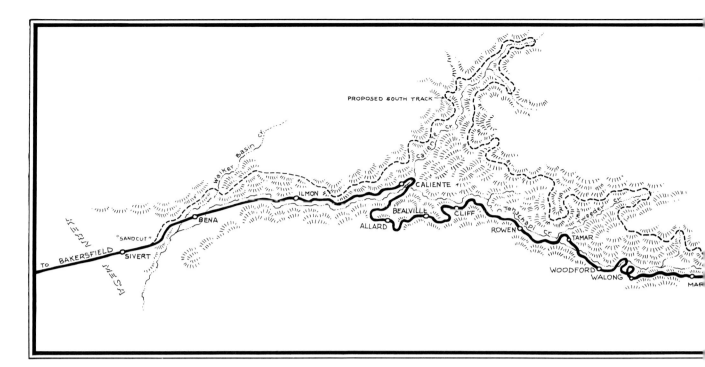

Facing a rising tide of traffic washing over the Tehachapi, railroad officials made plans to cope with the situation. With delays becoming excessive clearly something had to be done to expedite moves in this strategic bottleneck. The first order of business was to increase the capacity of the existing track. Old sidings were lengthened, second sidings installed at Caliente, Bealville, Rowen and Woodford. Many new passing tracks were built including Proctor, between Summit and Cameron and Lexin, formerly a spur between Rosamond and Mojave — both in 1901. Today Lexin is known as Ansel. Westward freight trains departing Bena would on occasion stall out on Sandcut hill. The usual procedure was to double the train to Wade (Edison after 1904), some six miles distant. To save time, a siding called Treves was built on level land just west of the top of the hill in 1903 to facilitate any doubling that might be necessary. This name was changed to Sivert on January 1, 1912, and is at the present time (1983) the site of the Sandcut crossover. By 1907, operations had escalated to the point where two more sidings were needed, at Taft (quickly renamed Magunden), and Fleta outside of Mojave. The siding on the loop itself was built in 1909 and named Walong in honor of District Roadmaster W. A. Long. Previously a spur called Fox had been located there. Sidings were built in 1910 at Grable (later LaRose), between Cameron and Warren, and at Allard, between Caliente and Bealville. In 1913, the spur at Cliff was extended into a siding.

Further improvements were effected in this period by the installation of an automatic block signal system utilizing Union Switch & Signal style B lower quadrant semaphores between Kern Junction and Mojave in 1905. At this time signals were also installed between Saugus and Tunnel. These were augmented by signals between Palmdale and Saugus through Soledad Canyon in 1908. Mountain District signaling was complete when the gap between Mojave and Palmdale, across the desert, was installed in 1909.

During the 1903 to 1913 period, the Southern Pacific investigated the question of electrification of the Tehachapi grade, as well as the Siskiyou and Sierra crossings. At this time similar electrification projects were being undertaken in Europe and the United States. Electrification of mainlines was the vogue. In a preliminary study, the mainline was to utilize a third-rail contact method with an overhead system in the yards at Bakersfield and Mojave. Third-rail was specified because of clearance problems in the many tunnels. In order to provide a flexible unit it was proposed to use an electric locomotive capable of handling a train unit of 500 tons, with as many electric engines per train as its weight would require. With the average freight train eastbound (towards Mojave) at the time weighing 2,000 tons (for which four Consolidations or their equivalent in Mallets were required on the north slope) it would appear that the electric locomotives were being figured to be roughly equal to the capacity of a Consolidation in mountain service.

The project never got off the ground. Many reasons were cited. The voltage limitations of the third-rail system and resulting impact on horse-power development was a significant factor. Although it was proposed to construct a power plant in the Kern River oil field near SP oil wells and water, it would have been costly to erect and

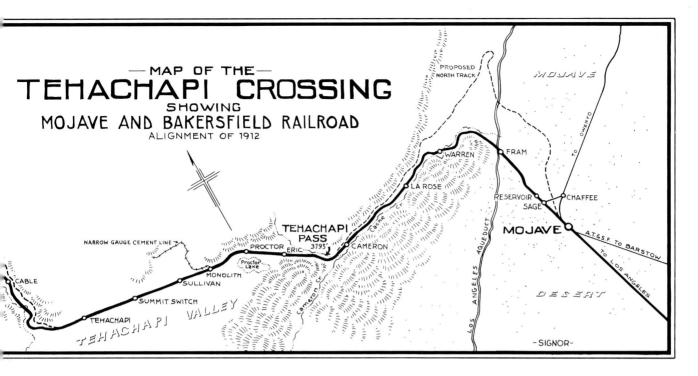

MAP OF THE
TEHACHAPI CROSSING
SHOWING
MOJAVE AND BAKERSFIELD RAILROAD
ALIGNMENT OF 1912

- SIGNOR -

maintain the transmission lines, contact system and other paraphernalia necessary for electric operation. The area was utterly devoid of available electric power. There was also the problems on how to handle Santa Fe's trains. Just too many questions to be ironed out satisfactorily. But perhaps the prevailing factor in the scrubbing of the idea, was the attitude of the operating department. The steam locomotive was strictly interchangeable, and could be moved from division to division, as the necessity for varying motive power capacity developed — by reason of crop movement or other factors. The electric locomotive would be limited to electrified trackage.

There the matter rested. The idea of electrification was never carried out on any of SP's mountain districts, although suburban passenger operations in the Oakland and Portland areas were eventually electrified.

Another panacea for heavy congestion was the installation of double-track. Unfortunately the terrain on the north slope of the Tehachapi, with its extremes in curvature and many tunnels rendered double-tracking virtually impossible. While the desert side of the pass was more readily adaptable to double-track, it shared the north slope's severe grades, and the grade was as much a problem as the capacity of the track. Accordingly, at the suggestion of Julius Kruttschnitt — then director of maintenance of way and operations — Southern Pacific in the spring of 1910 sent teams into the field, under the direction of William Hood, to locate a 1.5 percent line between the vicinity of Bena and Tehachapi, and from Cameron to Mojave.

This alignment, which became known as the Mojave & Bakersfield Railroad of 1912, departed radically from the existing line of track. Commencing at a point near Sivert, the survey began climbing to the east along the bluffs above Bena, Ilmon and Caliente, then up Caliente Creek several miles as far as Devil's Canyon, before looping across the creek and turning back. Another horseshoe was necessary in Montgomery Canyon before turning south and crossing the divide into Tehachapi Creek Canyon high above Marcel. The existing grade was then rejoined near the headwaters of Tehachapi Creek about a mile west of the station at Tehachapi. This line, 45 miles in length, was to have 5 sidings, 27 tunnels and 15 viaducts.

No alternate tracks were proposed from this point up and across the Tehachapi Valley until the narrows just west of Cameron. Here, the 1.5 percent line departed the existing alignment once again, following Cache Creek Canyon at a higher elevation for several miles before heading easterly into the desert near Warren. About five miles out, the line looped back in the direction of Mojave. This section, 15.4 miles long, was to have two sidings. In operation, the proposed line was to accommodate eastbound traffic only on the north slope and westbound traffic only on the desert side thereby providing uphill trains the advantage of a lesser grade.

In May of 1912, the scheme was laid before Santa Fe officials who heartily concurred that something needed to be done, although just exactly what it should be was a matter for dispute. The proposed grade would require heavy excavation on the north slope and quantities of land would have to be acquired — both costly propositions. Negotiations between the two roads, both cash short at the time, as to the merits of the project dragged into the following spring. One of the principal causes of congestion had been the shipments of oil with the SP dragging 5,000 barrels a day and the Santa Fe 12,500 barrels over the mountains in slow heavy trains. The construction of a petroleum pipeline between Bakersfield and Mojave would eliminate these trains and reduce traffic flow over the hill enough to forestall building a second track at a fraction of the cost. This plan made sense and a pipeline was authorized and constructed in 1913. Later when traffic levels again rose to the saturation point, a less costly plan of double-tracking as much as possible of the existing grade was adopted.

Rumors surfaced periodically in the *Bakersfield Californian* that the Santa Fe, wishing to secure its own line over the Tehachapi Mountains free of the restrictions imposed by working with the Southern Pacific, had surveyed and was intending to build an alternate line over the barrier between Bakersfield and Muroc. The reputed line approximated the 1897 Santa Fe Pacific proposal over Brite's Summit. It was said that the SP was none too happy about the idea and threatened to cancel Santa Fe's lease the day they broke ground on the project. Amazingly, these rumors fell short of what the Santa Fe management was actually contemplating.

Grapevine Canyon, a rugged and steep-walled crevasse leading to 4,213 foot Tejon Pass, about 40 miles due south of Bakersfield, had evaded any serious attempts at railroad location since the Southern Pacific's infancy. Because of the canyon's tortuous ascent, there had been the suggestion of a cog railroad in the late 19th century. There was also the veiled threat by Claus Spreckles of the Bakersfield & Los Angeles Railroad in 1898. In the late summer and fall of 1913, the *Bakersfield California* made scattered mention of yet another proposal. The Los Angeles & San Joaquin Valley Railroad Company, articles of incorporation of which were filed August 27th, proposed to construct 135 miles of railroad from Olig on the Sunset Railway Company southwest to Glendale by way of Tejon Pass — all of which was to be electrified. At first it was reported that the incorporators, T. E. Gibbon, W. C. Scheton, J. E. Stephens and J. R. Colburn Jr., were allied with the Santa Fe or Western Pacific. Later it was rumored to be the Union Pacific. At any rate, the scheme quietly faded from the public eye that fall without the slightest bit of surveying being done for the project.

In the early 1920's, however, the Santa Fe set about developing a new shorter route between Los Angeles and northern California. It was difficult for the road to compete with the Southern Pacific in this corridor with their line via Cajon Pass and Barstow fully 111 miles longer between Los Angeles and Bakersfield alone. A number of alignments were figured. Indeed, the entire region bordered by the east side of the San Gabriels and south side of the Tehachapi Range was criss-crossed with possible rights of ways. One line diverged from Summit on Cajon Pass northwesterly towards Gorman and Tejon Pass closely following today's SP Palmdale Cutoff — a distance of 239 miles. Another route departed Los Angeles following the SP Valley line through San Fernando, then to Castaic where it diverged through Elizabeth Lake Canyon, the Antelope Valley and Tehachapi Pass for Bakersfield — a distance of 162 miles.

The proposal that received the most attention, however, was the 2.2 percent Tejon Pass grade surveyed in the spring and summer of 1923 by L. F. Barnum and party. Briefly stated, this alignment commenced at Dayton Avenue in Los Angeles and closely followed the SP through the San Fernando Valley to Sylmar, then through Castaic, Gorman, Lebec, Tejon Pass, threaded Grapevine Canyon to Wheeler Ridge, and on to Bakersfield. The scheme envisioned 15 tunnels — the longest of which was to be 17,600 feet allowing entrance into the Piru Gorge from the south. In order to cut costs, modifications were tried in critical areas at 3.0 and 3.5 percent. This brazen scheme could shave the distance from Los Angeles to Bakersfield to 128 miles — a savings of 153 miles in all via Cajon Pass and Barstow. A considerable amount of time and money was spent on developing this line and the Santa Fe even went as far as to secure certain strategic parcels of property near Gorman and Lebec. It seems incredible that this plan would have been contemplated to such a degree. In the intervening years the why's and wherefore's of its conception and its eventual abandonment have been lost to obscurity.

While all these schemes to relieve congestion in the mountains were being proposed, traffic levels in the Tehachapi continued to rise unremittingly. The job of train dispatching on the Mountain District was complex. Telegraph offices for the movement of trains numbered ten in the Tehachapi in 1901, with seven more as far as Saugus. These were located at Bakersfield, Kern Junction, Pampa (Bena), Caliente, Bealville, Keene (Woodford), Girard (Marcel), Tehachapi, Cameron, Mojave, Rosamond, Lancaster, Palmdale, Vincent, Ravenna, Lang and Saugus. Traffic densities were increasing, however, and by December 1913, the *Southern Pacific Bulletin* was reporting a new record of 996 cars moved over the Tehachapi grade in 71 train movements in 24 hours requiring 182 train orders. It is interesting to note this was accomplished with the use of 81 locomotives including nine new SP Mallets, five new Santa Fe

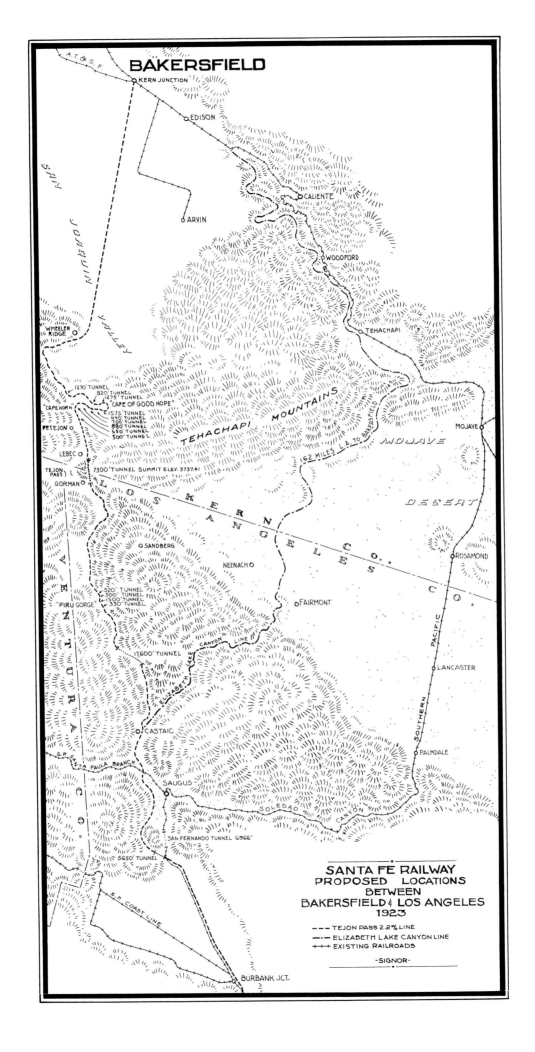

BAKERSFIELD

A.T.&S.F.

KERN JUNCTION

EDISON

ARVIN

CALIENTE

WOODFORD

SAN JOAQUIN HILLS

TEJON VALLEY

WHEELER
RIDGE

TEHACHAPI

TEHACHAPI MOUNTAINS

MOJAVE

1270' TUNNEL
820 TUNNEL
1275 TUNNEL
"CAPE OF GOOD HOPE"
1575 TUNNEL
440 TUNNEL
700 TUNNEL
880 TUNNEL
550 TUNNEL
500' TUNNEL

CAPE HORN

PETEJON

LEBEC

TEJON
PASS

GORMAN

7300' TUNNEL SUMMIT ELEV. 3737.41

162 MILES L.A. TO BAKERSFIELD

MOJAVE DESERT

LOS ANGELES CO.

KERN CO.

SANDBERG

NEENACH

FAIRMONT

ROSAMOND

VENTURA CO.

PIRU GORGE

520' TUNNEL
500 TUNNEL
1500' TUNNEL
330' TUNNEL

17,600' TUNNEL

ELIZABETH LAKE CANYON LINE

LANCASTER

PALMDALE

PACIFIC

SOUTHERN

CASTAIC

S.P. STA PAULA BRANCH

SAUGUS

SOLEDAD CANYON

SAN FERNANDO TUNNEL 6966'

5650' TUNNEL

S.P. COAST LINE

SANTA FE RAILWAY
PROPOSED LOCATIONS
BETWEEN
BAKERSFIELD & LOS ANGELES
1923

- - - TEJON PASS 2.2% LINE
-·- ELIZABETH LAKE CANYON LINE
+++ EXISTING RAILROADS

-SIGNOR-

BURBANK JCT.

Mallets, four new Santa Fe 2-10-2's, with the balance comprising heavy Consolidations plus the passenger engines.

By 1916, with the addition of telegraph offices at Edison, Sivert, Rowen, La Rose, Warren and Fram, the number of Train Order offices in the Tehachapi rose to 16. The company was forced to employ another dispatcher on each shift. In the fall of 1916, SP company records indicated that in a 24 hour period, an average of at least 50 train movements occurred between Bakersfield and Mojave — eight of them passenger — requiring 70 and frequently between 90 and 105 train orders per trick. The yards at Bakersfield and Mojave became choked with freight trains since it was considered unwise to release trains onto the district in closer than two-hour intervals in order to avoid conflicting with passenger trains. Sidings at Oban, Denis, and Berlin were laid during this period in response to the alarming increases in traffic. Berlin was soon renamed Paris out of sympathy for the French.

The war in Europe curtailed some passenger service, but freight traffic continued to spiral. The idea of double-track was staved off temporarily in 1913 by the installation of a petroleum pipeline and later by Federal control of the railroads. The problem was pressed once again by San Joaquin Division Superintendent F. M. Worthington who, in the summer of 1920, pointed out that in addition to the deluge of freight trains during the summer months, 16 passenger trains were regularly negotiating the congested rails of Tehachapi Pass in a 24 hour period. The delay to freight trains was intolerable, frequently taking 10 to 14 hours to move across the 68 mile district. Eight to ten hours for a light engine to return to Bakersfield from Summit was not uncommon. Apparently Worthington's pleas for action were convincing enough, because shortly thereafter, plans were prepared and funds made available to undertake double-tracking portions of the line.

The first section of second track to be laid in place was between Kern Junction Tower and Magunden, completed on February 12, 1922. This was followed by the section from Magunden to Sivert, completed in December 1923. Double-tracking had also been completed across the Tehachapi Valley between the town of Tehachapi and Cameron. It was at Cameron that the grade of the Mojave & Bakersfield line was to depart from the existing alignment. While the M & B RR grade on the north slope was a dead issue by this time, the merits of building the section between Cameron and Mojave were still being debated. Although local engineering and operating officials argued on its behalf, in the end, the second track was laid

beside the existing mainline between Cameron and Mojave. Work was completed on this section June 30, 1924.

The double-track couldn't have come at a more opportune time as traffic continued to rise to the extent that the *Bulletin* was able to report in September 1925 yet another record. That month 41,877 cars were moved over the Tehachapi Mountains averaging 1,396 cars daily. There was a total of 1,131 trains in the district that month with 400 refrigerator cars being moved westward daily out of Los Angeles. During this period, 350 to 400 train orders constituted a normal days work. On one day, September 20th, seven detoured Union Pacific passenger trains boosted the trains handled to 47 with a total of 110 separate train movements, including light engines. Worthington's successor to the superintendency of the division, A. F. Bowles, was led to remark in the *Bulletin* that, "The performance in the last two weeks in train operation, I will say, can not be excelled anywhere in the United States." The fact that the railroad was able to absorb this traffic was directly attributable to the second track and the emergence of the heavy 2-10-2 locomotives. The situation had improved so much that by early 1926, Southern Pacific crews were again running the whole 168 miles between Los Angeles and Bakersfield without changing at Mojave.

Through the foresight of Colonel Porter Turner, retired San Joaquin Division Chief Dispatcher (now deceased), a copy of the dispatcher's train sheet for a day in September 1927 was furnished to the Beal Memorial Library in Bakersfield and presented is a glimpse into the complexities of this fascinating and demanding joint-track operation.

DISPATCHERS RECORD OF
MOVEMENT OF TRAINS
BAKERSFIELD AND MOJAVE SUBDIVISION
SEPTEMBER 17, 1927
SAN JOAQUIN DIVISION TIMETABLE NO. 145

KEY

SP	—Southern Pacific	**Helper utilization code.**	
SFE	—Santa Fe		
mty	—empty car(s)	B-S	Bakersfield to Summit
lds	—loaded car(s)	C-S	Caliente to Summit
M	—unit of measure	M-E	Mojave to Eric
	1000 lbs.	B-T	Bakersfield to
p/u	—pick up		Tehachapi
s/o	—set out		
Dep.	—depart	Time	—Time required to
Arr.	—arrive		make it over district.

1st Trick Dispatcher — W. A. Glenn
2nd Trick Dispatcher — E. P. Gibson
3rd Trick Dispatcher — E. F. Braswell
Chief Dispatcher — Col. P. E. Turner

No. 60   **SP West Coast Limited**
3643 through, 3638 B-T. 13 cars 1691 Ms
Dep. Bakersfield 2:00 A.M.
Time — 2 hrs. 20 min.

No. 1-252   **SP Sunset Manifest Freight**
3767 through, 3638 B-S, 2624 C-S.
49 cars 4623 Ms
Dep. Bakersfield 2:45 A.M.
Time — 7 hrs. 15 min.

No. 26   **SP Owl**
3647 through, 2365 B-S. 10 cars 1450 Ms
Dep. Bakersfield 3:05 A.M.
Time — 2 hrs. 18 mins.

X 1239   Edison switcher   1239   6 mty
Dep. Bakersfield 4:15 A.M.

No. 2-252   SFE freight
1641 B-S, 3842 B-S, 1687 through.
53 lds 3 mty 2353 Ms
Dep. Kern Jct. 4:50 A.M. Time 6 hrs. 20 min.
—s/o 3   p/u 2 at Tehachapi,
p/u 1 at Monolith.

No. 3-252   SP work train
3674   8 cars 500 Ms
Dep. Bakersfield 4:50 A.M.
Arr. Tehachapi 9:15 A.M.

X 3676   Lite engine 3676, helper off No. 251.
Arr. Mojave 5:30 A.M. from Eric.

X 1635   Lite engine 1635, helper off X 1691 West.
Arr. Mojave 5:50 A.M. from Eric.

No. 1-262   SP Drag freight
3696 through, 3764 B-S, 2805 C-S.
44 lds. 4631 Ms
Dep. Bakersfield 6:15 A.M.
Time 6 hrs. 10 mins.

No. 2-262   SFE freight
3832 through, 3839 3834 B-S. 55 lds. 2393 Ms
Dep. Kern Junction 7:05 A.M.
Time 5 hrs. 50 min.

X 1675   SFE Lite engine 1675, helper off X 959 west.
Arr. Mojave 7:05 A.M. from Eric.

X 2784   SP Lite engine 2784, helper off No. 255.
Arr. Mojave 8:25 A.M. from Eric.

X 1635   SFE Lite engine 1635, helper off No. 9.
Arr. Mojave 8:32 A.M. from Eric.

No. 2   **SFE Tourist Express**
3701   6 cars 430 Ms
Dep. Kern Junction 9:10 A.M.
Time 2 hrs. 18 mins.

No. 320   SP Local freight
3689 18 lds. 1876 Ms.
Arr. Mojave 36 lds. 4094 Ms
Dep. Bakersfield 9:15 A.M.
Time 9 hrs. 50 mins.

X 2770   SP Lite engine 2770, helper off No. 321.
Arr. Mojave 9:30 A.M. from Eric.

X 1682   SFE Lite engine 1682, helper off X 1690 west.
Arr. Mojave 9:50 A.M. from Eric.

X 1675   SFE Lite engine 1675, helper off X 1681 west.
Arr. Mojave 10:20 A.M. from Eric.

No. 3-262   SFE freight
3849 through, 3846 3841 B-S.   56 lds 2626 Ms
Dep. Kern Jct. 9:30 A.M.
Time 5 hrs. 30 mins.

No. 4-262   SP Freight East Manifest 815
3709 through, 2367 3726 B-S.
46 lds 3 mty 4473 Ms
Dep. Bakersfield 10:35 A.M.
Time 5 hrs. 45 mins.

No. 58   SP passenger
4326   7 cars 681 Ms
Dep. Bakersfield 11:45 A.M.
Time 2 hrs. 30 mins.

No. 1-264   SFE freight
1677 through, 3844 3843 B-S. 56 cars 2639 Ms
Dep. Kern Jct. 12:01 P.M. Time 5 hrs.

X 2784   SP Lite engine 2784   helper off No. 263.
Arr. Mojave 1:35 P.M. from Eric.

No. 2-264   SP freight
3698 through, 2688 3638 B-S. 49 cars 4365 Ms
Dep. Bakersfield 1:55 P.M.
Time 6 hrs. 30 mins.

No. 3-264   SFE freight **GFX** Green Fruit Express
956 through, 3845 1676 B-S. 56 cars 2601 Ms
Dep. Kern Jct. 2:05 P.M. Time 7 hrs. 35 mins.

No. 4-264   SFE freight **GFX** Green Fruit Express
948 through, 3835 3840 B-S   56 cars 2625 Ms
Dep. Kern Jct. 2:30 P.M. Time 8 hrs.

No. 5-264   SFE freight **GFX** Green Fruit Express
1684 through, 3831 3830 B-S. 56 cars 2583 Ms
Dep. Kern Jct. 4:10 P.M. Time 6 hrs. 30 mins.

X 1239   SP Edison switcher 1239.
Dep. Bakersfield 4:15 P.M.

No. 52   **SP San Joaquin Flyer**
2366   6 cars 679 Ms
Dep. Bakersfield 5:10 P.M.
Time 6 hrs. 30 mins.

X 1635   SFE Lite engine 1635 with 1682, helpers
off X1688 west.
Arr. Mojave 5:10 P.M. from Eric.

X 1675   SFE Lite engine 1675, helper off x 978 west.
Arr. Mojave 5:15 P.M. from Eric.

No. 6-264   SFE freight GFX Green Fruit Express
1692 through, 3848 3838 B-S. 56 cars 2552 Ms
Dep. Kern Jct. 5:20 P.M. Time 6 hrs. 30 mins.

No. 1-258   SP freight
3690 through, 2369 3727 B-S. 37 cars 4345 Ms
Dep. Bakersfield 6:25 P.M. Time 7 hrs. 5 mins.

X 2784   SP Lite engine 2784, helper off No. 261
Arr. Mojave 7:15 P.M. from Eric.

No. 2-258   SP Freight East Manifest 916
2669 through, 3707 B-S, 2805 C-S.
49 cars 4621 Ms
Dep. Bakersfield 10:12 P.M.
Time 5 hrs. 43 mins.

X 1675   SFE Lite engine 1675, helper off X1693 west
and 1635, helper off X3833 west.
Arr. Mojave 10:20 P.M. from Eric.

No. 22   SFE Passenger
3700   5 cars 371 Ms
Dep. Kern Jct. 11:11 P.M.
Time 3 hrs. 54 mins.

X 3848   SFE Lite engines 3848 3838, helpers
          off No. 6-264
          Arr. Mojave 11:30 P.M. from Summit.

No. 56   SP **San Francisco—
          Los Angeles Passenger**
          Power not available. 8 cars 904 Ms
          Dep. Bakersfield 11:50 P.M.
          Time 3 hrs. 33 mins.

X 2369   SP Lite engine 2369, helper off No. 1-258
          Arr. Mojave 12:01 A.M. September 18
          from Summit.

X 2770   SP Lite engine 2770, helper off No. 251
          Arr. Mojave 12:05 A.M. September 18
          from Summit.

WESTBOUND

X 3803   SFE Lite engine 3803 1635 3835 3840.
          Dep. Tehachapi 1:35 A.M.
          Time 3 hrs. 55 mins.

X 956   SFE Lite engine 956 1683.
          Dep. Tehachapi 1:45 A.M.
          Time 5 hrs. 5 mins.

X 3849   SFE Lite engine 3849 1677.
          Dep. Bealville 3:38 A.M. Time 1 hr. 56 mins.

X 3669   SP drag freight
          3669 15 lds 19 mty 2304 Ms
          Dep. Tehachapi 3:50 A.M.
          Time 3 hrs. 50 mins.

No. 55   SP **Tehachapi**
          5018   9 cars 991 Ms
          Dep. Mojave 3:55 A.M. Time 2 hrs. 45 mins.

No. 251   SP freight West Manifest 816
          3707 through, 3676 M-E.
          41 lds 2 mty 4112 Ms

X 3698   SP Lite engine 3698, helper off No. 66.
          Dep. Tehachapi 4:00 A.M.
          Time 2 hrs. 50 mins.

X 1691   SFE freight
          1691 through, 1635 M-E.
          1 ld. 55 mty 1500 Ms

X 3698   SP Lite engine 3698 2805.
          Dep. Woodford 4:50 A.M.
          Time 2 hrs. 30 mins. 2805 cut Caliente.

X 5016   SP Lite engine 5016 2688 and 2365—
          helper off No. 26.
          Dep. Tehachapi 5:10 A.M.
          Time 3 hrs. 55 mins.

X 959   SFE freight
          959 through, 1675 M-E   2 lds 54 mty 1457 Ms
          Dep. Mojave 5:20 A.M. Time 6 hrs. 50 mins.

No. 255   SP Stock drag
          3675 through, 2784 M-E   7 lds 49 mty 2950 Ms
          Dep. Mojave 6:30 A.M. Time 6 hrs. 35 mins.

X 2678   SP Lite engine west 2678.
          Dep. Sivert 7:00 A.M. Time 47 mins.

No. 9   SFE **Mail & Express**
          1340 through, 1635 M-E   7 cars 480 Ms
          Dep. Mojave 7:14 A.M. Time 2 hrs. 31 mins.

X 1690   SFE Freight
          1690 through, 1682 M-E   9 lds 50 mty 1709 Ms
          Dep. Mojave 7:30 A.M. Time 7 hrs. 55 mins.

No. 321   SP local freight
          3676 through, 2770 M-E   9 lds 21 mty 2567 Ms
          Dep. Mojave 7:50 A.M. Time 12 hrs. 40 min.

X 1681   SFE freight
          1681 through, 1675 M-E   7 lds 49 mty 1728 Ms
          Dep. Mojave 8:10 A.M. Time 8 hrs. 36 mins.

X 2624   SP Lite engine 2624 to Caliente, helper
          off No. 1-252.
          Dep. Tehachapi 9:20 A.M.
          Time 3 hrs. 45 mins.

X 3755   SP Lite engine 3755, helper off 1-252.
          Dep. Tehachapi 9:30 A.M.
          Time 6 hrs. 15 mins.

X 3674   SP work train
          3674   1 car 70 Ms
          Dep. Tehachapi 10:10 A.M.
          Time 9 hrs. 7 mins.

X 3847   SFE Lite engines 3847 3848, helpers off
          No. 2/264 of 9/16.
          Dep. Woodford 10:52 A.M.
          Time 3 hrs. 27 mins.

No. 51   SP **San Joaquin Flyer**
          2366, 5 cars 570 Ms
          Dep. Mojave 11:13 A.M. Time 2 hrs. 20 mins.

X 3842   SFE lite engines 3842 1687, off No. 2-252
          and SP Lite engines 3764 and 2805, off
          No. 1-262. 2805 cut Caliente.
          Dep. Tehachapi 11:25 A.M.
          Time 6 hrs. 25 mins.

X 3839   SFE lite engine 3839 3834, helpers
          off No. 2-262.
          Dep. Tehachapi 11:55 A.M.
          Time 5 hrs. 55 mins.

No. 263   SP freight West Manifest 917
          3675 through, 2784 M-E   13 lds
          11 mty 6075 Ms
          Dep. Mojave 12:01 P.M. Time 5 hrs. 54 mins.

X 1239   SP Edison switcher 1239 14 lds. 660 Ms
          Dep. Edison 2:00 P.M. Time 30 mins.

X 3846   SFE lite engine 3846 3841 helpers
          off No. 3-262.
          Dep. Tehachapi 2:00 P.M.
          Time 4 hrs. 20 mins.

X 3844   SFE lite engine 3844 3843 helpers
          off No. 1-264.
          Dep. Tehachapi 4:05 P.M.
          Time 4 hrs. 55 mins.

No. 21   SFE
          3701   6 cars 430 Ms
          Dep. Mojave 4:25 P.M. Time 2 hrs. 40 mins.

No. 261   SP freight
          3753 through, 2784 M-E   8 lds.
          51 mty. 2486 Ms
          Dep. Mojave 5:40 P.M. Time 5 hrs. 30 mins.

X 1688   SFE freight
          1688 through, 1635 1682 M-E.
          54 lds. 2 mty 2157 Ms

X 2688   SP lite engine 2688 3638 helpers off 2-264
          and SFE lite engines 3845 1676 helpers
          off 3-264.
          Dep. Tehachapi 7:45 P.M.

X 1693   SFE freight
1693 through, 1675 M-E   1 lds.
55 mty. 1540 Ms
Dep. Mojave 8:35 P.M. Time 7 hrs. 20 mins.

X 3833   SFE freight
3833 through, 1635 M-E. 0 lds. 56 mtys.
1489 Ms
Dep. Mojave 8:40 P.M. Time 7 hrs. 21 mins.

X 1239   SP Edison switcher 1239   14 lds.
1 mty. 660 Ms
Dep. Edison 9:30 P.M.

No. 25   SP **Owl**
3643   8 cars 1123 Ms
Dep. Mojave 9:45 P.M. Time 2 hrs. 28 mins.

X 3835   SFE lite engines 3835 3840 helpers off 4-264.
Dep. Tehachapi 9:57 P.M.
Time 6 hrs. 27 mins.

No. 59   **SP West Coast Limited**
3647   11 cars 1501 Ms
Dep. Mojave 10:03 P.M. Time 2 hrs. 57 mins.

X 1679   SFE Supply train
1679 through, 1635 1682 M-E.
21 lds, 35 mty 1834 Ms
Dep. Mojave 3:20 P.M. Time 5 hrs. 50 mins.

X 978   SFE freight
978 through, 1675 M-E.
2 lds, 54 mty. 1575 Ms
Dep. Mojave 3:30 P.M. Time 5 hrs. 50 mins.

X 3776   SP lite engine 3776 2367, helpers off 4-262.
Dep. Tehachapi 3:40 P.M. Time 6 hrs.

No. 57   **SP Los Angeles—San Francisco Express**
3641   9 cars 978 Ms
Dep. Mojave 4:00 P.M. Time 2 hrs. 28 mins.

No. 251   SP freight
3708 through, 2770 M-E.
Dep. Mojave 10:10 P.M. Time 7 hrs. 30 mins.

X 3831   SFE lite engines 3831 3830 helpers off 5-264.
Dep. Tehachapi 10:50 P.M.
Time 6 hrs. 25 mins.

X 3727   SP lite engine 3727 helper off 1-258.
Dep. Tehachapi 12:40 A.M.
Time 5 hrs. 30 mins.

Even with the advent of double-track on a large part of the Tehachapi grade, the north slope between Sivert and Tehachapi was still a tremendous headache. Double-track from Sivert to Bena was completed October 31, 1928, then a series of interlocking plants were installed further up the mountain to expedite moves. Railroaders referred to these installations as "remote control," which is precisely what they were. By March 24, 1928, the telegraph operator at Caliente was able to control both the east and west switches at his station. That fall the telegraph office at Bealville contained levers that controlled the east and west switches at both Bealville and Cliff, as well as, the east switch at Allard. Similarly, by April 9, 1929, the Woodford operator could control the east and west switches at his station as could the operator at Marcel his. About the same time the operator at Tehachapi was able to control movements to and from the double-track, and the west switch of the number one siding where helpers often accumulated. Even as these measures were being carried out, however, the general economy of the country was teetering on the brink of a great depression. It would be fully ten years before traffic densities would again rise to the point these interlocking plants would be appreciated once again.

The nerve center of the San Joaquin Division Mountain District was the dispatchers office located atop the depot at Bakersfield. This view taken in February 1930, finds dispatcher Porter E. Turner at the right working the mountain desk. Chief dispatcher E. F. Wasem, standing at the left, confers with dispatcher Leon J. Baker on valley district matters. —
SOUTHERN PACIFIC

On this and the adjoining page are two views of the Southern Pacific station at Bakersfield as it appeared in 1916. The structure also houses the San Joaquin Division offices and dispatchers. — BOTH SOUTHERN PACIFIC COLLECTION

The Bakersfield & Sumner Street Railway, electrified in 1901, extended from the courthouse in downtown Bakersfield and terminated at the SP station. This view taken in the early part of this century, shows an electric car waiting in the middle of Baker Street, while men and equipment pose for the camera in the SP yard. The business car shed is on the left.
— KERN COUNTY MUSEUM

Shop goat No. 218 poses for the camera at Bakersfield on June 14, 1914. Originally built as Oakland Traction Co. No. 2, this Baldwin product was scrapped in 1919. — R. P. MIDDLEBROOK — A. S. MENKE COLLECTION

Bakersfield was a major locomotive repair point beginning about 1885 and continuing for as long as steam lasted. The San Joaquin Division store house in the foreground, dominates this view of the shops looking north. — KERN COUNTY MUSEUM

In the above scene, a variety of motive power radiates from the Bakersfield turntable in 1916. — VERNON SAPPERS COLLECTION (RIGHT) Two examples of heavy mountain locomotives decorate the "whisker" tracks the same year. The No. 4029 was a 57-inch drivered freight engine introduced to the district three years earlier. (LOWER) The No. 4206 with its 63-inch drivers was being tested in passenger service at the time. — BOTH R. P. MIDDLEBROOK - A. S. MENKE COLLECTION

Santa Fe's No. 963 is a representative of the road's 900 class 2-10-2 type locomotive. These engines were common to the Tehachapi grade throughout their working lives. — R. P. MIDDLEBROOK — STAN KISTLER COLLECTION

The Santa Fe depot in Bakersfield was located in the southern section of downtown. The station contained the familiar ticket office and waiting room, offices, and a large Harvey House dining facility.

The Santa Fe yard at Bakersfield looked as if it had ceased operation when this photograph was taken looking south toward the mountains. The roundhouse and light repair shops were located at the right. — KERN COUNTY MUSEUM

A double-headed freight departs Bakersfield for the Tehachapi Mountains in this 1905 view. — DONALD DUKE COLLECTION

In the above view, SP train No. 108 the *Los Angeles Express,* arrives off the valley run on June 22, 1916, behind high-wheeler No. 1533 and departs for Tehachapi (RIGHT) behind husky Ten-Wheeler No. 2326. — R. P. MIDDLEBROOK — A. S. MENKE COLLECTION

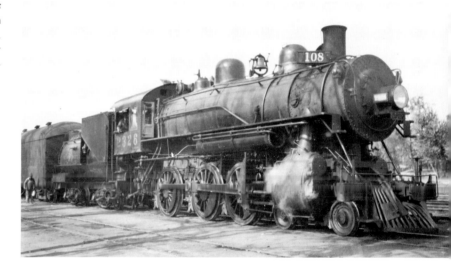

Freight trains required more elaborate switching at Bakersfield and the placement of helpers in the train. Mountain District regular No. 2942 is cut in a train at Bakersfield on June 20, 1916. — R. P. MIDDLEBROOK — A. S. MENKE COLLECTION

The switch is lined for the Santa Fe at Kern Junction in this view taken in 1916, a time when the mainline running toward the mountains was single track. The Sunset Railway interchange yard is behind the tower.
— SOUTHERN PACIFIC COLLECTION

A Santa Fe passenger train, perhaps the *Overland,* pauses at Kern Junction for train orders, circa 1905. The engineer takes these few extra minutes to double check his engine. — DONALD DUKE COLLECTION

Edison, seven miles south of Bakersfield, now the site of extensive citrus
cultivation, looks rather bleak in this
1916 view. — SOUTHERN PACIFIC COL-
LECTION

Extra No. 5017 west drifts downgrade through Bena in the late 1920's. These three-cylinder engines, tried for a while
in both freight and passenger runs on the Tehachapi grade, were not entirely successful. The district's extremes in
grade and curvature contributed to severe flange wear on the lead drivers. — R. P. MIDDLEBROOK — A. S. MENKE
COLLECTION

Bena depot as it looked in 1916. The
station is now on exhibit at the
Pioneer Village at Bakersfield. —
SOUTHERN PACIFIC COLLECTION

An SP freight, heavily laden with Kern County oil, works upgrade near
Caliente. — HERB SULLIVAN — TRAINS MAGAZINE COLLECTION

A string of light engines drift down through the
Caliente Creek narrows near Ilmon in 1902. This
section of track was particularly vulnerable during
storms and after a long series of washouts, the trestles
were eliminated by a line change in the 1930's. — GUY L.
DUNSCOMB COLLECTION

Caliente located at 1,291 feet above sea level, was at the foot of the heavy grade. In addition to being a water stop, helpers were cut in here at various periods of time. The name Caliente translates from the Spanish as "hot." This is perhaps understating the conditions prevailing at this location during the summer months. — SOUTHERN PACIFIC COLLECTION

A Caliente street scene, circa 1915. In addition to administering the affairs of the railroad here, local agent C. A. Mallachowitz, was also the local Justice of the Peace and dispensed justice in this little settlement of 50 souls for over 30 years. One might define this as an SP town! — KERN COUNTY MUSEUM

When new in 1913, Mallet No. 4037 negotiates the big curve at Caliente as she helps a freight up the north slope to Tehachapi. A short time later the big engine blew up at Edison killing her crew. — GERALD M. BEST COLLECTION

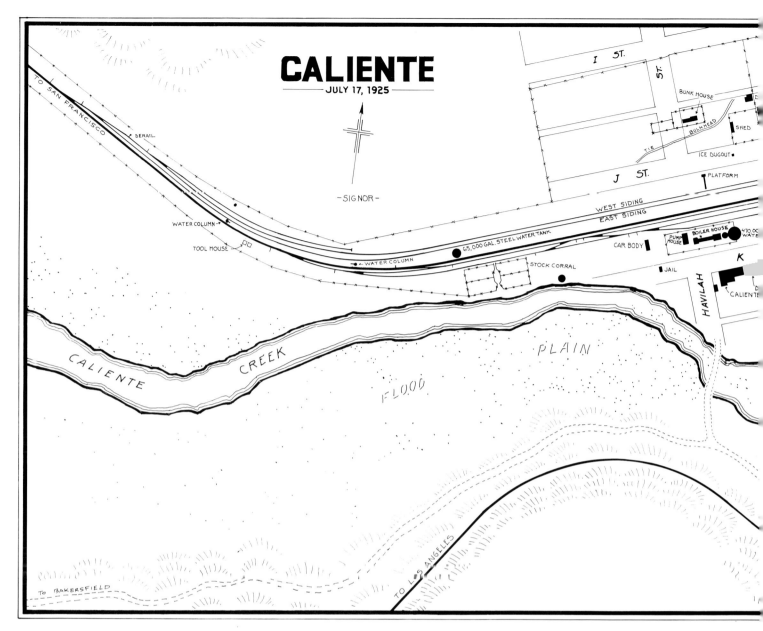

CALIENTE
JULY 17, 1925

- SIG NOR -

TO SAN FRANCISCO

DERAIL

WATER COLUMN

TOOL HOUSE

WATER COLUMN

I ST.

ST.

BUNK HOUSE

BULKHEAD

SHED

TIE

ICE DUGOUT

J ST.

PLATFORM

WEST SIDING

EAST SIDING

65,000 GAL. STEEL WATER TANK

CAR BODY

PUMP HOUSE

BOILER HOUSE

470,00 WATE

JAIL

K

HAVILAH

CALIENTE

STOCK CORRAL

CALIENTE CREEK

FLOOD PLAIN

TO BAKERSFIELD

TO LOS ANGELES

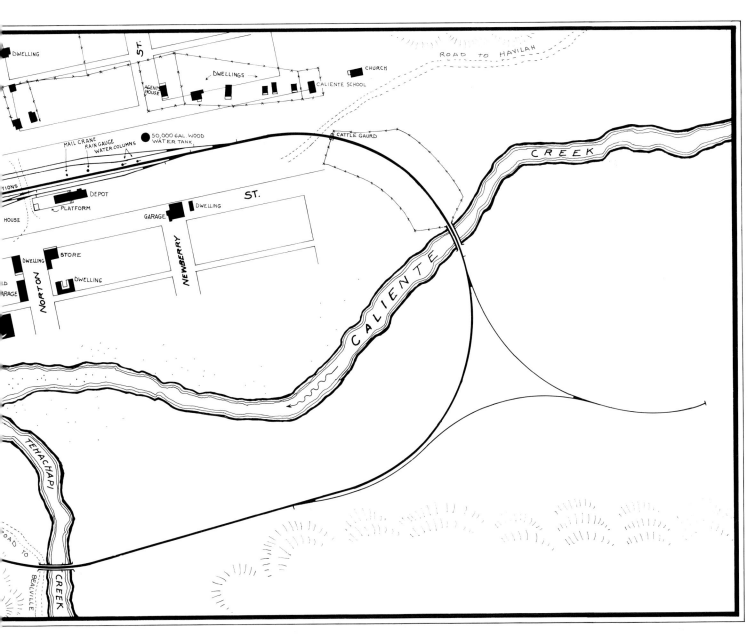

Prior to the emergence of Bakersfield as an engine terminal, it had been the custom to add helpers at Caliente. This practice was revived in July 1925 when the Santa Fe and Southern Pacific placed helpers at this location. The operation was not a success, however, and phased out within 10 years. Remains of the wye, built at this time, may be seen on the outside of the horseshoe in the photograph on the opposite page. — SOUTHERN PACIFIC COLLECTION (RIGHT) Helper crews stayed in the Caliente Hotel, but were forced to seek shelter in tents after it burned to the ground during January 1926. — OLA MAE FORCE COLLECTION

The train order office at Bealville, key B, as it appeared about 1916. The spot was named for Edward F. Beale who was superintendent of California's Bureau of Indian Affairs during the 1850's. In 1865, be became owner of the adjacent rancho El Tejon. — SOUTHERN PACIFIC COLLECTION

Bakersfield bound Southern Pacific helpers drift downgrade at Cliff, an aptly named siding built in 1913 at the edge of the Tehachapi Creek gorge. — GUY L. DUNSCOMB COLLECTION

While a Santa Fe passenger train pauses in the westward siding just above the crossover at Rowen, travelers take the opportunity to explore the oak-studded woodland that is the hallmark of Tehachapi Pass. — O. B. KATZ COLLECTION

A broken wheel was allegedly the culprit in this little mishap at Rowen in 1915. — F. A. NEJEDLY — OLA MAE FORCE COLLECTION

The telegraph office at Rowen, circa 1916. — SOUTHERN PACIFIC COLLECTION

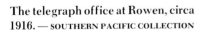

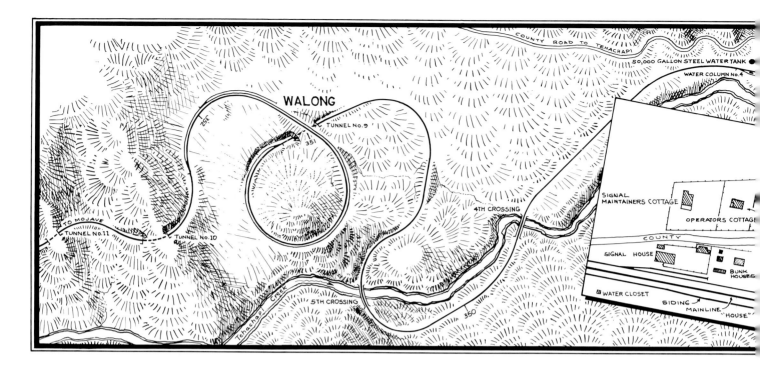

A panorama of Woodford as it appeared in the late 1920's. The horizon is dominated by 6,934-foot Bear Mountain. Note the passenger train which will shortly pass the telegraph station in the center of this scene. — OLA MAE FORCE
COLLECTION

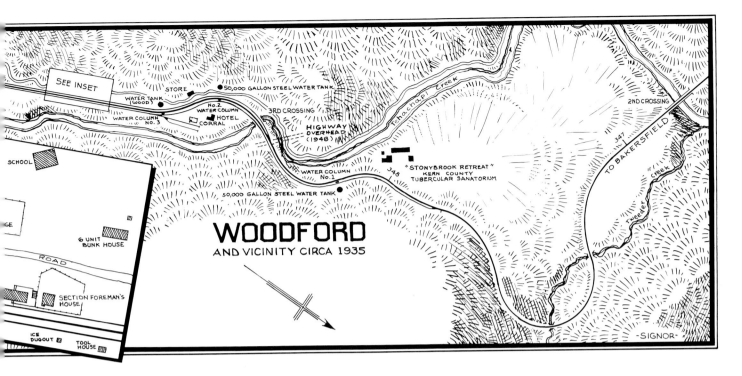

SEE INSET

SCHOOL

6 UNIT
BUNK HOUSE

ROAD

SECTION FOREMAN'S
HOUSE

ICE
DUGOUT

TOOL
HOUSE

WATER TANK
(WOOD)

STORE

50,000 GALLON STEEL WATER TANK

No.2
WATER COLUMN

WATER COLUMN
No. 3

HOTEL

CORRAL

3RD CROSSING

HIGHWAY
OVERHEAD
(1948)

WATER COLUMN
No. 1

50,000 GALLON STEEL WATER TANK

Tehachapi Creek

"STONYBROOK RETREAT"
KERN COUNTY
TUBERCULAR SANATORIUM

348

347

TO BAKERSFIELD

2ND CROSSING

Tweeds Creek

WOODFORD
AND VICINITY CIRCA 1935

-SIGNOR-

A Tehachapi landmark, the Stony Brook Retreat tubercular sanitorium, was built between Rowen and Woodford during 1918. — KELCY OWENS COLLECTION

The school house occupies a site between the county road, Tehachapi Creek and the railroad tracks in this view of Keene dated 1915. In the distance is Rock Spur, a quarry which provided material to build Kern County highways many years ago. This track became the lower end of Woodford siding in the 1920's. — KELCY OWENS COLLECTION

Confusion with the name Kern Junction led to changing the station of Keene to Woodford in 1910. — SOUTHERN PACIFIC COLLECTION

Over a foot of snow has fallen at Woodford as an eastbound Santa Fe passenger train moves up the long siding and past the depot. At 2,709 feet, Woodford was subject to occasional snow falls. — F. A. NEJEDLY - OLA MAE FORCE COLLECTION

A Santa Fe westbound passenger train rolls down off the loop in April behind heavy Mountain type locomotive No. 3703. The camp in the foreground housed C.C.C. workers building the highway over Tehachapi Pass known as the White Wolf Grade. — GERALD M. BEST

A Santa Fe freight train works its way around the Tehachapi Loop at Walong in the 1920's. There are five locomotives visible in the photograph. The lead engine is just passing over the tunnel at the center left, while three helpers cut into the train are in the foreground. With the aid of a powerful glass a pusher can be seen just emerging from the tunnel. — F. A. NEJEDLY — JAMES H. HARRISON COLLECTION

The head brakeman waits at the west switch of Walong for his train to depart for Bakersfield. A siding was built on the upper curve of the Tehachapi Loop in 1909 where a spur named Fox had previously been located. The name was derived from District Roadmaster W. A. Long. As train lengths and congestion on the hill increased, Walong siding was extended around the loop to the mouth of tunnel No. 9. — GUY L. DUNSCOMB COLLECTION

84

Santa Fe No. 3600, a one-of-a-kind Pacific type locomotive built by Baldwin in 1915, makes a rare appearance at Marcel in 1922. Unpopular with the men, the engine was top-heavy, turned over a lot, and spent most of its life at the company shops in San Bernardino. — F. A. NEJEDLY - OLA MAE FORCE COLLECTION

The Tehachapi Range extends to the horizon from a vantage point southwest of Marcel. In this scene, the railroad threads its way up the canyon at the bottom of the picture. — F. A. NEJEDLY — OLA MAE FORCE COLLECTION

The telegraph office at Marcel, on the left, is dwarfed by the mountains to the southwest. (BELOW) While at trackside Southern Pacific's prestigious *Owl* blasts upgrade in the same vicinity on December 1, 1911.
— BOTH F. A. NEJEDLY — OLA MAE FORCE COLLECTION

On May 14, 1915, tunnel No. 15 between Marcel and Cable caught fire resulting in a 90-foot plug in the middle of the bore with collapsed portals. The most optimistic reports estimated it would take at least six weeks to reopen the bore. It was decided to construct a shoofly around the tunnel for the duration. This was a precarious affair requiring a 450 foot trestle 85 feet high, as seen under construction in the view above, which was opened June 9 for traffic. Engineer M. A. Spier crossed the spidery trestle with some reservations on the first locomotive across the temporary line. During the blockade, the Coast Division absorbed all the traffic of both the Santa Fe and Southern Pacific. (RIGHT) Tunnel No. 15 was rebuilt in concrete and soon after a program was underway to concrete line all of the tunnels on the Tehachapi grade. — BOTH F. A. NEJEDLY — OLA MAE FORCE

A passenger engine takes the ditch at Cable in 1917. — F. A. NEJEDLY — OLA MAE FORCE COLLECTION

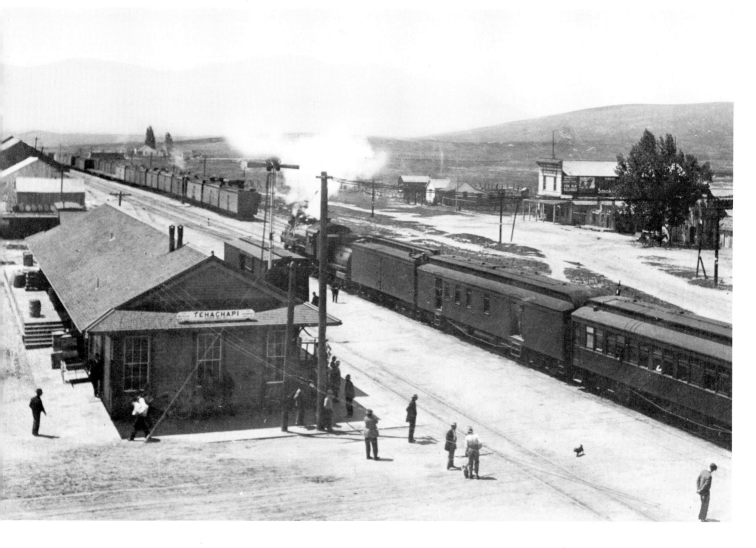

At 3,967 feet, Tehachapi was not quite at the top of the grade. This occurred a mile beyond at Summit Switch (4,028 feet) where a wye to turn helpers was located. In the days before the double-track, a staff system was utilized to move helpers between the two points. These views of the station at Tehachapi date from the second decade of the twentieth century. — F. A. NEJEDLY — OLA MAE FORCE COLLECTION

With thirsty helpers congregating at Tehachapi, two water tanks were required to keep tenders full. A third was added in 1917. — F. A. NEJEDLY — OLA MAE FORCE COLLECTION

During the Depression, the Santa Fe consolidated three trains Nos. 2-*The Navajo,* 4-*The California Limited,* and 22-*The Missionary* as a single schedule leaving San Francisco at 10:20 A.M. for Chicago. Railroad photographer, Gerald M. Best, captured this amalgamation at Tehachapi Summit at dusk on May 30, 1936 as No. 3521 assists road engine No. 3709.

Santa Fe's crack passenger train, the *Limited,* makes a station stop at Tehachapi in 1911. The big Mallets were briefly utilized in Tehachapi passenger service commencing in 1909. — F. A. NEJEDLY — OLA MAE FORCE COLLECTION

Santa Fe and the Mallet, a fleeting romance . . .

Examples of Santa Fe's brief and entirely unsuccessful Mallet Compound experiments congregate at Tehachapi. The first to use Mallets on the Tehachapi grade, Santa Fe introduced in November 1909 the 1301 class in passenger service. The engines then broke in on oil drags in October 1910. During June of that year, two engines of the 1700 class were assigned to Tehachapi service. (BELOW) Seen with dynamometer car No. 29 trailing, the No. 1701 was rated at 1,100 tons for oil and 1,050 tons for mixed service on the north slope. Neither one of these two classes proved satisfactory. The 1301 class engines were withdrawn soon after with the primary complaint begin excessive slippage of the front engine. This problem plagued the 1700 class as well, which with modifications — most notably a large sand dome forward, continued to operate on the district as the 1798 class. (BOTTOM VIEW) Probably the most successful of the breed were the four engines of the 3296 class produced in 1911 from 1950 class Consolidations. Examples of these last two classes survived in helper service on the grade into the early 1920's. The No. 3296, shown at the lower right, was recorded on film at Tehachapi on September 27, 1921. The last of these unique engines was broken up in 1924. — (LOWER RIGHT) R. P. MIDDLEBROOK — STAN KISTLER COLLECTION, ALL OTHERS F. A. NEJEDLY — OLA MAE FORCE COLLECTION

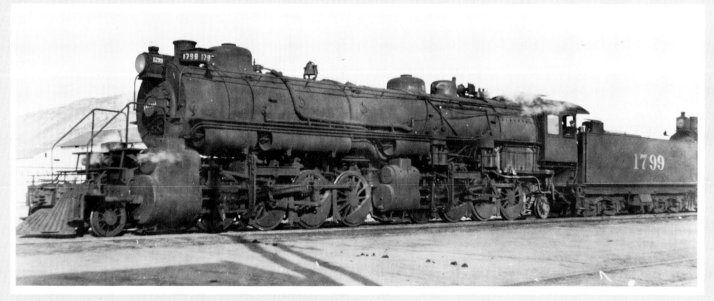

Although the Santa Fe introduced the Mallet to the Tehachapi, the Southern Pacific soon followed their lead. When the Santa Fe gave up their experiment in disgust, SP's distinctive cab-forward Mallets were establishing an impressive record. (ABOVE) Two of these impressive machines await orders in the snow at Tehachapi in 1920. Prior to their introduction, the SP relied principally on their fleet of Harriman Common Standard Consolidations. In the view below, seven of these locomotives drop down through Marcel on a wintery day in 1911. Special instructions later prohibited more than five Consolidations or two Mallets from descending the mountain coupled together. —
BOTH F. A. NEJEDLY — OLA MAE FORCE COLLECTION

In the summer of 1907, the City of Los Angeles erected a large cement plant along the railroad 2.5 miles east of Summit to supply the needs of the then building Owens Valley aqueduct. The site, initially called Aqueduct, soon became known as Monolith. Following the aqueduct project, the plant was operated on a small scale by the city until 1920. It was then sold to the Monolith Portland Cement Company who expanded the operation considerably and continue to operate the plant today. — LOS ANGELES DEPARTMENT OF WATER & POWER

A narrow gauge railroad 5.25 miles in length connected the plant with limestone deposits necessary for the preparation of cement. — LOS ANGELES DEPARTMENT OF WATER & POWER

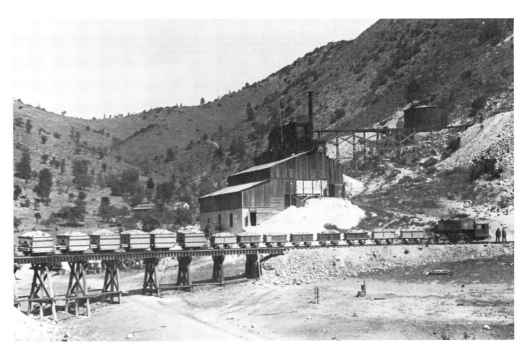

Cameron was named for George Washington Cameron who, with his brother, operated a station for stages and freighters in the 1860's and early 1870's at this location. The Southern Pacific established a telegraph station at this point — key Ca — in 1888. This picture of the place dates from 1913. — SOUTHERN PACIFIC COLLECTION

The south slope of the Tehachapi grade could be extremely treacherous. Every bit as steep as the north slope, but lacking the curves, this section had an ominous reputation as a "racetrack" and the tragedies associated with it were numerous. In these views of No. 49, the *San Joaquin Flyer,* has derailed following the striking of a cow at the big curve near the top end of Cameron. The only casualty, helper engineer Virgil Newbill who was found with the Johnson bar of engine No. 9517 piercing his chest. — F. A. NEJEDLY — OLA MAE FORCE COLLECTION

Warren telegraph as it appeared during the busy war year of 1917. — F. A. NEJEDLY - OLA MAE FORCE COLLECTION

Santa Fe inspection car No. 149, possibly a product of Hall-Scott built during 1911-12, pauses at Warren. — F. A. NEJEDLY — OLA MAE FORCE COLLECTION

Misunderstood orders are to blame for this "cornfield meet" at Warren in 1919. — F. A. NEJEDLY — OLA MAE FORCE COLLECTION

A giant of one age meets the vanguard
of another at Woodford in 1948. —
JAMES H. HARRISON COLLECTION

96

3

Years of Transition 1930-1955

As railroad operations in the Tehachapi Mountains passed the half century mark, the full effects of the economic crash of 1929 were felt. Compared to the performance levels of the late 1920's, the railroad business for the most part of the 1930's was anything but encouraging. As the economy plunged into decline, all railroads reacted accordingly by retrenching and trimming operations and operating costs wherever they could. The San Joaquin Division Mountain District was no exception. Many men were furloughed. Agencies and stations were closed wherever possible. Some passenger schedules were also dropped.

On the Southern Pacific, the lowest point, as far as passenger trains go, was reached January 31, 1932 when the *Owl* and *West Coast* were consolidated over the Valley Line leaving just three first class schedules each way in the Tehachapi. Santa Fe schedules were similarly cut. In January 1935, No. 23, the *Grand Canyon* westbound and No. 2, the *Navajo* eastbound were all the road could offer for passenger accommodations in the mountains. This was down from an all-time high of eight in 1917.

As an indicator of freight operations within the same territory, tonnage handled between Bakersfield and Mojave slid from 19 million tons in 1925 to 15.2 million in 1935, of which the Santa Fe shouldered less than half. While lumber, oil and manufactured goods were in a strong decline in

this period, the seasonal perishable rushes continued unabated each summer and early fall, thus boosting an otherwise appalling level of traffic. The stirring image of one block (solid train of refrigerator cars) after another of grapes, rushing East during the season, remains clear in the minds of railroaders forced to endure the horrible night of the Depression.

It was not train operations, but storms of savage intensity, which were the hallmark of railroading on the Mountain District in the 1930's. In the fall of 1932, Tehachapi Pass suffered the worst flood in the history of the railroad's presence in the area. The storm, which caused the disaster, had started as a tropical tornado at the Isthmus of Panama. It then pursued an unusual course northwest with diminishing intensity finally breaking over the mountains of southern California on the afternoon of Friday, September 30, 1932.

Rain had fallen in the Tehachapi for several days prior to this episode. On Wednesday the 28th, about two inches of rain fell in a short time causing 1.5 feet of water to flow alongside the SP station at Tehachapi. The rushing waters washed out 500 feet of side track at the west switch, besides causing minor washouts between Tehachapi and Monolith, and elsewhere on the mountain. The storm seemed to subside with only light showers occurring on Thursday the 29th. Then a downpour of cloudburst intensity broke over the pass around 4:00 P.M. on Friday the 30th dumping 4.39 inches of rain in slightly more than four hours. Con-

97

siderable damage occurred, at this time, to the station and yard trackage at Tehachapi. Farther down the north slope the results were catastrophic.

As the downpour continued, the water in Tehachapi Creek rose and debris plugged the seventh railroad crossing of the creek midway between Tehachapi and Cable, just east of milepost 358. Water began to back up and eventually the seventh crossing, consisting of a concrete arch and fill gave way. Water surged down the creek bed at an estimated 20,300 cubic feet per second to the sixth crossing, just west of the west switch at Cable. This crossing now became plugged with tons of debris. Eventually a portion of the bridge gave way taking steel girders down to the fifth crossing below the Walong loop at milepost 350.5. Here the process was repeated once again as it was at the fourth crossing about a quarter of a mile father down the canyon. The water was now rushing with an intensity better than 28,500 cubic feet per second.

Just below the fourth crossing lay the yard at Woodford where two trains were being held due to the alarming reports coming over the wires concerning the storm. A Santa Fe eastbound 40-car freight, first 818, was stopped in the No. 1 siding next to the rising creek, while an SP eastbound, second 818, was lined in behind it. Second 818, with cab-forward No. 4110 on the point and two helpers cut into its 66-car train was right up against the Santa Fe's caboose with its train strung across the third crossing at the lower end of the yard. As the water descended in a wall reportedly more than 30 feet high, the destruction and loss of lives at Woodford was awesome. While the train crews were at the depot attempting to secure orders, the side wash from the raging creek undermined the

No. 1 siding about 100 feet east of the depot rolling the helper on the Santa Fe freight — a 200 ton 2-10-2 No. 3834 — into the raging torrent without a trace. The Woodford depot itself escaped serious harm, but a nearby gasoline filling station and cafe located on what was then the main highway, were swamped and totally destroyed taking a dozen or more customers to their deaths.

Just west of the depot, SP No. 5036, a 4-10-2, was cut in 29 cars ahead of the caboose on second 818. The locomotive sat squarely on the concrete arch which made up the third crossing of the creek. The waters backed up against the structure undermining the fill on either side. The helper engine and several cars toppled into the flood along with two railroad men. Brakemen Harry Moore was swept away and drowned, but fireman Enos Brown was miraculously rescued in a tree 200 yards down stream. His only injury, a broken jaw, did not prevent him from yelling loudly for help. The engineer on the No. 5036, A. H. "Pinkey" Ross, who had been at the cafe at the time, was lost when it was destroyed. His body was later found at Ilmon. In addition to the members of the train crew and those in the cafe that perished, concern was expressed over a boxcar said to have contained 21 hoboes which was also tossed into the swift moving currents.

Below Woodford, the water continued on down the mountain taking out the second crossing just above Rowen in a like manner. Three patients at the Kern County Tuberculosis Hospital at Keene perished as the flood swept past their location. Farther down the canyon, as the wall of water approached the sleepy settlement of Caliente, it gathered in a force nearing 37,400 cubic feet per second. The deluge disintegrated the first crossing

On Friday, September 30, 1932, a tropical storm dumped 4.39 inches of rain over the Tehachapi Mountains in slightly more than four hours time. Flood waters destroyed all seven railroad crossings of Tehachapi Creek. This is the remains of a concrete arch viaduct and fill comprising the 7th crossing and was the first to go. — DONALD DUKE COLLECTION

At each crossing the water was momentarily held by debris allowing the flood to gain in intensity. By the time it reached Woodford, the flood was cresting at better than 30 feet. Portions of two trains were swept from the rails at this location. Engine No. 5036, entrained on an uphill freight and stopped squarely on the 3rd crossing at the time, toppled into the raging torrent. — In the view above, the No. 5036 after the raging water rescinded. (RIGHT) The debris covered No. 5036 prior to its removal from the flood scene. — BOTH DONALD DUKE COLLECTION (BELOW) Her engineer, A. H. "Pinky" Ross was caught, along with a dozen others, having a cup of coffee at the nearby El Rita store. — F. A. NEJEDLY - OLA MAE FORCE COLLECTION

Piers of the 2nd crossing were swept away. Note the debris covered box-car at the right. — DONALD DUKE COLLECTION

The onrushing waters disintegrated the 1st crossing of Tehachapi Creek then fanned out to engulf the sleepy settlement of Caliente under two feet of swiftly moving waters, as shown in the above scene. (LEFT) Mrs. Nell Cooper, an SP telegrapher, and her granddaughter lost their lives when the flood suddenly swept up her cottage and deposited it across the Southern Pacific mainline. — BOTH DONALD DUKE COLLECTION

The exact whereabouts of Santa Fe 2-10-2 No. 3834 was unknown for several days. During the flood, the heavy engine had rolled into raging Tehachapi Creek at Woodford and was found buried under 10 feet of silt and debris 150 feet downstream. It was located by the aid of a magnetic needle, and it took more than 30 days to recover the engine. The bell and headlight were never found. — BOTH OLA MAE FORCE COLLECTION

of Tehachapi Creek on the high side of the loop at Caliente then fanned out to engulf the town under two feet of swiftly moving water. A local woman, Mrs. Nell Cooper, who was also an SP telegrapher, lost her life along with her granddaughter. The water lifted her cottage and deposited it squarely across the SP mainline. The elapsed time between the failure of the sixth crossing and the time the flood hit Caliente was about three hours.

Farther down the canyon, below Caliente, the combined strength of Tehachapi and Caliente creeks created a flow approaching 39,000 cubic feet per second. In the narrow defile above tunnel No. ½ over a mile of line was washed out.

On the south slope of the mountain on the desert side of Tehachapi Pass, Cache Creek handled the bulk of the runoff. The cement plant at Monolith sustained some damage and minor washouts occurred during the height of the storm at Eric and Cameron. So intense was the downpour that flood waters engulfed portions of the mainline between Mojave and Lancaster and a lake one-mile long and one-half mile wide was formed six miles south of Mojave — its surface thick with floating debris.

In a little over three hours over 31 miles of railroad had been completely crippled. At least 15 people lost their lives and an estimated 60 were missing. Reports were slow in coming in from the devastated area since all means of communication — the railroad, highway and telegraph wires — had been severed. For the duration of the emergency, all traffic was routed via the Coast Line. Train No. 52, the *San Joaquin Flyer,* managed to get through Caliente while the flood was raging farther up the mountain, but was stranded at Bealville as bridges on either side of the train were washed out. The passengers of No. 52 were taken to Los Angeles by bus.

101

Acting quickly, railroad officials organized and rushed men, materials and equipment into the area to begin the task of rebuilding. At its peak nearly a thousand men were on the job. As inspection teams sifted through the mess the following morning, the full impact of the storm's fury was realized. Every crossing of Tehachapi Creek was lost. Whole sections of the railroad had been swept away. Slides blocked the right-of-way at many points, but unquestionably the worst damage was sustained at Woodford.

A great deal of time was needed to extricate the two engines from their watery graves. Indeed the exact whereabouts of the Santa Fe 2-10-2, which was buried under 10 feet of silt and debris, was not known for several days. The water and crude oil compartments of its tender were the only portions of the No. 3834 visible. They had broken loose from the tender frame and were carried 250 yards down stream. Officials made several attempts to locate the engine with little success.

Ten days following the flood the Bakersfield High School class of mineralogy, hearing of the railroad's difficulty, volunteered the use of a magnetic needle suspended in a ring used to locate iron deposits. It proved too small to be of genuine service. Malcolm M. Galbraith, an engineer in the employ of the Los Angeles Department of Water & Power, learned of the predicament and volunteered the use of the department's needle. Quite a bit larger, this one had been used previously to locate $100,000 worth of electric generators buried under 30 feet of sediment following the collapse of the St. Francis dam east of Santa Paula. After a couple hours of testing with this device, the unfortunate engine was located and excavation started. The ultimate resting place of the No. 3834 was 150 yards downstream from where it had fallen in. Shooflies were constructed around the site of each disaster so the railroad could be placed back in service. It took fully one month to recover the Santa Fe engine. At that, many of its parts were never found — including the bell.

After considerable around-the-clock efforts the Tehachapi line was reopened for service on October 14, 1932. Work continued for many months thereafter, with the total cost of repairs to the railroad approximating $581,050.

Due to this flood and the previous history of washouts in the narrow canyon between tunnel No. ½ and Caliente, temporary structures were placed in this section and plans laid for a complete line change. Actual work on the 1.78 mile modification commenced April 30, 1936. On September 26, 1936 the work was completed and the first train —third No. 60, the *West Coast Limited* — was allowed over the track which was laid at a higher location than the old grade with no crossings of the creek.

The Caliente helper operation, already adversely affected by the introduction of larger power, was abandoned outright. This was largely due to the line change which by reason of being shorter than the old alignment, created a grade nearly as severe

Early in 1938, the Mountain District once again suffered at the hands of nature. In a 24-hour period ending March 3rd, 6.03 inches of rain fell over southern California. Soledad Canyon was particularly hard hit. This was the situation March 5th at the 11th crossing of the Santa Clara River about a mile west of Lang. — D. K. MCNEAR COLLECTION

A central construction camp was set up near the 3rd crossing. Hundreds of men were at work on the restoration effort. The camp may be seen on the bluff in the center of the view above. (RIGHT) With the waters of the Santa Clara River cresting at 16 feet in the narrows, tunnel No. 18 was transformed into a giant culvert.

— BOTH D. K. MCNEAR COLLECTION

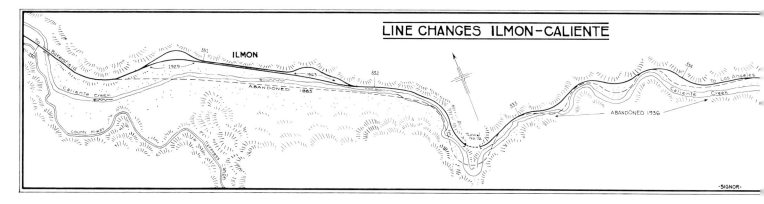

LINE CHANGES ILMON-CALIENTE

as any found on the north slope of the Tehachapi. Accordingly, in July 1937, the last vestige of this operation, the Caliente wye, was taken up.

Heavy storms once again struck the Mountain District early in 1938. For 19 days in January and February SP's Portland, Shasta, Western and Sacramento divisions were disrupted by epic storms. Then, several weeks later, southern California was ravaged by one of the most severe rainfalls in its history. A six day storm that began manifesting itself February 27th over the region from Santa Barbara to the Mexican border dumped 11.06 inches of rain in Los Angeles. The real tooth of the storm broke over the region March 2nd, dumping 6.03 inches of rain in a 24-hour period. Swollen streams caused considerable damage as the storm reached its climax. All rail conections into southern California were severed, including those routed over the Tehachapi, Cajon and Beaumont passes. All telephone and telegraph wires were down. The Ridge Route Highway (the main highway route through the center of California) was closed by slides. The *Owl* and *San Joaquin* of March 1st were held at Bakersfield because of the gloomy reports coming in from the San Joaquin Mountain District. On the nights of March 2nd and 3rd, stub trains were operated out of Oakland Pier as far as Bakersfield. All rail services in and out of Los Angeles came to a standstill.

Within the Los Angeles Terminal area alone things were in chaos. By the afternoon of March 2nd the swollen Los Angeles River had taken out the key double-track Dayton Avenue bridge. Several hours later the Arroyo Seco bridge on the north bank was swept away effectively cutting off entrance into the city from the north. Alhambra Avenue Roundhouse and Shops were out of commission due to high water. Flat cars were shoved into the river bordering Taylor Yard to divert the flow. Ultimately the river cut into railroad property at this location more than 60-feet in places.

On the San Joaquin Valley Line things were every bit as bleak. At tunnel No. 25, near Newhall, the west portal was obscured by a slide 600 feet long and 15 feet deep. Farther up the line the Santa Clara River in the Soledad Canyon region was running wild and cresting at 16 feet in the narrower cuts. The high water was carrying destruction all along its path to the sea. Railroad officials were

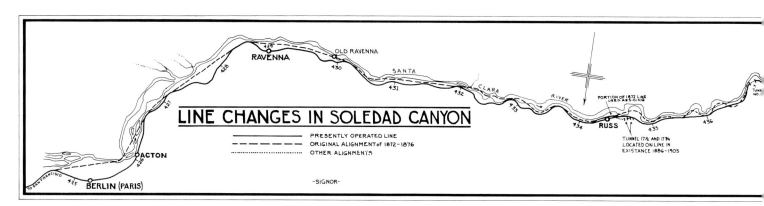

LINE CHANGES IN SOLEDAD CANYON

uncertain just how much damage was being done since all wires were down between Bakersfield and Los Angeles. One of the last reports coming in indicated the loss of two Mallets in a washout at China Flat near Ravenna. In the Tehachapi Mountains both Caliente and Tehachapi creeks were rising rapidly. There were slides everywhere on the pass, especially a large one at tunnel No. 12 near Marcel. The westbound main track at Tehachapi was in the process of being washed away.

As reports were coming into the General Offices in San Francisco the afternoon of March 2nd, a special train was dispatched with engineering officials aboard who would direct restoration efforts in the afflicted areas. Another special, carrying operating officials, was dispatched later in the evening — both specials taking the Coast Line. Each train made it as far as Montalvo, 32 miles south of Santa Barbara before being abruptly halted. Here a 32-span steel bridge over the wild running Santa Clara River was threatened and the structure had been rendered unsafe to cross. It was not until the evening of March 4th that the bridge was considered safe for the passage of trains.

The railroads in and out of Los Angeles were at a virtual standstill by March 3rd. The daily morning report for the following day, prepared by the chief dispatcher of the Los Angeles Division, indicated nothing had moved on the division in the previous 24 hours.

A shoofly was placed in operation around the fallen Arroyo Seco bridge near downtown Los Angeles, on March 5, thus reopening the Coast Line. The Valley Line was not quite so easily repaired. On the same day, an inspection party of engineers and maintenance men, traveled through Soledad Canyon on foot to survey the extent of damage in that section. It was apparent this leg of the San Joaquin Line had taken the brunt of the storm. The damage in the Tehachapi was moderate compared to the carnage in Soledad Canyon.

Fully 13 miles of railroad, between Ravenna and Lang, had been battered by the waters of the Santa Clara River. In the section of railroad between Russ and Lang, the destruction was particularly severe. Five steel bridges were washed out and three others completely buried in silt and debris. Tunnel Nos. 18 and 19 near milepost 437 had been converted into giant culverts and were clogged with debris. Over 3,000 feet of track one-mile below Ravenna, was gone without leaving a trace. Four additional miles of railroad, between milepost 434.5 and milepost 438, were also totally washed away requiring complete rebuilding. Wild animals, used in movie making, normally harbored in a compound near Ravenna, were running loose.

In order to return the railroad to complete operation as soon as possible, track and bridge gangs were rushed in from the Coast, Western, Sacramento and Tucson divisions to expedite the rehabilitating of the damaged portions of the Soledad Canyon line and elsewhere in southern California. Private contractors — actually anyone with a Caterpillar tractor or similar piece of equipment — were hired to rebuild damaged or destroyed fills. At the peak of reconstruction, 2,000 men were employed in the storm devastated area.

On March 7th, the Tehachapi Line, between Bakersfield and Mojave, was reopened for service. SP's Valley Line passenger schedules still stub ended at Bakersfield with SP's subsidiary Pacific Motor Trucking handling milk, mail, baggage and express between there and Los Angeles. Passengers continued their journey by bus. The Santa Fe was allowed to resume normal operations across the

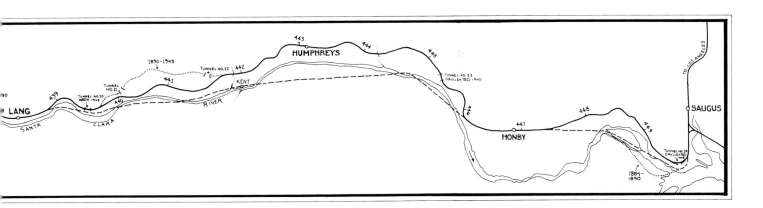

During the storm, five steel bridges were lost. Three other bridges were buried under silt and debris. (ABOVE) Both highway and railroad suffered at the 2nd crossing near Russ. (LEFT) Work is underway on a line change at the 6th crossing. —

district to Barstow.

At 10:30 P.M. on March 14th, twelve days after the line was closed in Soledad Canyon, the last spike was driven on a temporary line and the route reopened for traffic. The most expensive repair centered between Ravenna and Lang, where in the restoration effort about five miles of line changes were made. None of the three remaining tunnels in this area were eliminated at this time although later, in 1944, tunnel No. 17½ was daylighted. A major characteristic of this new work was the elimination of all but one of the eleven crossings of the Santa Clara River that were left after the "water proof" line changes of 1890. Although the emergency was over, the railroad had learned a bitter lesson. Clearly, one did not attempt to bridge the Santa Clara and expect the structure to last. Huge new river channels were excavated in the Santa Clara and lined with a concrete bed so that only one crossing in the entire canyon was necessary.

During the next several years and up through 1945, a number of similar line changes were made to ease curves. In 1945, tunnel Nos. 20, 21 and 22 were eliminated when a new three mile line change was built between Lang and Humphreys. Tunnel No. 23, a mile and one-half west of Honby was daylighted in 1942, and tunnel No. 24 near Saugus eliminated by a line change in 1943. The net effect was the relieving of some restrictions in this heavily trafficked corridor.

Traffic through the area had been on the upswing since the late 1930's. By this time, sufficient passenger business was returning to justify expansion of schedules. On February 2, 1936, SP's *Owl* and *West Coast* once again became separate trains in the Tehachapi Mountains. A short time later, the Santa Fe was able to return two trains to the Barstow-Bakersfield run, No. 2, the *Scout* and No. 9, the *Navajo*. Then, in July of 1938, the Santa Fe inaugurated the *Golden Gate* streamliners running between San Francisco-Oakland and Bakersfield connecting at Bakersfield with trains for the East.

The Southern Pacific was the first of the two railroads to inaugurate a streamliner over the Tehachapi Mountains. With the success of their *Coast* and *Noon Daylight* trains, a decision was made in late 1939 to run one of similar design down the Valley Line. Equipment was ordered closely patterned after the Coast Line trains. On July 4, 1941, two new *San Joaquin Daylight* trains were placed in service. Each consisted of six chair cars, a diner, a tavern-coffee shop car, a parlor-observation car and a baggage-mail car. These two trains were essentially an upgrading of the old *San Joaquin*, retaining the old train Nos. 51 and 52. The streamliner traversed the Tehachapi westbound about midday and eastbound in the late afternoon. Special motive power for the trains was arranged. In the valley, three P-10 Pacific's equipped with skyline casings and *Daylight* skirting were utilized. Five Mountain type locomotives, Nos. 4350, 4352, 4353, 4361 and 4363, had their cabs and tenders painted in *Daylight* red and orange, and were assigned to the mountain run.

Freight traffic was on the increase as the 1930's came to a close. The perishable business, which remained strong during the depression, received a shot in the arm with the development of the Central Valley Water Project — specifically the Friant-Kern canal. This waterway opened up vast acreage in the lower San Joaquin Valley which had previously been unsuitable for cultivation. The White Rose of California, a smooth well shaped potato, was found to be well suited to the sandy soil of Kern County. With water available, the White Rose was destined to become the county's number one crop. By July 1939, the SP claimed 4,132 cars of potatoes were shipped out of the Edison-Arvin district — most of it going north, then east on the Overland Route. In the next few years, however, the Santa Fe was to corner a sizeable share of the potato traffic. The May-through-July potato rush over a period of years became a significant factor in traffic densities over the Tehachapi.

Sugar beets were another crop introduced with the availability of water. Handled almost exclusively by the Southern Pacific, the beets were loaded in "racks" — wooden cages with tapered bottoms and trap doors — two to a flat car. These often weighed upwards of 100 tons per car when fully loaded. A solid train of the "roots," as they were called, made excessive demands on its crew. This was due to the age of the equipment and weight restrictions — upwards of 5,000 tons per train. Braking became the principal problem. Solid sugar beet trains descending either slope of Tehachapi Pass were required to do so at a speed of 12 miles per hour. This required the setting of virtually all retainers on the train. Enormous clouds of blue smoke from the hot brakeshoes were the result. On one occasion, this phenomena created quite a scene. According to H.D. "Rock" Padgent, an engineer of considerable reputation, "We had orders to head in at Ravenna" with a heavy train of sugar beets, "and the smoke was so thick you couldn't see the second unit. By the time we got stopped, two county fire trucks had responded thinking the canyon was ablaze. But when the smoke cleared, all they had was a sugar beet train."

The emergence of the fast merchandise train, in response to the ever increasing competition from highways, made its appearance in the late 1930's. The Santa Fe inaugurated such a train in the late 1920's between Chicago and California known as symbol train No. 33. In April 1940, in answer to increasing competition, a similar train, No. 99, was placed on the schedule offering fifth morning delivery between St. Louis and Richmond. The Southern Pacific established "Zippers" Nos. 339 and 340 on the timecard about the same time.

These were first class schedules catering to the merchandise trade — the first of their kind on the Valley Line. The "Overnights" had already been in operation on the Coast Line since 1935. The significance and preferential scheduling of these new trains was soon engulfed, however, in a rising tide of traffic generated by hostilities on a global scale.

On December 7, 1941, the United States was plunged into war with Japan and Germany. With the immediate threat occurring in the Pacific theater, Southern Pacific and Santa Fe lines in California were quickly choked with priority war related traffic as men and materials moved toward Pacific Coast ports of embarkation. At this time, the energy and skill of railroaders working the Tehachapi grade was put to the test. The Mountain District grappled with the greatest job in its history. Railroad men furloughed for the better part of the 1930's suddenly had all the work they could handle and a good deal more.

Existing schedules were pushed to include ten sections or more of a single numbered train. Troop trains, of course, held priority. During the first three months of 1943, passenger traffic on the Pacific Lines of the Southern Pacific was more than double the corresponding period of World War I. Troop movements were to increase to more than four times heavier than a corresponding period in 1917-18. Even the "freight only" Jawbone saw special movements in the early years of the war. Trainloads of domestic Japanese were shipped to Owenyo where they were loaded into trucks bound for internment camps at Manzanar. Among the hottest war related special movements were the bomb trains. Short, amply powered and heavily guarded, these special movements were given rights over all trains and made the distance from Los Angeles to Bakersfield on the SP in less than eight hours. Mojave became a center of top priority activity due to the construction of military bases at Rogers Dry Lake and Inyokern on the Jawbone Branch. Sentries were posted at tunnels, bridges and junctions all across the district as a protection against any would be saboteurs.

The remote control systems set up in the late 1920's on the north slope and under utilized during the 1930's were now sorely taxed. Problems with crews departing Bakersfield dying on the 16-hour law before ever reaching Tehachapi were caused by the heavy congestion of trains. So heavy was the traffic density in this section of the hill that two dispatchers were used each trick. One handled the 29-mile section between Bakersfield and Bealville, while the other covered the railroad between Bealville and Tehachapi including the double-track through to Mojave. Two operators were stationed at Mojave, one to deal with the SP dispatcher and handle trains both east and west of town, and another whose duties included dealing with the Santa Fe dispatchers and copying messages. During the last years of the war, a train order office was established at East Mojave to deliver orders to eastward trains. There were now three operators per trick at Mojave. During 1941 and 1942 frequently 100 train orders were copied in an eight-hour shift, with as many as 72 tissues often being delivered to a single train with helpers. At this time the Tehachapi district was widely regarded as the heaviest train order job in the country.

With so many orders on the clip board, there was always the danger of "overlookin' your hand" (misreading the orders and forgetting about some important opposing train). Stories of harrowing experiences due to this oversight were associated with the busier times on the mountain. Sometimes deliberate liberties were taken to keep the railroad fluid. If a train wouldn't clear at a designated point, a flagman was sent out and the rear helper would take a portion of the train and drop back down to the next siding using the opposing train's head rights. At times of phenomenal density, the railroads didn't even try to run trains against each other. Rather they would move trains across the district in fleets of one direction or the other.

Woe be unto the inexperienced railroad man thrown into this dispatchers nightmare. Telegraphers were particularly vulnerable. As the story has it, a boomer operator who thought he was good — but was also suspected of hitting the bottle a little — confidently assumed the duties of 2nd trick train order operator at Tehachapi late one evening in 1942. The day man went up town to the hotel to lay down. Several hours later he was awakened by an alarming amount of whistles blowing in the local yard. Rushing down to the depot to see what was the matter, he discovered the once confident boomer quite shaken and unable to perform his duties. What's more, westbound trains were backed up from the office at Tehachapi clear to Mojave and the yard was choked with helpers waiting to return down the hill. The trainmaster soon arrived on the scene and sent the poor man out for coffee while he and the regular dayman sorted out the mess and got trains on the move again. The unfortunate telegrapher was discharged later that night, a victim of the intense pressures that went hand in hand with running a single track railroad where 100 train movements a day was rapidly becoming commonplace. Westbound trains awaiting clearance onto single track were the man's undoing — eastbound movements were easier to clear since they were entering double track.

Returning helpers complicated an already exceedingly busy situation to the point of saturation. To alleviate the problem, to some extent, it was the practice to run gangs of light helper engines back down the mountain in single movements. One Sunday, early in November 1942, a record helper movement was achieved. This day one helper after another reached Summit, was cut out and drifted back to Tehachapi pulling in the clear on the No. 3 siding to await orders and clearance back to Bakersfield. It was early evening before there was a break in oncoming traffic and by that time even track No. 2 was filled to capacity with returning helpers. There were 24 in all in the lineup, with representative examples of Santa Fe's 900, 1600 and 3800 class 2-10-2's intermixed with SP Mallets, 2-10-2's and 4-8-2's — nearly a half a mile long. When assembled and ready to leave they totalled 100,000 horsepower. Each engine had a crew — 48 men in all — and each crew received a copy of all train orders required for the run — nine each — totaling 216 tissues. Off down the hill, this record movement made an impressive sight and even appeared in *Ripley's Believe It Or Not*. This practice

Accumulated helpers, trapped at Tehachapi due to the war time congestion of traffic, drift downhill at Caliente in 1942. Eleven locomotives appear in this view; the record was 24, but the installation of C.T.C. in 1943 all but eliminated such spectacles. — F. A. NEJEDLY - OLA MAE FORCE COLLECTION

was generally frowned upon because of excessive weight on bridges but during the war, it sometimes became necessary.

With SP's Pacific Lines so vital to the war effort, the installation of Centralized Traffic Control (C.T.C.) on its heavily congested corridors became a priority. Early in 1942, C.T.C. was installed on the 16.6 miles of single track mainline over Cuesta Pass on the Coast Division. Later that year C.T.C. was in place on the Shasta Division between Redding and Black Butte. Simultaneously that summer signal crews began converging on the Tehachapi Mountains with the work beginning at Bena. As each section was completed it was placed in service. Slowly the gap of train order territory shortened as one by one train order offices were closed, at Caliente, Bealville, Woodford, and Marcel. Just twelve months later, on June 1, 1943, the C.T.C. was complete and fully functional (32.3 miles) from Bena to Tehachapi. The office at Tehachapi remained open for some time afterward, however, to issue run-lates to eastward trains entering the double-track. This allowed freight trains to run ahead of late first class trains.

With the new system in place, operating officials hoped to step up train movements by 50 percent, if not more. Certainly the traffic was there to test the system. On the single track north slope, the machine registered an average of 60 movements in 24 hours with 100 occurring on peak days. All in all, freight tonnage totals on Tehachapi Pass had swelled from a depression low of 15.2 million tons to a wartime peak in 1945 of 50.5 million tons shared equally by the Santa Fe and Southern Pacific. The latter's Saugus Line peaked in 1945 at 24.5 million tons.

The bulk of SP's wartime traffic was shouldered by the cab-forward locomotive. Even though the Southern Pacific had shipped all of these distinctive engines to other divisions in the early 1920's, their operation on the Mountain District proved quite successful. When new orders for this type of power were delivered by the Baldwin Locomotive Works, many were assigned to the Tehachapi run. In 1928, locomotives Nos. 4100 through 4109 were delivered. These engines were followed in 1929 and 1930 by 41 more bringing the series up to No. 4150. Enough of these (4100-4124) heavy 4-8-8-2's — the equivalent of nearly three Consolidations or not quite two 2-10-2's — assigned to the district were to have a significant impact on operations. This was especially true in light of a wholesale downturn in business. In the lean years of the early 1930's, the 4100's were powering virtually all through freight trains, as well as, some helper assignments in the Tehachapi.

The helper terminal at San Fernando was a casualty of larger engines and the general scarcity of traffic. The helper terminal at Caliente undeniably suffered from this development, too. With business on the increase, as the decade wore on, and the economics of running larger trains in order to cut cost, the SP saw the need for consistent helper operation on the grades between Mojave and Los Angeles. Lancaster, for a short time during the late 1930's, became home base for cab-forward helpers. One engine was generally handled with three crews on a rotation basis. The Lancaster helper worked west up to Ansel, or on occasion as far as Mojave, but more often than not worked east up to Vincent. While the engine was based at Lancaster, it would be added to a train anywhere convenient on the floor of the desert. Saugus replaced San Fernando as home base for helpers working the east end of the Mountain District. During the war years, just about any type locomotive under steam could be found working out of Saugus. The Saugus helper assisted westbound tonnage from Sylmar to Vincent, but occasionally could be found cut in at San Fernando or even Burbank. Some trips might even find the helper working through to Mojave. Eastbound assignments were generally confined to the stiff climb from Palmdale up to Vincent, or from Saugus to Tunnel. Fruit blocks off the Santa Paula Branch frequently required assistance and on many an occasion a Saugus helper would be added on the branch at Fillmore, and stay with the train to the top of the grade at Tunnel.

The pace of all helper operations on the San Joaquin Mountain District quickened as the full impact of the war was felt. At one point during the war, there were 44 helper turns on the Bakersfield engineer's assignment board; 15 at Mojave; 6 at Saugus. On eastbound trains operating out of Bakersfield, the traditional cutting off of all helpers at Summit ceased with the delivery of the 4200 series 4-8-8-2's received from Baldwin in 1942-43. As more of these big locomotives were received from the builder, it became the standard practice to run through at least two of these "Mallets" (a road engine and swing helper cut in) on most trains between the terminals of Bakersfield and Los Angeles. The necessary short helpers were added in the Tehachapi or where needed. While every locomotive that would steam was thrown at the mountain in the busy war years, it was the 4100 and 4200 series cab-forwards that were the backbone of steam power operations in the Mountain District. This claim even extended to passenger service.

As the passenger business continued to swell, train consists became too heavy for the 2300 series Ten-Wheelers, even the modern heavy versions. SP

The San Joaquin Division Superintendent conducts business from an office above the station as do the dispatchers. Centralized Traffic Control was installed on the mountain in 1943 between Bena and Tehachapi. (RIGHT) "Pop" Gaylan works the "button job" not too long after this modern equipment was installed. — SOUTHERN PACIFIC COLLECTION (BELOW) Having lost its helper, train No. 51 pauses just short of Baker Street in Bakersfield during March 1947. Shortly the Oakland bound *San Joaquin Daylight* will work its way north. — DONALD DUKE

Mountain District passenger schedules were then placed in command of 4300 series 4-8-2's and 4400 series 4-8-4's. Often the 4300 or 4400 would receive the helper assignment and the latest of the big cab-forwards would be the road engine. East out of Bakersfield, the helper would be cut at Summit. West out of Los Angeles Union Passenger Terminal, the helper would stay with the train all the way to Eric on a 236 mile "short" passenger turn-around job. After being cut off, the helper would drift back to Mojave where the crew would stop to eat, then double-head back to Los Angeles on another passenger run. In later years this operation was simplified by having the helper double-head across the entire district in both directions on passenger runs.

Something of a distinction in "Mallet" operation — and in passenger service for that matter — occurred on the *Owl* during heavy periods. Where else, but on the Tehachapi run, could one witness the spectacle of two 16-drivered Mallets routinely double-heading across an entire district on a passenger assignment.

Of the SP's passenger trains, only the *San Joaquin Daylight* regularly negotiated the Mountain District without the aid of the cab-forwards. The usual practice was to double-head a 4300 against a 4400 road engine out of Los Angeles on train No. 51. Upon arrival at Bakersfield, the 4300 was cut off and coupled to the point of No. 52 later in the day. The train was then double-headed back to Los Angeles. But even the *Daylights* were not immune. Economy, in the form of a Mallet, reared its ugly head in the early part of 1953 when the train had shrunk in size due to off-season loadings.

Although still too heavy for a single 4-8-4, the addition of the helper or second engine to the *San Joaquin* seemed an unnecessary extravagance. The solution was to assign a single 4200 to the run. Somewhere in the desert east of Mojave on its maiden run, the higher speeds of the streamliner caught up with the big engine and a rod was thrown. The following afternoon more conventional power was returned to the point of No. 52 operating out of Bakersfield, although from time to time in emergencies, a Mallet was seen on the train.

Working with so many helper and engine crews over such a long and punishing district created a spirit of comraderie among the men regularly working the mountain. Everyone had a job to do and there was a method in the way things were done. Double-heading out of Los Angeles on the passenger runs with a Mallet against the train and a 4300 with a large Vanderbilt tank as the helper dictated a certain way of doing things, especially with only a single water plug at many places along the line. Both engines would work hard out of Los Angeles on the steady pull up to San Fernando. Here the 4300 might take water if unusually low, but if not, water was then taken at Ravenna. The grade peaked midway through the lengthy San Fernando tunnel and while in the bore, the Mallet would do all the work so no one would get gassed. The Mallet would take water at Saugus and both engines would work hard up Soledad Canyon to Vincent. The helper would do most of the work across the floor of the desert and take water at Lancaster. The road engine would water at Mojave and so on.

The number of brakemen required on both Santa

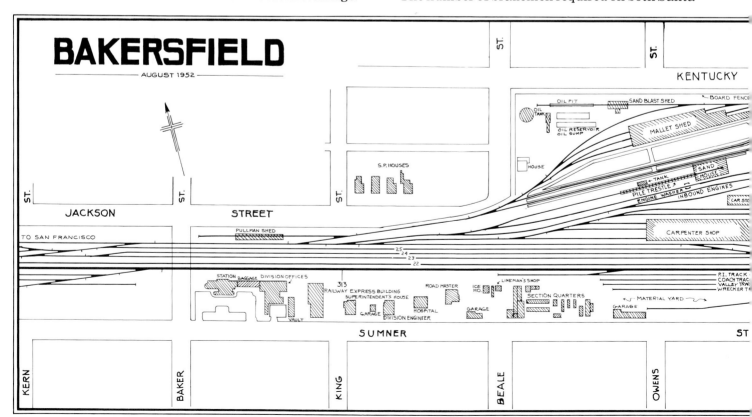

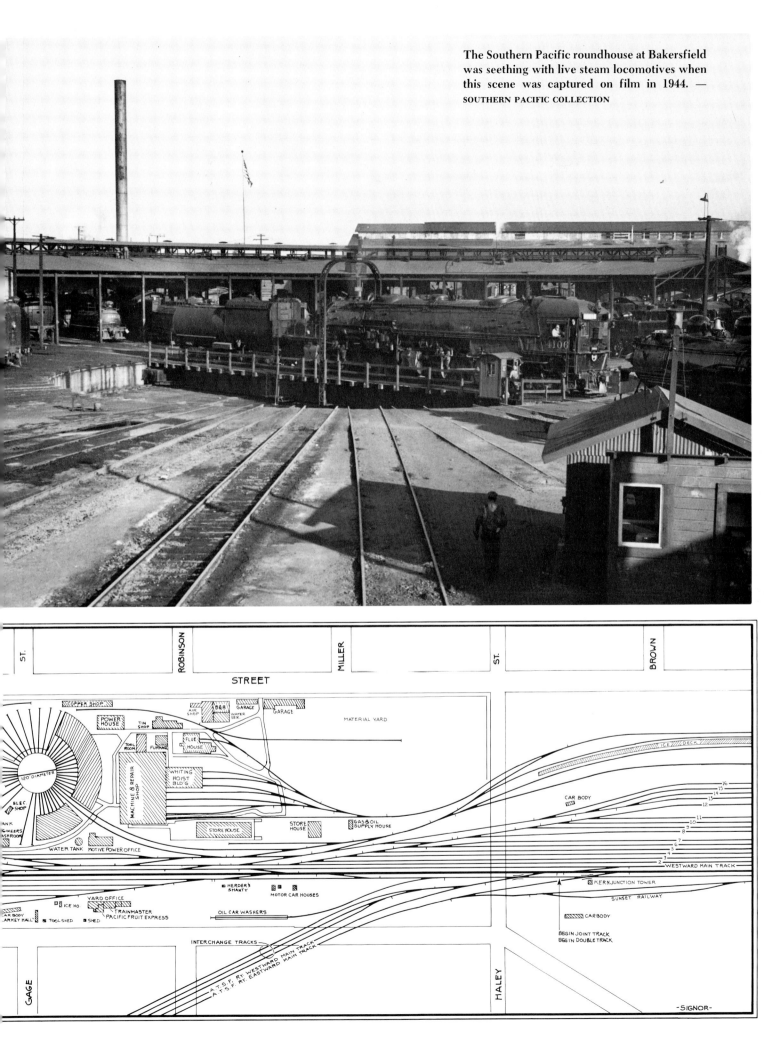

The Southern Pacific roundhouse at Bakersfield was seething with live steam locomotives when this scene was captured on film in 1944. — SOUTHERN PACIFIC COLLECTION

Southern Pacific maintained this ice deck at Bakersfield to accommodate the tremendous volume of perishable business generated in the lower San Joaquin Valley. The plant could freeze 400 tons of ice daily. — SOUTHERN PACIFIC COLLECTION (LEFT) A similar facility over at the Santa Fe yards in Bakersfield provided fully-iced and pre-cooled refrigerator cars for local packers such as this potato shed switched by the Santa Fe in the Arvin district — SANTA FE RAILWAY

Fe and SP trains in the mountains between Kern Junction and Mojave were thus; 1-49 cars, two men; 50-57 cars, three men; 58-72 cars, four men; 73-87 cars, five men; 88-102 cars, six men, and seven men were required on trains with 103 to 117 cars. Most trains, however, never exceeded 80 cars. Fourteen men operating a four-engine freight train up the north slope of the Tehachapi was an exercise in teamwork and communication in the days before radios. A freight train, generally 72 cars in length, would be in four parts down in the yards at Bakersfield when an eastbound train was called. As the engines emerged from the roundhouse ready track, each one would take its place in the train; the road engine on the east end at Mt. Vernon Avenue, the first swing helper against his cut, and the second swing against his cut. The rear of the train was made on the short tracks near the depot or sometimes west of Baker Street. When the rest of the train was together, the rear helper would then drag this cut up to make the train. The carmen then made an air test.

When the highball was received from the herder at Mt. Vernon, whistle signals and highballs by hand or lantern were passed down the train. The helpers, starting from the rear forward, would then shove the train out of the yard and do most of the work until the train was up to Sandcut. The road engine did some of the work up from Ilmon and through the narrows to maintain speed, but it wasn't until the train was out of Caliente that all the engines were working at capacity for the hard pull to the top.

Water stops on the north slope were a necessary evil. There were two water plugs at Caliente and water might be taken by SP engines conveniently spotted if the train was stopped for some reason. Santa Fe 900 and 1600 series 2-10-2's possessing 8,500 or 9,000 gallon tanks working up hill watered here out of necessity. The general use of larger capacity tenders, especially in the post-war years, rendered Woodford the only major water stop on the north slope of the Tehachapi. SP's No. 340, the hot merchandise train, running with Mallets equipped with 22,000 gallon tanks would run the water hole at Woodford and take it at Lancaster instead (if the water was above the fourth rung on the tank as the train passed Rowen). Otherwise virtually all freight trains watered at Woodford. In the San Joaquin Division timetable special instructions for the Tehachapi Subdivision, considerable space was devoted to procedures required when taking water at Woodford. Because of the complexity of the operation, it was truly a matter of pride to see how fast the chore could be accomplished.

Working upgrade into Woodford, the road engine would reduce throttle and let the helpers shove it to spot at the No. 1 water plug near the east switch. When stopped, the first swing helper would cut away and drop back down to the No. 2 plug just below the section houses. When this engine was stopped, the second swing helper would cut away and drop back to the No. 3 plug located in the curve above the third crossing of Tehachapi Creek. When this engine was stopped, the rear helper would cut away and drop back down to the No. 4 plug about 20 cars above the west switch. After each engine had taken its fill, the train was put back together, commencing with the first swing helper moving against the head end, with the rear helper bringing up the final section to make the train. While all this was being done, the brakemen were busy securing and unsecuring portions of the train by means of handbrakes according to the special instructions. With air restored, an air test was made and when completed and authorization to leave Woodford was received, the helpers, starting from the rear forward, would lean against the train to start it. The entire operation, done on the crooked tracks in the canyon, was accomplished by hand, lantern, and whistle signals. The Santa Fe trains, of course, shared in the ritual of taking water at Woodford and for them the same rules applied. An hour and a half could be consumed in the operation, but as little as 20 minutes to perform the job was claimed on occasion. It was a matter of pride to see how fast it could be accomplished and the taking of water at this wide spot in the road on the north slope of the Tehachapi was an art.

Santa Fe's late steam freight operations in the Tehachapi Mountains were characterized by the consistent use of Santa Fe type motive power designs — some dating back to the very beginnings of the road's operation in the area. All innovations and experimental power were left to the more "competitive" Los Angeles-Chicago mainline. Massive 2-10-2 workhorses in the 900, 1600 and 3800 classes continued to work the Mountain District much as they had done throughout the first three decades of the twentieth century. Enough of these engines were delivered to relegate the 2-8-0 Consolidations to yard and branch service. War-time emergencies, however, placed some of these aging engines into temporary helper service on the mountain. Santa Fe engines were well maintained and it was generally conceded by both Santa Fe and SP men alike that the 3800 class had the loudest and sharpest exhaust of any engine on the hill. They also had the best whistles too!

Crews working on Santa Fe's Mountain District were based at Bakersfield, turned at Barstow and, up until 1949, were under the jurisdiction of the Arizona Division. During the busy war years, as many as 80 mountain engine crews appeared on the Bakersfield assignment board. The Santa Fe maintained no helper crews, but called the men in turn for various positions on the train. The first man out was on the road engine all the way to Barstow; the second out on a helper as was the third and fourth man if necessary. The normal procedure was to have one road engine and two short helpers to Summit Switch on eastbound trains. From there it was easy for a single engine to handle the train all the way to Barstow. Rich Hill, a seven-mile rise along Rodgers Dry Lake east of Mojave, could offer some resistance but was easily overcome. Westbound out of Barstow, trains were operated with a single locomotive to Mojave with a 3800 series 2-10-2 nearly always holding down the assignment. With these engines equipped with 15,000 gallon tanks or better, the water stop at Muroc was frequently omitted. At Mojave, during the heavy war years, as many as 15 crews were maintained by the Santa Fe to work the helpers. While helpers were placed on a westbound train, the road engine would stop to fill its tank. Then it was off to do battle with the Tehachapi grade.

The Santa Fe had a strong valley perishable business each season. Their Green Fruit Expresses were the fastest freight trains on the mountain. A GFX with two 3800's shoving would often pass an SP train outside of Bakersfield. Its helpers would then be half way back down the hill from Tehachapi before the SP train it had passed earlier was up to Woodford. Occasionally, when a high market price was to be gained by the shipper, Santa Fe would expedite special perishable trains even more rapidly than usual. Fast mountain engines were hot and ready to go when these trains, limited to about 20 express reefers, arrived on the mainline at Bakersfield from the growing areas. The lading might consist entirely of strawberries, early potatoes, or even plums. On occasion it was asparagus — this train being referred to as a "Grass Special." In a matter of minutes the power was swapped and the train would be off. With passenger train priority, the specials moved quickly over the Mountain District.

Santa Fe passenger schedules were handled by the 3700 class 4-8-2's and 3751 class 4-8-4's as mainline power and conventional 2-10-2's as helpers. During times of heavy troop movements, examples of the 79-inch drivered 3450 class 4-6-4's would run up and down the Valley Line to Bakersfield. Some lighter Pacifics were often used. But the Santa Fe kept the northern California extension off limits to its larger classes of steam power. The road's famous 3776 and 2900 class 4-8-4's, to the best of everyone's recollection, never saw the oak-studded hills of the Tehachapi. Such was not the case for the mighty 5001 class 2-10-4's. While these engines were not used in the Tehachapi per se, at least one trip up that way was well documented.

Santa Fe's modern steam operations in the Tehachapi Mountains were punctuated by early and consistent use of a revolutionary new form of motive power. It was at the Santa Fe's insistence that a 5001 class 2-10-4 was pitted against an Electro-Motive 5,400 horsepower four-unit FT diesel

Electro-Motive demonstrator No. 103 rounds the loop on a test run over the district during January 1940. With a Santa Fe dynomometer car in tow testing the performance of the diesel locomotive, the test engine took, 2,200 tons from Barstow to Bakersfield in five hours and four minutes without the aid of a helper. — F. A. NEJEDLY — OLA MAE FORCE COLLECTION

The *San Joaquin Daylight* with retainers smoking on all 16 cars, drops downgrade near tunnel No. 10. These two Mountain type locomotives, Nos. 4352 and 4363, are equipped with skyline casings. At one time each of these engines had *Daylight* skirting and their cabs and tenders painted in red and orange for the mountain run.
— H. L. KELSO - JEFF MOREAU COLLECTION

OVERLEAF

The *San Joaquin Daylight* led by two 4300's especially painted for the train, drop down through Allard in the spring. This colorful painting was executed by railroad artist Rod Richard Aszman.

118

locomotive in carefully monitored tests between Barstow and Bakersfield. The results of these tests, which occurred in January 1940, were not favorable to the steam powered contender. The diesel, demonstrator No. 103, handled 2,200 tons across the district westbound in five hours and four minutes. The 2-10-4 took 51 minutes longer and required the services of a helper from Mojave up to Eric. Eastbound, the diesel turned in another impressive record taking 1,800 tons unassisted to Barstow in six hours and six minutes. This was the first appearance of a road diesel locomotive in the area and the forerunner of a new age in railroading in the Tehachapi Mountains.

Santa Fe officials were impressed. Not only had the diesel performed well in the Tehachapi, but everywhere on their far-flung system. The advantage of a locomotive requiring no water on a railroad running through the arid southwest where water was scarce and loaded with alkali, was a large plus. The Santa Fe placed a large order and the first of the new freight FT's began arriving in the fall of 1941. Deliveries continued through the war years at the same time the SP was receiving their new cab-in-front Mallets. The first units to be delivered were assigned to the eastern lines of the Santa Fe system. As the new power continued to arrive, their territory was gradually expanded from Winslow, Arizona, west to San Bernardino and Bakersfield. The diesels began turning up in the Tehachapi in 1943 on GFX perishable trains and expedited troop movements. Numbered in the 100 series, the FT's were used as the road engine and steam continued to be used as helpers. After the war, the diesels were assigned to the territory and became a regular feature, especially during the potato rush. Eleven four-unit sets of the 100 class were modified in the summer of 1946 for passenger service. These diesels were rebuilt to include steam generators, 90 miles per hour gearing, and new passenger paint schemes. They saw service in the Tehachapi, as well as their replacements — the 16 class F3's and 51 class ALCO PA's, when they were delivered in the late 1940's.

The Southern Pacific was late to embrace the diesel. It wasn't until 1947 that the railroad began taking delivery of road freight units. By this time the 5,400 horsepower FT had been upgraded and a new model offered in its place — the 6,000 horsepower F3. Numbered in the 6100's (for cab units) and 8000's (for boosters), these engines began running on the San Joaquin Mountain District intermittently in the summer of 1948 to qualify the crews. Six four-unit sets were assigned to the district on October 1st of that year.

As with any learning experience from something new, there were teething pains and many long and arduous trips undertaken while getting to know the new power. Sarcastic crew callers upon awakening a crew for duty, would remark "You've got a diesel, bring a lunch." Yardmasters wouldn't dare place empty cars on the head end of a train powered by the diesels, their manual transition[1] would pull the guts right out of a car. This fact was amply demonstrated by one of the first test trains with the F3's run in the district. Departing Los Angeles just ahead of No. 55 with a full train, five brakemen and a cab full of officials, the diesels did well on the pull up through Sylmar. The grade peaked within the confines of tunnel No. 25, and once the diesels had surmounted it, they raced forward breaking the train in two within the dark and lengthy bore. This caused much consternation on the part of those involved and created serious delay for No. 55 and several opposing trains.

Stories of this nature got wide circulation, but the management was still impressed. There were too many good points to be overlooked. A run eastward to Tehachapi could be made often with a single Mallet helper and westward no helper was required at all from Los Angeles clear through to Bakersfield. Water stops were eliminated as was a considerable amount of delay attributed to working retainers. Turning time at the terminals was drastically reduced as was congestion due to less frequent use of helpers.

By the spring of 1949, although passenger service was still 100 percent steam, enough of the four-unit F3's were delivered for the Southern Pacific to optimistically dieselize its San Joaquin Division Mountain District freight operation. This arrangement was short lived however. The F3's ability to lug at low speeds was hampered by its traction motor gearing. A 62:15 ratio was utilized giving the locomotive a 65 miles per hour maximum speed and a minimum effective speed of 15.5 — significantly higher than normal mountain operations required. In this capacity, the steam helpers were better suited and shortly the Mallets returned to the Tehachapi and the F3's were transferred to Texas where their speed capability could be better utilized.

Both the Santa Fe and Southern Pacific began taking deliveries in 1949 of the next stage in freight diesel development, the F7. New engines of this model continued to arrive in vast quantities through 1950 and 1951. The SP's versions, which continued in the same numbering blocks as the F3's, were now delivered with a lower gear ratio (65:12) rendering the top speed 50 to 55 miles per hour. The effective minimum speed, however, was reduced to

---

[1]In short an electrical function similar to the switching of gears in a transmission.

12 — a rating more suitable for drag mountain service — and examples of SP's F7's began to filter into the Tehachapi operation, although this time on a more gradual basis than with the F3's.

The Santa Fe, however, with their ranks of F7's (200 Class) growing, now sought to dieselize their western operations with a vengeance. Enough 200 class units were delivered by the summer of 1950 to place them on the point of virtually all freights in the Tehachapi. The 100 class FT's were now replacing the steam helpers. A stable of 3800 class 2-10-2's was still maintained at Bakersfield for pusher service on the north slope, but their ranks were steadily thinned. The final blow to the 3800's came late in 1950 when the Santa Fe began taking delivery of General Motors GP7 1,500 horsepower road switchers. Numbered in the 2650 series, these diesels were assigned to the Tehachapi helper service fresh from the factory. Their arrival effectively killed the fire on the last Bakersfield 2-10-2's.

With the exception of an occasional 4-8-4, Santa Fe passenger schedules were now being handled routinely by the 16 class F3's, delivered between 1946 and 1949 and the 51 class ALCO PA's delivered between 1946 and 1948. The 90-class passenger diesels received from Fairbanks-Morse in June 1947, were tried in the Tehachapi, but were not a success. Amazingly enough, the units were not equipped with sanders. Frequent slipping down on the hill caused the engine's overspeed device to trip shutting the engines to idle. A trip with the 90 on the mountain was looked upon with dread by the firemen who would, of necessity, be stationed at the overspeed lever in the engine room until the summit was achieved.

Total dieselization of Santa Fe Mountain District operations was expected any day now. Even the SP was making significant gains in this regard. But events across the Pacific were to give the steam locomotive one last reprieve in the Tehachapi Mountains. War broke out in Korea in June 1950 dragging with it a pledge for military assistance from the United States. With this commitment came the familiar glut of military traffic in the Tehachapi Mountains. Hitting as it did during the busy perishable season, all available motive power was pressed into service. Santa Fe's 3800's made their last stand in helper service that summer and they were not returned to service the following season. It was during these hostilities that the road operated its last steam power on the mountain — in passenger service. The engines used were not the traditional 2-10-2's, 3700 class Mountains or 3751 class Northerns, but members of the seldom seen 3450 class 4-6-4's. Engines Nos. 3450 and 3459 became a common sight on main trains (*main* line troop *trains* as referred to by the rails) during the first years of the war. At this time, even the 84-inch drivered No. 3460 piloted a troop train into Bakersfield, but was quickly turned and sent back to Barstow. It is believed that during July 1952, the last 4-6-4 rolled across the district closing this chapter of Santa Fe operations in the Tehachapi even though the war continued for another year. Southern Pacific, however, continued to rely heavily on its brace of steam power.

A wartime *San Joaquin Daylight*, with engine No. 4429, rolls into Bakersfield sans helper. On this day the train had only three headend cars, four coaches, and a diner. — ROY GRAVES — BANCROFT LIBRARY COLLECTION

In a daily ritual, the incoming valley power on No. 52, the *San Joaquin Daylight,* is cut off and routed through the pocket track to the roundhouse. A set of freight F7 diesels, wait patiently beyond the switch for the run up the hill. Although the mountain run of the *San Joaquin Daylight* was dieselized late in 1952, 4-8-4's continued to handle the train north of Bakersfield until September 1956. — DONALD SIMS

Steam was still king at Santa Fe's Bakersfield roundhouse, but the diesels were beginning to appear. An FT can be seen on the ready track in the lower left corner of the aerial view shown above. — KERN COUNTY MUSEUM (LEFT) Mountain helper engines ring the turntable at the Santa Fe roundhouse in Bakersfield. — R. O. STOLZENFELS

The Santa Fe Railway joins the SP's Mountain District at Kern Junction Tower in Bakersfield. Since the SP was there first, Santa Fe employees staff and maintain the structure. In these views, taken in December 1947, Charles A. Griffith pulls the levers while David B. Halan copies orders which are picked up by Santa Fe trains entering the joint line. — ALL KERN COUNTY MUSEUM

The Southern Pacific had the first regularly scheduled streamliner over the Tehachapi line. Their *San Joaquin Daylight* was unveiled July 4, 1941. A heavy version of this train with 20 cars is seen climbing Sandcut Hill three years later. — JAMES H. HARRISON COLLECTION (LEFT) Santa Fe's *Golden Gate* train gets underway at Bakersfield during World War II. The road was the first to regularly operate a streamliner into Bakersfield, inaugurating the service during 1938. — R. O. STOLZENFELS

The rear helpers of train 1-814 are shoving hard as the head end crests Sandcut during May 1938.
— F. C. SMITH - STAN KISTLER COLLECTION

Helpers are a dispatcher's curse, but they add interest to the operations in the Tehachapi. "Everything but the kitchen sink" is represented in this string of 15 locomotives looping round at Caliente during 1942. — F. A. NEJEDLY - OLA MAE FORCE COLLECTION (RIGHT) Wartime emergencies dictated drastic measures, steam and diesel helpers, two trains worth, take the same curve in 1950. — STAN KISTLER

With the worst of the heavy grade behind, a westbound SP freight train slips through Caliente during April 1952. Southern Pacific and Santa Fe crews alike agreed that the flats of Caliente always looked like heaven when they worked a hard-to-handle-train down the hill. — STAN KISTLER

The ascent of the north slope of the Tehachapi starts in earnest on the high side of Caliente. (RIGHT) Train No. 24, the *Grand Canyon,* knuckles into the grade during February 1949. — DONALD DUKE (BELOW) While farther up the grade, the rear brakeman gets a full view of two cabforward pushers assisting an eastbound freight. — SOUTHERN PACIFIC - TRAINS MAGAZINE COLLECTION

Train No. 52, the *San Joaquin Daylight*, leaving Bakersfield for the mountains presented a striking scene. The long string of brilliantly colored equipment contrasted with the earth tones of the rugged Tehachapi country in the long shadows of the late afternoon. Railroad photographer Stan Kistler masterfully captures the beauty of this daily event in December 1952 as the *Daylight* works upgrade in the ravine between Ilmon and Caliente. (OPPOSITE PAGE-TOP) The *Daylight* approaches the portal of tunnel No. 2. (OPPOSITE PAGE-LOWER) Later the streamliner streaks across the Tehachapi Valley, near Summit Switch, at 60 miles-per-hour as the mid-winter sun fades into twilight.

Southern Pacific No. 4434, one of the original *Daylight* 4-8-4's with single headlight, slowly steams up to the water plug at Caliente during the mid-1950s. The locomotive is handling an excursion train from Los Angeles to Bakersfield, and is now on the return leg of the trip. — DONALD DUKE

Santa Fe's daily accommodation, the *Grand Canyon,* works uphill above tunnel No. 1 behind stylish ALCO passenger engines during December 1952. — STAN KISTLER

An SP freight, running as first section of No. 812, picks up orders at Bealville in 1940. The train order office here was closed during the late spring of 1943 following the installation of C.T.C. — FRANK PETERSON - DONALD DUKE COLLECTION

Santa Fe extra No. 139 east grinds upgrade at tunnel No. 2 on May 17, 1947. Shoving hard are 2-10-2's Nos. 3841 and 3850. The diesels had replaced steam as road engines on the point of most Santa Fe trains by this time. — BOTH DONALD DUKE

Fireman R. O. Stolzenfels has camera in hand as his train drops down grade in the Tehachapi during World War II. (BELOW) Holding the siding, Stolzenfels' train clears the Santa Fe extra No. 3845 east at Rowen.

The second section of Santa Fe train No. 23 approaches the east switch at Rowen on December 21, 1951. Road engine No. 3760 is assisted by F7 No. 253 and booster — added at Mojave. The two units in dynamic braking mode could hold the entire train of 10 cars to 25 m.p.h. on the descending grade. — PHILLIPS C. KAUKE

133

Southern Pacific extra 6123 west whines down the north slope of the Tehachapi. The F3, on one of its first runs over the district in 1948, negotiates a rare stretch of tangent track at Rowen. — SOUTHERN PACIFIC COLLECTION

Train 1-814, trailing the drawbar of cab-forward No. 4100, takes siding at the west end of Woodford. — R. H. KINDIG - GUY L. DUNSCOMB COLLECTION

Cab-forward No. 4202 and 4-8-4 No. 4440 work upgrade in the remote Caliente Creek narrows en route to Caliente. The train is a wildflower excursion from Los Angeles. Note the California poppies in the foreground. (LEFT) Three Santa Fe ALCO PA's charge the mountain grade which begins in earnest at Caliente in 1954 with the *Grand Canyon Limited.* — BOTH DONALD DUKE

Four water plugs were strung out the length of the Woodford siding and it was a rare freight indeed that didn't stop to take water there. (ABOVE) An eastbound, having taken its fill, departs Woodford during May of 1944. The center track is the mainline while the rails on the right are the house track or short siding. Water plug No. 3 is in the foreground. — JAMES H. HARRISON COLLECTION (LEFT) The advent of diesels like FT No. 127 slipping by plug No. 2 near the 3rd crossing of Tehachapi Creek changed all this. — V. C. CIPOLLA COLLECTION

Up until the installation of Centralized Traffic Control, the 24-hour train order office at Woodford figured heavily in Tehachapi operations. — ROY GRAVES - BANCROFT LIBRARY COLLECTION

The season perishable rush was a time of great congestion in the Tehachapi. This was due largely to Santa Fe traffic of potatoes from April to September. Santa Fe could move anywhere from six to eight *GFX* (Green Fruit Express) trains over the mountain within a 24-hour period. (ABOVE) Two 2-10-2's hustle a 15-car *GFX* through Woodford during 1946. — DONALD DUKE (LEFT) A year later FT's were on the point of these expedited trains. — JOHN LAWSON - WILL WHITAKER COLLECTION

A Southern Pacific wildflower excursion train to the Tehachapi Mountains blasts past the station at Vincent. With no wells close by, water cars supplied this outpost at the summit of the Soledad Canyon grade. — DONALD DUKE

Santa Fe F-units still handled this mainline assignment over the Tehachapi when No. 235-C rolled through Bena, bound for Bakersfield in 1965. — GORDON GLATTENBERG

Telegrapher Frank Nejedly sits amidst the tools of his craft in the operator's bay at Woodford in 1937. From left to right, his tools include a pole with hook used to hang out a lantern at night in order to flag trains (Woodford being a flag stop), train order delivery hoops, train order signal levers, venerable old L. C. Smith typewriter for typing train orders, dispatcher's phone, telegraph sounder, remote control switch indicators and levers, and the standard railroad clock. The display board, center of scene, indicates a meet is in progress with westbound SP extra No. 3711 which is framed in the window, and an unknown eastbound. Frank was born December 6, 1882, began his railroad career on the Denver & Rio Grande, but was working 2nd trick telegraph at Warren on the SP by 1907 — a position he held for 8 years. He worked other places on the mountain — Cameron, Bealville, Marcel, Tehachapi, and Mojave — before settling down at Woodford in 1922. Upon the closing of Woodford in 1943, Frank took a job at Rosamond until he retired in 1947. Over the years Frank distinguished himself by becoming resident photographer and historian for the Tehachapi country. Indeed, many of the rarest illustrations in this volume are his work. — SOUTHERN PACIFIC COLLECTION.

It was widely regarded among railroaders that Santa Fe's 3800-class 2-10-2's had the sharpest and loudest exhaust of any engine working the Tehachapi grade. The best whistles too! Time is running out for the breed, however, as the No. 3849 lugs eastbound tonnage over the 5th crossing of Tehachapi Creek in this 1949 view.
—DONALD DUKE

The celebrated Tehachapi Loop has attracted photographers for years. (RIGHT) Joseph Muench caught Santa Fe train No. 9, the *Scout,* approaching tunnel No. 9 in the late 1930's. — DONALD DUKE COLLECTION (BELOW) The locomotive and caboose of an eastbound SP freight line up perfectly for the company photographer in 1944. An 80-car train of 40-foot cars would do it every time. — SOUTHERN PACIFIC - DONALD DUKE COLLECTION

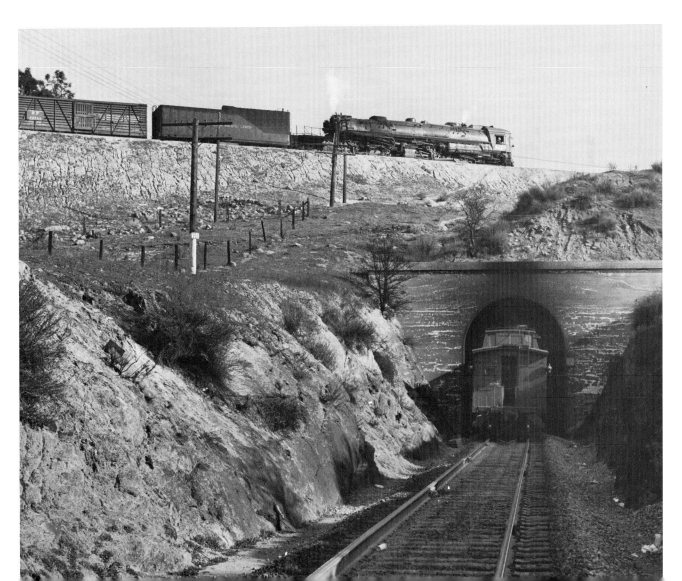

During a February blizzard in 1945, Santa Fe's *NCX* prepares to depart Walong following a meet with an eastbound. Although the Tehachapi Mountains are generally associated with the warm to scorching weather of spring and summer, snow regularly falls at this elevation and lower each winter season. — PHILLIPS C. KAUKE

Extra No. 4196 has just passed through the tunnel as it prepares to round the loop en route to Tehachapi. Santa Fe No. 1690 waits patiently for the green. — H. L. KELSO - JEFF MOREAU COLLECTION (RIGHT) Cab-forward helper assists a freight around the loop. — JAMES H. HARRISON COLLECTION

The exhausts of a four-engine freight, intensified by cold weather, trace the circumference of the loop during the winter of 1940. — F. C. SMITH -STAN KISTLER COLLECTION

Diesels have just taken a "Kaiser perishable" pipe train around the loop in the late 1940's. JAMES H. HARRISON COLLECTION (LEFT) Lots of train activity crowds the scene a few years later at the east switch of Walong. — DONALD DUKE

The basic layout of the loop can be ascertained by studying the two photos on this page. Nearly two miles of railroad can be traced in the lower photo yet the distance as the crow flies between the extremeties is a mere 2,200 feet! The difference in elevation from railhead to railhead at the center of the loop is 77 feet. — BOTH DONALD DUKE COLLECTION

The tradition of operating special trains each spring over the San Joaquin Mountain District came about in the late 1940's. During April and May, the unspoiled and wildly beautiful Tehachapi country comes alive with California poppy, lupin, baby blue-eyes, mustard and a myriad of other species of wild flowers carpet the rich green slopes. Taking advantage of the season, the Railway Club of Southern California, the Railroad Boosters, Pacific Railroad Society, and other rail enthusiast groups organized special trains designed to appeal to the "poppy pickers." Yet judging by the strength of the photo line as one such outing pauses at the loop in 1954, it was the hundreds of rail enthusiasts that made the excursions a success. — DONALD DUKE

A set of FT's, with the aid of a steam generator car, move an eastbound troop train between Walong and Marcel during the summer of 1946. — DONALD DUKE

A freight running as No. 811 snakes down through tunnel No. 11 in April 1940. This short bore, lacking both portals and interior lining, was day-lighted along with nearby tunnels Nos. 12 and 13 in 1943. — WALTER THRALL - DONALD DUKE COLLECTION

The head brakeman and fireman take advantage of the comfort afforded by an open window and short sleeves as Southern Pacific extra No. 4233 east blasts upgrade through Marcel on a hot summer day during 1946. Spring switches at both ends of Marcel create two single direction sidings. The track adjacent to the roaring Mallet is the eastward track. Santa Fe No. 964, a 2-10-2, pauses at the west switch of the westward siding. — DONALD DUKE

The paint job on this set of FT's, barely three years old, is showing marked signs of wear as Santa Fe extra 132 west pauses at Marcel in 1946. — PHILLIPS C. KAUKE

During the late summer of 1953, Southern Pacific assigned 17 ALCO 1,600 horsepower road switchers to the Tehachapi. Ideally suited for mountain drag service, these six-axle RSD-5s replaced the last steam helpers based at Bakersfield. (RIGHT) Two of these locomotives having helped an eastbound to the summit, drift down through Caliente on December 27th of that year. (BELOW) The No. 5301 tows the east mountain local through the siding at Cable the same day. — BOTH STAN KISTLER

The section of track between Cable and Tehachapi, now double-track with reverse signal C.T.C., was for many years single track. A late-season *GFX* negotiates this stretch during October 1945. Up ahead are the four FT units No. 147 followed by dead-heading steam generator car No. 9000.
—PHILLIPS C. KAUKE

The first section of Santa Fe's *Grand Canyon* overtakes a Southern Pacific freight 2-806, at the east switch at Cable. — WILLIAM D. MIDDLETON

Santa Fe F7's began showing up in the Tehachapi during 1950. Extra No. 210 passes Southern Pacific helper No. 4237 waiting on a siding at Cable. — STAN KISTLER

151

A Southern Pacific train powered by ruggedly-geared F7's, pass the west switch at Tehachapi in May 1954. A string of foreign line reefers trail the motive power. — JAMES H. HARRISON COLLECTION

Santa Fe extra No. 227 west crests the summit of Tehachapi Pass at 50 mile-per-hour. — RICHARD STEINHEIMER

A late season *GFX* running as 2nd No. 812, with 4-8-2 No. 3726 up front and 2-10-2's Nos. 3830, 979 and 3831 shoving hard at various intervals throughout the 68-car consist blasts toward summit during October of 1941. The Santa Fe shared second and third class schedules with the Southern Pacific from World War I up until the installation of C.T.C. Thereafter the Santa Fe's trains ran extra. In displaying markers for a following section, rule No. 19 of the Special Instructions stipulated that the Southern Pacific use green, while the Santa Fe should use yellow, a procedure in effect until the late 1960's. — PHILLIPS C. KAUKE

A heavy *Grand Canyon* train is caught in the late afternoon light streaking across the Tehachapi Valley. The GP7 helpers will be removed at Mojave. Trailing the ALCO passenger locomotives is rare Fairbanks-Morse "Erie Built" No. 90 which, in 1952, was seeing its final runs over the Mountain District. — STAN KISTLER

During each Christmas season special trains were operated by the Southern Pacific to accommodate a burgeoning express business. One of these trains called the "Santa Claus Specials," steams upgrade at Cameron in the 1940's. — V. C. CIPOLLA

In 1946, four 100 class freight diesels were modified for passenger service by the Santa Fe. (RIGHT) A pair of these units streak by the camera near Warren assisted by a 2-10-2. Enough additional passenger power was delivered by 1950 to have the four returned to freight service. (BELOW) The road's steam power was by then, for the most part, withdrawn from the district. In what is undoubtedly one of the last runs of a Santa Fe steam engine in the Tehachapi, Hudson type No. 3450, moves four cars of a Navy officers special through Cameron during the summer of 1953. The special is running as the 2nd section of No. 7, the *Fast Mail & Express.* — BOTH V. C. CIPOLLA

A 21-car troop train, held in check by 2-10-2 No. 3854, glides into Mojave during the summer of 1946. — FRANK J. PETERSON - DONALD DUKE COLLECTION

By the summer of 1949, diesels were becoming increasingly common in the mountain operation. Four unit sets command many assignments. This string of freight units is rated at 2,500 tons on the south slope of the Tehachapi. — T. M. HOTCHKISS

Train No. 24, the *Grand Canyon,* pauses at Mojave behind a set of F3's. Nine of the 11-car cars making up the train are handling head end business consisting of mail, express, and company business. — JOHN LAWSON - W. C. WHITTAKER COLLECTION

Extra No. 3250 west smokes it up at the west end of tunnel No. 29 at Searles. Signal No. 4268 is one of two block signals on the Jawbone Branch. The other protects the opposite end of the bore. — DONALD DUKE

A single RSD-5 handles the Lone Pine Local near Saltdale. The ALCO's were banned from the branch after officials began to worry that they might set the Searles tunnel afire. — RICHARD STEINHEIMER

During the Memorial Day weekend of 1952, a special "Owens Valley Holiday" was operated over the Oweyno Branch by the Railway Club of Southern California. The main interest was SP's famous narrow-gauge at the end of the line, but a photo run-by was obligingly staged at the south entrance to the Searles tunnel. — V. C. CIPOLLA

"Mudhen" No. 4012 working a Searles Turn is reflected in a pool of irrigation water at Cantil. An oasis in a barren desert, Cantil, 23 miles from Mojave, was one of two water holes on the entire Jawbone Branch. The other was at Haiwee, 81 miles down the line toward Lone Pine. — N. D. HALLAMORE COLLECTION

This frame structure served as the telegraph office and agency at Searles, junction of the Trona Railway, for many years. — W. C. WHITTAKER COLLECTION

Mr. Farrow takes his call . . .

The call boy pounds on the door of room No. 23 of the Quincy Hotel in Bakersfield disturbing Southern Pacific engineer Bascom Farrow. It's 1:00 A.M. and Farrow, a Mountain District hoghead since 1907, is taking his last call prior to retirement — 2:45 A.M. on duty for No. 60, the *West Coast Limited*. A bite to eat amidst late night revelers and fellow rails, and it's down to the roundhouse. — ALL WARD KIMBALL

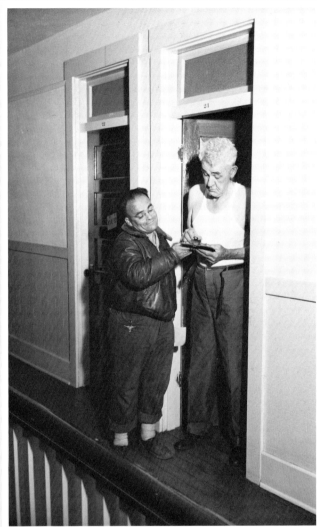

2:45 A.M. on duty . . .

3:45 A.M. out of town . . .

Out of his street clothes and into his Lee jumper, Farrow fills out the register. His power for the night — AC-10 No. 4246. Up front Ten-Wheeler No. 2350 will provide help up the hill. Clip board filled with orders, hand on the throttle — No. 60 is ready to depart on time for the mountains. — ALL WARD KIMBALL

Over the hill
on No. 60 . . .

BRIAN BLACK

162

ROBERT HALE

Mojave 5:45 A.M. . . .

The herder has done his work and No. 60, having lost its helper during the night, takes the crossover at the west end of Mojave and glides to a stop at the depot. Farrow glances back along his charge in the pre-dawn light.
—BOTH WARD KIMBALL

A veritable army of overall-clad rails, assigned to westbound freights 2nd and 3rd No. 801, wait patiently in the clear as No. 60 races through Saugus at 7:35 A.M. Down the line is Los Angeles and for Farrow a waiting pension. — WARD KIMBALL

A few years later, Saugus bustles with activity. Train 1st No. 803 waits in the westward siding for a train rolling in on the mainline to the left. In the pocket, at the right, a 4300 helper awaits another assignment. — RICHARD STEINHEIMER

An evening of train watching at Glendale in the early 1950's was rewarding. In addition to a steady parade of trains moving to and fro on the Coast Line, trains routed the "Valley" line also passed the location. This included three Bakersfield bound passenger trains easily identified by their schedule number — and the giant cab-forwards up front. (TOP-OPPOSITE) First to depart at 5:00 P.M. was the *Owl*, No. 57, rolling into town at sunset in 1952. — NOLAN BLACK (ABOVE) The *West Coast* was due to leave at 6:50 P.M. — DICK STEINHEIMER. Several hours later, the night mail, No. 55, would get underway. (LEFT-OPPOSITE PAGE) The *Mail*, awaits a 9:40 P.M. highball for the mountains in May 1954. Train No. 55 had the unique distinction of being the last train to be hauled over the Tehachapi grade by a steam locomotive in revenue service. — STAN KISTLER

Burbank Junction Tower, at milepost 471.6, has for many years been the point at which the San Joaquin Mountain District trains depart Los Angeles Division trackage. Running orders are obtained for the single-track run to Mojave by each westbound train. (LEFT) The engineer of a freight running as 3rd No. 807, reaches for the "flimsies" at Burbank Junction in the early 1950's. — RICHARD STEINHEIMER (ABOVE) The tower itself has since been razed and replaced by a simple metal structure. — DON SIMS

The *Owl* drops down Soledad Canyon near Russ in the later years of steam operation. During heavy periods, the *Owl* regularly ran with two cab-forwards. Where else but on the San Joaquin Division Mountain District of the Southern Pacific could one witness the spectacle of two sixteen-drivered articulateds being routinely double-headed across an entire district on a passenger run? — DON SIMS

Train No. 51 steams out of tunnel No. 18 near Lang during February 1946. The 4300 series Mountain will double-head with the 4-8-4 all the way to Bakersfield. — DONALD DUKE

The operator at Lang hands up orders to scheduled freight No. 801 creeping up the siding. — RICHARD STEINHEIMER (LEFT) Lang, the site of the "Golden Spike" driving in 1876, was for many years an important train order station at the mouth of Soledad Canyon. The station was closed in 1967. — DON SIMS

Ravenna, ten miles farther up the line, was an important water stop and train order station deep in the bowels of Soledad Canyon. — JOHN LAWSON - WILL WHITTAKER COLLECTION (BELOW) A westbound freight having taken water here, departs on the mainline during November 1939. The track adjacent to the station shown above, had a capacity of 36 cars and was designated by timetable as No. 2 track. — T. M. HOTCHKISS

First trick telegrapher C. B. Lary poses in front of the Vincent station in 1944. — SOUTHERN PACIFIC COLLECTION

Santa Fe 2-10-2 No. 3927, leased by the SP during a power shortage in 1951, crests the summit at Vincent on a westbound freight. The poorly fired engine holds the mainline. Spring switches at either end of Vincent provided eastward and westward sidings of 97-car capacity. A wye was available to turn helpers. — V. C. CIPOLLA

The crew of eastbound freighter No. 804 snare their orders as first the head-end power, the helper, and finally the caboose pass Vincent. —
ALL RICHARD STEINHEIMER

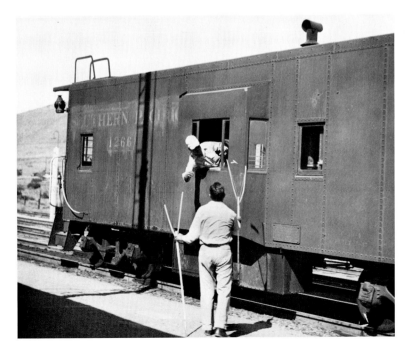

The first section of the *West Coast Limited* charges down off Ansel Hill in 1939, ahead stretched across the floor of the Antelope Valley, lay 20 miles of tangent and comparatively flat railroad. — FRANK J. PETERSON - DONALD DUKE COLLECTION

Ansel Hill, three miles of one percent or better grade, presents a problem for train No. 815 tackling the hill on a cold November morning during 1941. Assisting Consolidation No. 2557 and 2-10-2 No. 3690 on a 51-car train is miscast Pacific No. 2408. Such sights would soon raise no eyebrows. In the chaos following Pearl Harbor, anything and everything would be thrown at the Mountain District's formidable grades. — BOTH PHILLIPS C. KAUKE

Recently reassigned from the Texas & New Orleans, GS-1 No. 702 leads a nine car *San Joaquin Daylight* out of Mojave in 1953. — DONALD DUKE

The Mojave depot, divested of its second story in the 1930's, presents an interesting scene in 1951. Baggage carts crowd the platform — indicative of the junction's importance as a regional mail handling center. — JOHN LAWSON - WILL WHITTAKER COLLECTION

The detour . . .

Epic storms in the Sierra and over the entire State of California, in mid-winter 1952, closed several key rail lines in the state. January 11th, Western Pacific's Feather River Canyon line was taken out by major slides. SP's Donner Pass line was taken out by heavy snows on the 13th. Even SP's Coast and Soledad Canyon lines succumbed to slides and flooding on the 16th. The joint-track line over Tehachapi remained open, however, making possible a rather lengthy detour. The first train to take advantage of it was Western Pacific's *California Zephyr,* departing Oakland for Mojave on January 13th. The detour continued from Mojave to Barstow on the Santa Fe then east on the Union Pacific to Salt Lake City. The SP followed suit and Overland schedules began taking the detour on the 14th. For one day, January 16th, SP's Coast and Valley Line schedules detoured via Tehachapi and Barstow, then over Cajon Pass into Los Angeles. One by one, the various lines were returned to service with the Donner Pass line last to be placed in operation. In the interim a number of unusual trains moved over Mountain District rails.

In the view above, Southern Pacific's combined *Overland Mail,* No. 21, and *Gold Coast,* No. 23, departs Mojave for the mountains running as extra No. 4257 west on January 18th. (RIGHT) Santa Fe 4-8-4 No. 2910 had brought in a train from Barstow. The 2900's were rare in this part of the country and never seen in the Tehachapi. — BOTH A. C. PHELPS

Western Pacific's westbound *California Zephyr* detours through Mojave January 22nd. The streamliner is running as the 4th section of Santa Fe train No. 23, the *Grand Canyon.* — PHILLIPS C. KAUKE

Detoured *City of San Francisco,* running as the 3rd section of Santa Fe train No. 23, passes the water tank at Bealville on January 19th. — PHILLIPS C. KAUKE

177

Looking south in March 1952, 4,183-foot Soledad Mountain rises in the distance behind the engine facility at Mojave. Mikados Nos. 3237 and 3266 are about to leave for Owenyo on a Jawbone Branch excursion. — STAN KISTLER

Women invade the roundhouse at Mojave during the second World War. — F. A. NEJEDLY - OLA MAE FORCE COLLECTION

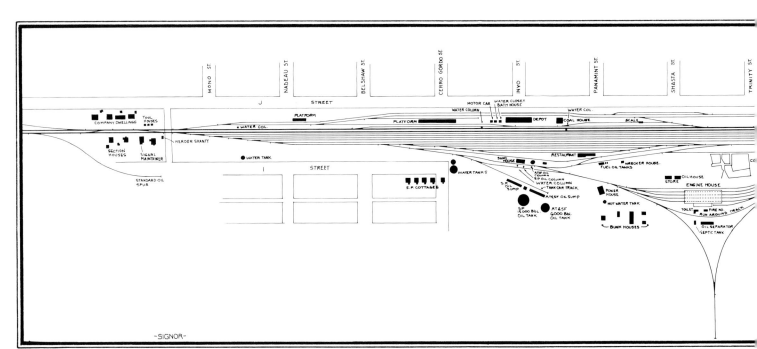

During World War II, both the Santa Fe and Southern Pacific assigned crews to Mojave to man helpers needed on the stiff 13 mile climb to Eric. Crews bunked across from the depot at the Kensington Hotel where the cockroaches were so big they reportedly needed saddles. In a frequent occurrence, both Santa Fe and SP helpers prepare to assist a freight, in this case an SP, out of Mojave. The year is 1941. — F. C. SMITH -STAN KISTLER COLLECTION

Beefy 2-10-2 No. 3838 shoves a train out of Mojave. — V. C. CIPOLLA

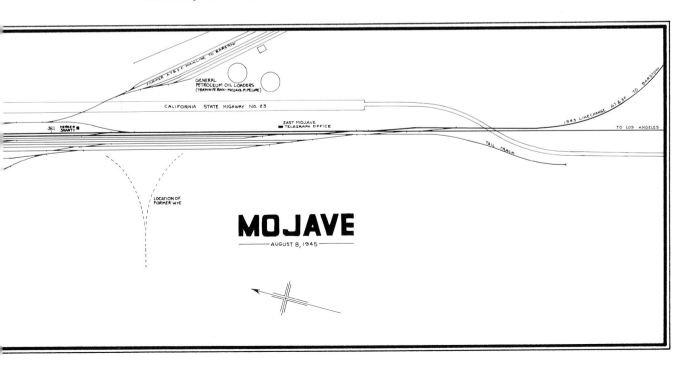

MOJAVE
—— AUGUST 8, 1945 ——

Helper No. 1638 assists extra No. 3842 west on the 2.2 percent grade west of Mojave. Seventy cars back, 2-10-2 No. 1686 shoves against the caboose. The train is making six miles-an-hour on this bone chilling morning in January 1942. — PHILLIPS C. KAUKE

Santa Fe fireman W. O. Schaefer snapped these shots from the tender deck of 2-10-2 No. 974 shoving a deadhead equipment train through Warren during 1946. — PHILLIPS C. KAUKE COLLECTION

Having turned on the wye at Eric, No. 974 prepares to crossover to the eastbound mainline and head back to Mojave. — W. O. SCHAEFER - PHILLIPS C. KAUKE COLLECTION

An SP westbound with through Mallet helper blasts through Eric in 1944. — TRAINS MAGAZINE COLLECTION

The earthquake

It was during the summer of 1952 that Tehachapi was suddenly thrust into the limelight as the forces of nature struck without warning. At 3:52 A.M. July 21st, a major earthquake (California's second largest at the time) ripped across central Kern County with a force of 7.5 on the Richter scale. The quake left 14 dead and a wide swath of destruction in its wake. All rail, highway and telephone arteries between the lower end of the San Joaquin Valley and Los Angeles were severed. Better than 50 aftershocks a day continued to shake the ground.

At Tehachapi, eleven people lost their lives in the chaos that ensued. SP's water tank toppled, not a building in town escaped damage — many were totally destroyed. The moment the quake struck, the C.T.C. system on the north slope of the Tehachapi was knocked out. The machine in Bakersfield became inoperable and all signals still standing out on the line went to their most restrictive indications. With that, all railroad operations on the mountain came to an abrupt halt. In those terrible 25 seconds major damage was inflicted upon eleven miles of railroad between Caliente and Rowen.

As officials of the San Joaquin Division began to sift through the rubble that morning it was found that the railroad was in a shambles. Nowhere had such an important rail link been so thoroughly crippled without warning in such a short period of time. Water tanks at Caliente, Bena and Tehachapi had collapsed. Rails in many places were shifted and badly out of alignment. An SP water line running down the mountain as far as Bena was broken. Near tunnel No. 1, above Caliente, 100 feet of fill had dropped away from the rails leaving them suspended four feet in the air. Commencing at tunnel No. 3, above Bealville, the heaviest damage was encountered. Here the railroad was built in a great loop around the perimeter of Clear

Creek Canyon piercing four tunnels in the process. An arm of the treacherous White Wolf fault passing through the area on an east-west axis had moved during the quake and the results were awesome.

The east end of tunnel No. 3 suffered considerable damage. Fully 200-feet of the heavily reinforced 23-inch concrete side walls were pushed in and the arch was broken in places. One rail was found twisted into an s-shape with one of the curves pushed under the wall of the tunnel yet neither the wall nor the rail was broken. Tunnel No. 4, originally 300-feet east of tunnel No. 3 was several feet closer due to the earth's movement. As a result, the rails between the two tunnels had been pushed into sharp curves and were 22 feet off center. Tunnel No. 4, itself, was badly cracked. At one point the rails were four feet above the floor. Long jagged fissures, several hundred yards in length, zig-zagged along the earth's surface 160 to 190-feet above the tunnels.

The track between tunnel Nos. 4 and 5 was covered by slides in places and a long fill in the vicinity had been shaken down three feet. The west portal of tunnel No. 5 was broken up and the inside and arches for 600-feet, were damaged in varying degrees. Beyond that point and about 360-feet apart, two plugs completely blocked the tunnel. Rail in the bore were so badly contorted that 500-feet of it was never found. The concrete lining between the two plugs was damaged beyond repair but amazingly, the east 200 feet of tunnel No. 5 was only slightly damaged. Tunnel No. 6 was partially blocked by a cave-in and the track between it and tunnel No. 5 was twisted.

Beyond this zone damage was prevalent, but not as severe. The walls of tunnel No. 7 were cracked and its sides bulged. No. 8 had its portal cracked and three boulders weighing up to 60 tons each were found at its west end. All 12 tunnels showed signs of movement. From Tehachapi down past Sandcut the earth beside the tracks, in cuts and fills, had been shaken down from a few inches to several feet from the ballast line outward.

Clearly it was a disaster of momentous and costly proportion. A half dozen trains were caught in the tumult. At Caliente, the water tank collapsed on a standing freight train. The handfull of passengers on the westbound mail train No. 55, with AC No. 4268 and eight cars, had miraculously escaped disaster in the tunnels just above Bealville. The train was stranded at Allard along with a Santa Fe freight. SP train No. 60, the *West Coast*, with No. 4289 and No. 4352 for power, 13 cars and 150 passengers, made it to Marcel before the C.T.C. went out. Although shaken, the train remained on the rails and after a thorough inspection of the track, No. 60 was allowed to flag on up the grade eventually arriving in Los Angeles over three hours late. It was the last passenger train from Bakersfield to Los Angeles for over 26 days.

The emergency failed to halt passenger service on the San Joaquin Route. Only two schedules, Nos. 59 and 60, the *West Coast*, were annulled. SP's *San Joaquin Daylight*, the *Owl* and the mail trains maintained their regular schedules north of Bakersfield, Santa Fe's runs made a similar schedule adjustment. Passengers, baggage, mail and express were shuttled between Bakersfield, Los Angeles, and Barstow (Santa Fe) by bus or truck. The regular schedules of arrival and departure times at Los Angeles Union Passenger Terminal were maintained.

While reconstruction in the Tehachapi was under way, operating personnel performed the momentous task of diverting the bulk of two railroad's north-south traffic over the SP's Coast Line. Westbound trains were routed over the Santa Paula Branch between Montalvo and Burbank Junction via Saugus. Eastbound freights and all passenger trains ran over the regular Coast Route via Santa Susana pass giving the railroad the equivalent of double-track through the area. Trains were limited to 75 cars or the tonnage equivalent as far north as Watsonville Junction. Earlier in July, the Santa Fe had been running 8 to 10 trains a day over the Tehachapi with about 650 cars, while the SP was dispatching 12 trains with 850 cars daily. During the height of the emergency, the Coast Route handled a daily average of 24 trains compared to eight before the quake, and 1,702 cars compared to 651. The peak came on August 10th when 1,886 cars travelled the Coast. These figures excluded eight scheduled passenger trains, an extra passenger and local freights.

Soon after news of the disaster reached the Southern Pacific General Offices in San Francisco, a special train consisting of No. 4361 (Mountain type 4-8-2), business cars *Sunset, Del Monte, Santa Barbara* and a rider coach, was dispatched from Oakland with SP President D. J. Russell, Operating Vice-President J. W. Corbett, and Chief Engineer E. E. Mayo aboard. By mid-afternoon of the 21st, the party arrived at Bakersfield where the officials were briefed on the disaster and then taken to the end of track for a closer look. It was obvious that tunnel No. 5, which had been the most difficult and time consuming to originally construct in 1875, was going to be the principle impediment to reconstruction of the line. Within hours, however, the group had decided on a course of action for restoring the line to service. Corbett and Mayo were assigned to supervise it.

To implement the plan, Southern Pacific called on the services of the Morrison-Knudsen Company,

contractors on many of the larger construction projects in the nation. Early the following morning they had bulldozers on the scene slicing away at the top of the mountains above tunnel No. 3. Eventually more than 100 bulldozers and dirt carry-alls were on the job. Men and machinery mobilized from all over the west by the railroads and contractors moved to the site. Some 176 maintenance-of-way outfits were moved in from all divisions of the SP, as well as, from the Santa Fe and the Western Pacific. By the morning of July 22nd, scores of cars containing ballast, water, bridge timbers, signal equipment, and other materials were rolling toward the Tehachapi. Within 36 hours bulldozers had carved out more than five miles of winding but serviceable access roads over the rugged terrain in the area. Jamming sidings on both sides of the devastation were 95 maintenance-of-way cars as the reconstruction effort reached its peak.

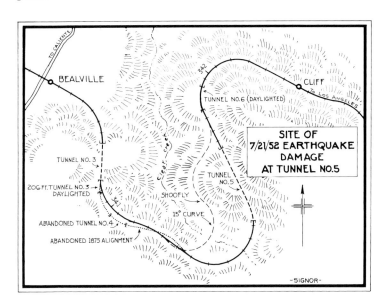

An emergency command post was set up in radio-equipped caboose No. 1311 parked at Bealville. Men out on the job communicated with it by means of 15 walkie-talkie sets. Instructions and messages were relayed to and from Bakersfield through the caboose. An emergency supply of water in tank cars was made available to the community of Tehachapi, cut off from normal supplies by the quake — even the local streams had mysteriously dried up. Tehachapi depot was made an emergency Post Office. Work trains fed materials to the work force from both ends of the damaged portion. On the west end, the work train was handled by an SP cab-forward 4-8-8-2 and on the east end by a Santa Fe four-unit F7. Heavy engines were assigned to aid in tamping freshly laid ballast.

The contemplated reconstruction of the line included the daylighting of the east end of tunnel

A major earthquake struck the Tehachapi region July 21, 1952 inflicting great damage upon the joint-track line. (ABOVE) Near tunnel No. 1, 100-feet of fill dropped from the rails. (BELOW) The east 200-feet of tunnel No. 3 was badly damaged and eventually daylighted. (RIGHT) The track between tunnel No. 3 and tunnel No. 4 was 22 feet off center and savagely twisted. —
ALL SOUTHERN PACIFIC COLLECTION

Destruction at Tehachapi was wide spread. The SP water tank collapsed taking water lines that supplied the town along with it. The SP made available strings of water-filled tank cars for emergency domestic and railroad use. Later the water tank at Ravenna was trucked to Tehachapi as a replacement. — SOUTHERN PACIFIC COLLECTION

The most serious problems involved tunnel No. 5 (RIGHT) The interior was a shambles and completely plugged necessitating a major rebuilding. — SOUTHERN PACIFIC COLLECTION

Radio equipped caboose No. 1311 parked at Bealville served as a communications center relaying messages from Bakersfield to crews at work on the mountain. — SOUTHERN PACIFIC COLLECTION

Because of the severity of the problems in tunnel No. 5, work started August 2nd on a shoofly around the bore. The top view, taken in May 1938, illustrates the conditions of tunnel No. 5 prior to the quake. — F. C. SMITH - STAN KISTLER COLLECTION (RIGHT) Hoards of machinery slice into the hillside to create the shoofly. — SOUTHERN PACIFIC COLLECTION (BELOW) The results of their efforts are still in use nearly three months after the quake. — F. C. SMITH - STAN KISTLER COLLECTION

On the first day of operation, August 15, an eight-unit Santa Fe light engine negotiates the 15 degree curve at the bottom end of the shoofly. — SOUTH-ERN PACIFIC COLLECTION (RIGHT) Curiously, the C.T.C. panel at Bak-ersfield was split in the same location where the quake had severed the line. — RICHARD STEINHEIMER

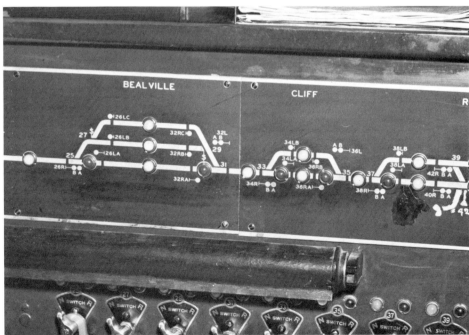

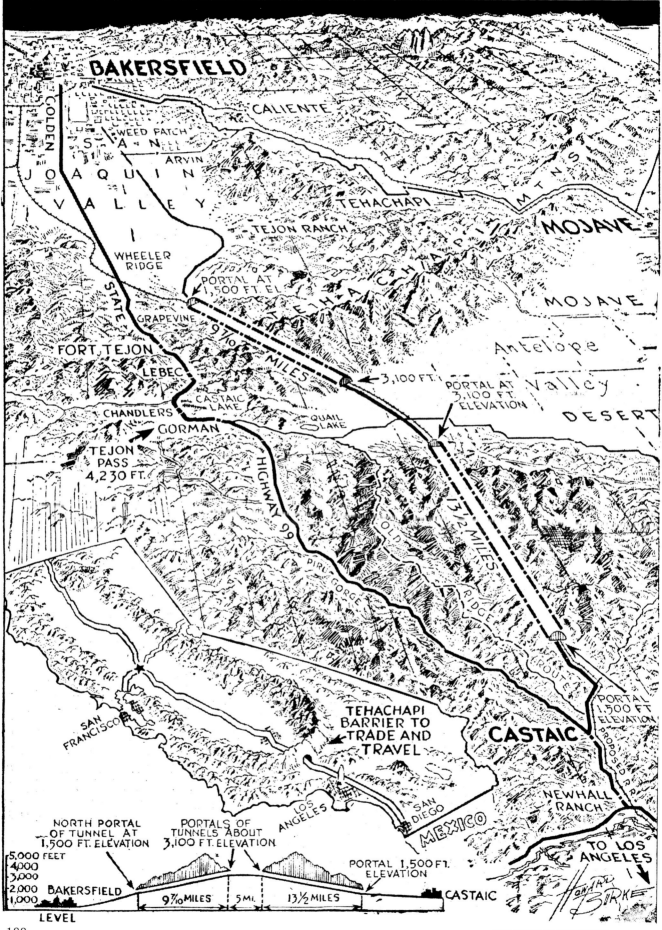

BAKERSFIELD

CALIENTE

WEED PATCH

S A N

ARVIN

J O A Q U I N

TEHACHAPI

MOJAVE

V A L L E Y

TEJON RANCH

WHEELER RIDGE

MOJAVE

PORTAL AT 1,500 FT. EL.

STATE

GRAPEVINE

9 7/10 MILES

Antelope

FORT TEJON

3,100 FT.

PORTAL AT 3,100 FT. ELEVATION

Valley

LEBEC

DESERT

CHANDLERS

CASTAIC LAKE

GORMAN

QUAIL LAKE

TEJON PASS 4,230 FT.

HIGHWAY 99

13 1/2 MILES

PIRU GORGE

OLD

RIDGE

SAN FRANCISCO

ROUTE

PORTAL 1,500 FT. ELEVATION

TEHACHAPI BARRIER TO TRADE AND TRAVEL

CASTAIC

PROPOSED R.R.

LOS ANGELES

SAN DIEGO

NEWHALL RANCH

MEXICO

TO LOS ANGELES

NORTH PORTAL OF TUNNEL AT 1,500 FT. ELEVATION

PORTALS OF TUNNELS ABOUT 3,100 FT. ELEVATION

PORTAL 1,500 FT. ELEVATION

5,000 feet
4,000
3,000
2,000
1,000

BAKERSFIELD

9 7/10 MILES   5 MI.   13 1/2 MILES

CASTAIC

LEVEL

No. 3, the complete daylighting of tunnel Nos. 4 and 6 and the repair and reconstruction of tunnel No. 5. For almost two weeks it was assumed that this tunnel could be repaired by the time that the rest of the railroad was rebuilt. Unfortunately, reports from deep within tunnel No. 5 were not so optimistic. On August 2nd, the decision was made to build a shoofly around the tunnel so that traffic could be restored since the tunnel wouldn't be ready. The shoofly — a tortuous 4,358 feet of track — was easily the most spectacular phase of the reconstruction work. Morrison-Knudsen hauled 250,000 cubic yards of earth in 150 hours from two giant cuts to make a new fill 132 feet high across Clear Creek Ravine. Part of the earth came from a cut about 100 feet into the mountainside along tunnel No. 4 to make room for the curve leading into the shoofly. This curve was a tight 15 degrees. At the opposite end of the temporary alignment was a 14 degree curve leading back on to the existing grade. The shoofly was ready for operation in 13 days. Because it was 690 feet shorter than the original line, it was necessary to construct it on a gradient of 2.37 percent.

On August 15, the 26th day after the earthquake, a Southern Pacific westbound freight train consisting of 100 Oregon lumber empties wound slowly down the mountain and over the shoofly. Two days later, the Los Angeles bound *San Joaquin Daylight* snaked up the grade — the first passenger train to make the trip since early on July 21st. The repairs to tunnel No. 5 took an additional three to four months to complete. For the duration, eastbound tonnage freights departing Bakersfield were reduced by 250 tons from normal limits in order to compensate for the excessive gradient and the drag of the curves on the shoofly.

In the end, tunnel No. 5 was restored to service and the temporary track around it abandoned. Today, as reminders of those terrible moments in the summer of 1952, stands the remains of tunnel No. 4 and the huge earthen fill over Clear Creek Ravine that carried the shoofly. Passing through tunnel No. 5 today, the sounds reverberating off its walls are entirely different than those encountered in the other tunnels — the floor being cement throughout its length. The total cost of reconstructing the Tehachapi line was estimated at $2,500,000.

There were those who used this great tragedy to advance their own scheme — that of the construction of a giant tunnel through the Tehachapi Range. During the 1940's, the idea of a huge tunnel connecting the Los Angeles area with the San Joaquin Valley was brought forth by Charles W. Jones, an engineer with the State Highway Department. In order to eliminate the tortuous grades of

the "Grapevine" — forerunner of today's Interstate 5 Tejon Pass crossing — a 25.3 mile tube entering the mountains six miles north of Castaic, Los Angeles County, and emerging at Grapevine in Kern County was advised. Consisting of two double-deck bores, the tunnels would have an estimated $350,000,000 cost. A much more feasible scheme was devised by Dr. Cecil Dunn, Professor of Economics at Occidental College. He advanced the idea of two shorter tunnels, one entering the mountains six miles north of Castaic and emerging 13.5 miles farther north, followed by five miles of open running with the second tunnel entering the mountains near Gorman and emerging at the foot of the Grapevine in a 9.7 mile bore. This would have made the crossing of the San Andreas Fault on the surface and the problems of ventilation greatly simplified. The revised estimates for the project now totaled a mere $60,000,000.

In 1950, advocates of the tunnel (including the trucking industry) formed a San Joaquin Valley Tunnel Association to arrange for preliminary surveys, funding and other details. The Tehachapi earthquake of July 1952 served to heighten interest in the project. The whole affair would be a toll route with provisions made for water canals, electric transmission lines and railways as well as highways. Electrification of the railroads using the tunnel was deemed advisable. While the SP and Santa Fe stood to shave considerable mileage from the run over Tehachapi Pass, little would be gained in tonnage per train — the maximum grade was to be a fraction above two percent. The railroads gave no public expression of their interest in the proposed Tehachapi tunnel, the State Highway Department found it improbable to construct and the matter quietly subsided from view.

With the earthquake episode behind them, the two railroads once again settled down to the business of railroading in the Tehachapi Mountains. On the Santa Fe, all service was now handled by diesels. For the Southern Pacific, 1953 was a momentous year in this regard. The Korean War was winding down eventually leading to a cease-fire and the SP was experiencing a sharp downturn in war-related business. More and more new diesels were becoming available. Diesels were now on the head end of virtually all SP freights on the district. As a direct result of this development, the Mojave helpers were eliminated. Only steam helpers remained at Bakersfield.

Several models of diesel motive power from various builders were tried with different degrees of success in the Tehachapi. Baldwin, for over a century a builder of steam motive power, was developing diesel-electric locomotives. In February 1950, a four-unit 6,000 horsepower "Shark Nose" diesel, similar to the F7, was tested in the Tehachapi. Although the SP failed to buy any of these units, soon thereafter they purchased from this builder AS-616 1,600 horsepower road switchers. Samples of these locomotives were tried in the demanding Tehachapi helper service. One of these units, the No. 5238, soon after its arrival on the district, was involved in a tragic incident on the north slope the night of August 22, 1952.

Shoving behind the caboose of train No. 1-802, engine No. 5238 was 250 feet from the west portal within the confines of tunnel No. 3. At 2:35 A.M. a knuckle broke between the fourth and fifth car of the train resulting in an emergency. With the memory of the earthquake fresh in the minds of the crew — indeed the train was strung out on the shoofly at the time — all hands in the tunnel abandoned the train. The crew beat a hasty retreat to the outside without applying sufficient hand-

brakes or even applying the independent brake on the helper. Soon the knuckle was replaced and the head end was back together again. When the air was restored, the brakes began to release on the train. The slack ran out with considerable force breaking the knuckle ahead of the helper and separating it and the caboose from the train. The No. 5238 and caboose, now running away, drifted back down grade at times approaching 25 mile-per-hour. At the east end of Allard, the runaway struck the standing engines of Santa Fe Extra 230C East causing much damage to track and equipment and injury to the head end crew of the opposing train.

These Baldwin units were effective as helpers but their services were required in Oregon along with the SD7 road switchers. These EMD locomotives also were briefly tested on the grade. The final blow to the Bakersfield-based steam helper operation was delivered in late summer of 1953

COMPARATIVE RATINGS IN TONS STEAM-DIESEL

— SOUTHERN PACIFIC —

CLASS	TYPE	TERRITORY/DIRECTION			
		Eastbound Bakersfield— Mojave	Westbound Mojave— Bakersfield	Eastbound Lancaster— Saugus	Westbound Saugus-Lancaster
C	2-8-0	675	775	850	775
MK 2,4	2-8-2	525	600	625	600
MK 5,6	2-8-2	600	675	750	675
MK 7-9	2-8-2	650	750	825	750
F 1	2-10-2	675	775	850	775
F 3-5	2-10-2	750	875	975	875
SP	4-10-2	900	1050	1175	1050
AC 4,5	4-8-8-2	1250	1450	1600	1450
AC 6-12	4-8-8-2	1350	1550	1700	1550
DF 1,2	(4)F3	2800	3400	3500	3400
DF 3-5	(4)F7	3275	3550	3700	3550
DF 1-12 (62:15 gear ratio)	F7	700	850	875	850
DF 101-108, 110-112	AS 616	850	925	975	975
DF 124-125	SD9	1000	1100	1200	1175
DF 115, 119, 123 126	RSD-5	1250	1350	1425	1425

— SANTA FE —

CLASS	TYPE	TERRITORY/DIRECTION			
		Eastbound Bakersfield- Mojave	Westbound Mojave— Bakersfield	Eastbound Mojave— Barstow	Westbound Barstow Mojave
3800,3900	2-10-2	1020	1150	4750	3000
(3800-3829 60 tons less Mojave to Eric, 50 tons less Bakersfield to Summit)					
900/1600	2-10-2	850	900	3500	2500
100	(4) FT	2100	2150	6800	5020
200 (ballasted)	(4) F7	2800	3400	—	—

when 17 ALCO RSD-5 1,600 horsepower diesel road switchers arrived on the property. These six-axle locomotives (Classes DF-115, Nos. 5294-5307 and DF-119 Nos. 5336-5339), with a continuous rated speed of 5 mph, were ideally suited for drag Tehachapi helper service. They summarily replaced the last of the Mallets in this capacity. Reflecting the new order of things in the Tehachapi Mountains, the wye at Eric, rendered expendable by the elimination of the Mojave steam helpers, was abandoned and removed on August 12, 1953. That November, a major rearrangement of the roundhouse at Bakersfield was completed providing diesel fueling, servicing and ready tracks.

Like the Santa Fe, the last SP steam operations in the Tehachapi Mountains were accomplished with engines not normally seen in the area, and in passenger service. As the age of steam was drawing to a close, the SP had four scheduled passenger trains each way across the Mountain District. The first of these trains to dieselize was the *Owl*, in June 1952 using slow freight units in sets of four. The *San Joaquin Daylight* followed, utilizing ALCO PA and PB locomotives on the Mountain District commencing in the latter part of 1953. The valley portion of the runs were not dieselized until September 14, 1956. Then the *West Coast* received the slow-geared four-unit freight diesels leaving only Nos. 55 and 56, the lowly night mail trains — and former *Tehachapi* — with their Mallets.

It was on the night mail that the last stand for an SP steam engine was made in the Tehachapi Mountains. The honor was not to go to a Mallet, however. In May 1954, the Southern Pacific lost the mail contract on the train to an experimental vehicle, the highway postal bus. The bus performed essentially the same work as the train, followed the same route on parallel roads and even employed R.P.O. clerks to sort out the mail en route. The net result was the downgrading of the train to four or five cars. The train was frequently annulled, sometimes as many as six days out of seven. Gone was the Mallet and in its place were much lighter Mikados, Nos. 3318 and 3271. These locomotives are remembered as being frequently used on the mail trains at this time. Application was sought for abandonment and seven months after the mail contract was lost, on January 9, 1955, Nos. 55 and 56 were abandoned. The 80 year heritage of Southern Pacific steam operation in the Tehachapi Mountains and high deserts of southern California came to and end.

Santa Fe train No. 24 is running a little heavy on this spring day in 1950 requiring the services of 4-6-4 No. 3458. Kern Junction is the location of this photograph. — PHILLIPS C. KAUKE

Santa Fe extra No. 5946 east blasts
out of tunnel No. 9 at the very center
of the loop. — TED BENSON

4

Contemporary Operation 1955 - Present

Even though the San Joaquin Division Mountain District operation had been essentially all diesel for some time, the last run of SP's night mail in January 1955 with its solitary 3200 class steam locomotive conveniently marked the end of one era and the beginning of another. It would be 20 years before the canyons of the Tehachapi Range would again echo the exhausts of a living steam engine. The rusting hulks of SP 2-10-2's, Mallets and other mountain engines which had accumulated in the yards at Bakersfield, for the traffic surge that never materialized, were now hauled over the hill dead-in-train destined for the blast furnaces of Kaiser Steel at Fontana. The familiar old symbols of the steam age and their operating requirements began to disappear along with them.

The passenger train and all of its attendant operations was another tie to the past. While they remained in the wake of total dieselization, in the course of the next 15 years, the ranks of passenger trains traveling over Tehachapi Pass would be thinned to extinction.

At the close of World War II, the Southern Pacific was operating eight first class passenger schedules over the Mountain District — Nos. 51 and 52, the *San Joaquin Daylight,* Nos. 55 and 56, the night mail trains, Nos. 57 and 58, the *Owl* and Nos. 59 and 60, the *West Coast.* The Santa Fe scheduled four trains between Barstow and the San Francisco area, Nos. 23 and 24, the *Grand Canyon,* and Nos. 1 and 2, the *Scout.* In the next two decades there was considerable pressure brought by railroad management to discontinue all passenger trains. The railroads were quick to point out the relative unprofitability of passenger service as compared to the more lucrative and less time sensitive freight operations. Travelers were also abandoning trains in favor of the convenience of their own automobiles. The government contributed to the problem by cancelling mail contracts which helped subsidize the service.

The Santa Fe established a bus connection between Bakersfield and Los Angeles with the introduction of their *Golden Gate* trains during July 1938. This service, in direct competition with SP schedules, cut trip time by more than half while traveling between the two points over the Ridge Route highway, rather than by the more circuitous rail route via Tehachapi, Mojave and Saugus.

Other bus operators took to the roads between these points at various times.

In the post-war years, the Santa Fe did some schedule jockeying of their Tehachapi runs. On June 8, 1947, North No. 7 (westbound), the San Francisco section of the *Fast Mail & Express* was inaugurated between Barstow and Oakland replacing No. 1 in the timetable. Then on February 20, 1949, another change occurred when No. 4, the *California Limited,* replaced No. 2 between Bakersfield and Barstow. There the schedules remained for awhile. In June 1953, however, President Fred Gurley of the Santa Fe announced plans to operate a new San Francisco-Chicago streamliner. One year later, on June 6, 1954, the first *San Francisco Chief* trains departed their respective terminals. On the West Coast, the inaugural ceremonies took place at Oakland Station. Several days prior to the first run, the equipment for the train was displayed at San Francisco. In a 30 minute ceremony, Hopi Chief Taptuka christened the new train with holy earth collected in a private religious ceremony at San Francisco Peaks near Flagstaff, Arizona. He was aided by David Talewiftema, and four Hopi ceremonial dancers, all garbed in colorful raiment. The trains, utilizing the numbers 1 westbound and 2 eastbound, were a success from the outset. The new train and schedule afforded Santa Fe patrons generous views of the rugged Tehachapi country as seen from the new full-length dome which was included in the all Budd equipped trains. Eastbound the run from San Francisco was accomplished in 47 hours and 10 minutes, westbound took ten minutes longer. No. 1 was in the Tehachapi at dawn and No. 2 in the early evening.

At the time the *San Francisco Chief* was introduced, train No. 4 was deleted from the schedule. In its place North No. 8, the *Fast Mail & Express,* was added between Barstow and Bakersfield with this schedule being extended to Richmond at a later time. For a short while the Santa Fe maintained six passenger schedules over the Tehachapi, something the road hadn't accomplished since the early 1920's. Trains Nos. 23 and 24 were later cut back to operating only between Bakersfield and Barstow, then dropped entirely from the schedule the following year. Meanwhile, plans and schedules were changing at the SP, but none of an optimistic nature.

SP's long range plans for the mid-1950's were based on transportation analysts predictions that within the decade passenger schedules could be reduced to one train on each of the road's major routes. The analyst's predictions regarding the Tehachapi line were chillingly accurate. As has been previously mentioned, in late 1954, SP's mail trains, Nos. 55 and 56, lost their mail contracts and

were discontinued the following January. Applications to discontinue Nos. 59 and 60, the *West Coast,* were filed as early as August 1956, but it was December 7, 1960 before these two trains were quietly removed from the schedule. The next train threatened with discontinuance was the *Owl,* Nos. 57 and 58. Originally placed in service December 18, 1898, the *Owl* was the longest continually operated passenger schedule in the Tehachapi Mountains. By the early 1960's, the SP claimed an annual loss of $312,000 on the train and abandonment followed. The last runs of the *Owl* departed their originating terminals April 11, 1965, thus ending a career spanning 66 years of service. In their last days, the trains were a mere shell of their former greatness. The usual consist on the last runs was a handfull of head-end cars and coaches with a single sleeper tacked on the rear.

By this time, the remaining passenger schedules of both roads were hanging by a thread. The United States Postal Service, continuing their policy of diverting the mail away from trains, cancelled their contract with the Santa Fe on train Nos. 7 and 8 early in 1967. The last days of the *Fast Mail & Express* were even more pitiful than those of the *Owl* with the once lengthy trains being reduced to a single locomotive unit and a rider coach. Total abolishment of the trains came in November 1967. On September 29, 1967, the Postal Service struck again as the last Railway Post Office (R.P.O.) was run on SP's Nos. 51 and 52. Thereafter, the road fought long and hard to discontinue these trains but to no avail. At the very least, the SP wanted to eliminate the *San Joaquin Daylight* south of Bakersfield and aggressively pushed a bus connection between their depot at Bakersfield and Los Angeles. Such service had been established after the demise of the *Owl* utilizing Santa Fe's buses. There now remained only four passenger schedules regularly listed over the Tehachapi Mountains — Santa Fe's *San Francisco Chief* and SP's *San Joaquin Daylight.* Seemingly the bottom was reached, but soon even these skimpy schedules were gone.

Congress spurred on by complaints from the general public and special interest groups to save the passenger train from extinction in this country, organized a quasi-governmental corporation in the early 1970's. An organization called the National Railroad Passenger Corporation (AMTRAK), was established to take-over all intercity passenger service in the United States during the spring of 1971. A map was prepared showing all the routes to be retained in this abbreviated national system. The San Joaquin Valley Line was not among them. Although groups from the affected areas lobbied long and hard prior to May 1, 1971 when

AMTRAK took over, passenger service over the Tehachapi Range was completely abandoned — after nearly a century of operation — and to this date has never been revived.

While passenger service in the post-war period was on the decline, freight traffic continued to gain in importance. Freight trains were not as time sensitive and generated more revenue per operating dollar. A post-war building boom created a tremendous demand for lumber and forest products. The Southern Pacific was well situated to transport these products, from the forests of Oregon and the northwest to destinations in the rapidly developing southwest. Lumber became the number one commodity shipped over the SP in 1949 outdistancing perishables which had held that position for years. In freight train operation, revenue is in proportion to the distance the commodity is carried. To take advantage of this formula, the SP continued their policy of diverting Oregon traffic south for the long haul across the Sunset Route — a policy long in effect. This course was reflected in the trains regularly operating over the Tehachapi grade. As always, there were more loads moving east than west (south than north) on the Pacific Coast. The Tehachapi represented the principal obstacle to be overcome on the long journey south from the Pacific Northwest.

A prime example of this diverted traffic occurred with the long distance lumber hauler the *PSSE* (Portland Sunset East) which was operated daily through to El Paso with 6th day arrival in St. Louis via SP's Texas & Louisiana and Cotton Belt subsidiaries. This train, if adhering to its advertised schedule, was on the Mountain District during the night. Other schedules carried eastbound traffic as well. The *T&L-SSE* operated daily from Roseville, California, through to El Paso with 5th day delivery at St. Louis or Memphis. The *EPE* (El Paso East) operated daily with primarily lumber traffic from Roseville to El Paso then via Tucumcari and the Rock Island Railroad to Chicago. These two trains traversed the Mountain District in the evening.

Los Angeles and southern California also experienced phenomenal growth following World War II and along with it a demand for the basic construction materials. To keep the flourishing housing industry in this region supplied with lumber, the SP operated the *PNL* (Pacific Northwest Los Angeles) daily from Portland contemplating a 4:00 P.M. arrival in Los Angeles on the 3rd day. An *Advance PNL* was also run daily about five hours earlier.

Perishable traffic on the San Joaquin Division was big business. In 1954 the SP reported shipping 1,538 cars weekly in the potato season (April to September); 829 cars of grapes weekly (July to March); 123 cars weekly of Valencia oranges (April to June); and 245 cars of Navel oranges weekly (November to February). Although the bulk of SP's Valley perishable crop traffic was dispatched north to Roseville, then east across the Overland Route (out of necessity), some traffic was placed on eastward trains departing Bakersfield for the mountains. The train which normally handled this traffic was the *VXE* (Valley Extra East) which originated at Roseville and picked up at manufacturing and canning centers down the valley such as Lodi, Stockton, Modesto and Fresno. The *VXE* was normally dispatched out of Bakersfield in the evening.

Westbound on the Mountain District, the *NCP* (North Coast Perishable) was the long-standing hot perishable and merchandise train having been introduced in the late 1940's. The *NCP* offered third morning delivery in Portland and was scheduled to operate in the Tehachapi in daylight with a 4:15 P.M. arrival in Bakersfield. It was the *NCP* which accommodated the banana traffic in later years, and other priority shipments between southern California and the Pacific Northwest. In advance of this train, Los Angeles would originate the *VXW* (Valley Extra West) with traffic destined for Roseville. The *VXW* was due to arrive in Bakersfield around sunup. One final train, the *TMW* (Tehachapi Manifest West) departed Los Angeles in the morning with short traffic destined for points on the Mountain District and south of Fresno. SP's westbound traffic in the area was traditionally empties, either refrigerator cars or Oregon lumber empties. The latter were dispatched in random trains, usually quite lengthy, and referred to as *XMUGS*, or empty Eugenes.

Mountain District originating traffic continued to be concentrated at Edison (perishables, mostly oranges and potatoes), Monolith (cement) and Searles on the Jawbone Branch (potash). In 1955 a branch was laid from the tail of the wye track at Mojave northeast on a maximum two percent grade 10.2 miles to Creal. The Oak Creek Branch, as it was named, was laid in response to the opening of a huge cement plant by the California Portland Cement Company. Livestock shipments, which were once an important part of the Tehachapi operation, experienced a strong decline in the post-war years and were eliminated entirely by 1960. A later development, the growing of sugar beets in the Antelope Valley, necessitated the placing of a beet loader at Rosamond in the early 1960's.

Increasing competition from trucks utilizing recently upgraded and federally subsidized Interstate highways led the SP to develop a super-expedited train. Piggybacking or TOFC — truck trailers riding on railroad flat cars — was first

195

Recently delivered SD9's take eastbound tonnage through Humphreys on the Soledad Canyon line. Forty-four of these capable mountain engines were assigned to the Tehachapi run in 1956. — DON SIMS

introduced on the system in 1953. The railroad inaugurated August 18, 1958, the *Starpacer* to cater to this business. Running at passenger train speed, the *Starpacer* originated at Los Angeles, departing that terminal at 12:01 A.M. with an arrival in Portland within 30.5 hours. This shaved an incredible 21 hours off the next best freight schedule on the run, the *NCP.* The new train was placed in the first class column of the timetable and it ran across the Mountain District as train No. 375. The published schedule showed an arrival time in Bakersfield at 5:15 A.M. making the 168 mile run in five hours and 14 minutes. The train was an immediate success. Its initial schedule of operation consisted of a Tuesday through Saturday departure from Los Angeles. The schedule was eventually expanded to seven days a week.

Operating in the opposite direction, the *TFC Special* was soon placed in service on a similar schedule making the distance from Portland to Los Angeles in 31.5 hours, with a departure from Portland on Monday, Tuesday, Wednesday and Saturday. The schedule contemplated a 12:25 A.M. departure east out of Bakersfield. Although operated with first class priority, the *TFC Special* received no published timetable schedule and was

known simply as the Extra East — a train well respected by operating men nonetheless. In the late 1960's, the train was assigned its own schedule on the Mountain District. Reviving an old number from the past, the *TFC Special* was given the number 340 between Bakersfield and Los Angeles, a number once born by a valley "Zipper" of the early 1940's.

With the success of the *Starpacer,* the SP introduced the *Advance Starpacer* in 1965. This train handled much the same traffic, but provided an earlier cutoff time at Los Angeles with an earlier arrival time at Portland. Following its introduction, the train was run frequently as the first section of train No. 57, the *Owl,* but on April 12, 1965, the *Owl* was removed from the schedule. That October the *Advance Starpacer* was assigned a first class schedule of its own and was given the No. 365 over the Mountain District.

The Santa Fe was every bit as active as the Southern Pacific in traffic development on their northern California line — the bulk of which had to be moved over the Tehachapi. As has already been mentioned, the Santa Fe encouraged the growth of agriculture along its lines in the San Joaquin Valley. The seasonal perishable rushes were a time

196

of great activity and congestion in the Tehachapi largely due to the Santa Fe. The road commanded the lion's share of the potato traffic, originating 30,000 reefers in the valley during 1952, virtually all of which moved south over the Tehachapi. On peak days, during the potato season from April to September, Santa Fe could move anywhere from six to eight 100-car spud trains over the mountain in 24 hours. The trains, called *GFX's* (Green Fruit Express), received four-unit diesel road engines and two-unit helpers to the Summit on a contemplated schedule of 107 hours to Chicago.

During the summer of 1953, the Santa Fe instituted an extremely fast perishable schedule between Bakersfield and Chicago. Limited to 29 cars, train No. 62 — for its 62-hour schedule — left Bakersfield nightly handling anything from grapes to plums, nectarines, asparagus, or strawberries on a 6:00 P.M. cutoff.

The Santa Fe was in direct competition with the SP on the north-south corridor along the Pacific Coast. Trains *NCX* (Northern California Extra) and *SCX* (Southern California Extra) handled traffic between the San Francisco Bay area and southern California via Barstow. There was also a brisk business between southern California and the Pacific Northwest. The "Inside Gateway," in direct competition with the all-SP route, accomplished the same end by alternative routing. Gateway trains moved via the Santa Fe from Los Angeles to Mormon Yard (Stockton), Western Pacific from Stockton, to Bieber, and the Great Northern from Bieber northward to the Columbia River. The principal train north on this route was the *SWG* (Santa Fe, Western Pacific, Great Northern) which, in direct competition with SP's *NCP,* offered 3rd day delivery of manifest freight in Seattle/Portland, and 4th day delivery in Vancouver. Southbound, the *GWS* competed with SP's *PNL.* Both the *SWG* and the *GWS* were in the Tehachapi in the afternoon. The *Expediter,* Santa Fe's answer to the *Starpacer,* originated at Los Angeles on Monday, Tuesday, Wednesday, and Friday with a 10:00 P.M. cutoff. It was routed via the "Inside Gateway" handling merchandise and autos. This train was in the Tehachapi in the pre-dawn hours and could be distinguished by having a caboose at each end — to facilitate quick turning at Barstow — and the frequent use of passenger engines as power. Although the *Expediter* enjoyed

During February and March 1961, twenty RSD-5's assigned to the Bakersfield-Tehachapi freight pool were upgraded into low-hood DL-702's. These in turn became Tehachapi regulars for most of the 1960's. Seen frequently on the point when new, as shown below near Humphreys in 1961, the 7000's were bumped to helper duties by new larger power and lived out their final years as heavy service yard engines. — DON SIMS - SOUTHERN PACIFIC COLLECTION

a modicam of success, the introduction of SP's *Advance Starpacer* in 1965 led to the ultimate discontinuance of this train. One other regular "Gateway" train, the *CAL*, handled drag freight south along the coast. Illustrative of its low priority on the Santa Fe, the *CAL* was scheduled to take 28 hours from Mormon (Stockton) to Los Angeles.

In addition to the *GFX* perishable trains, the Santa Fe Valley Division originated other eastbound trains, the *OAF* (Oakland Forwarder) offering 5th day delivery between Richmond and Kansas City/Chicago for the merchandise and TOFC and the *BK* (Bakersfield Kansas City) for drag freight destined to the same points. The *BTX* (Bakersfield Texas) offered 4th day delivery from valley points to Texas.

Westbound on the Santa Fe's transcontinental line, was train No. *59*, inaugurated in January 1948. By July 1, 1952, the train offered a 103-hour schedule from Chicago to Richmond with 6th morning delivery at San Francisco. This was later differentiated by train *SF59* which originated at Chicago/McCook, and *S59* which was a run-through off the New York Central System at Streator, Illinois. Train *49* provided Kansas City-Richmond service, and train *99* offered fifth morning delivery at Richmond from St. Louis. The *QSF* (Quanah, Acme & Pacific — San Francisco) provided west Texas-Richmond service for merchandise and TOFC (Trailers On Flat Cars).

Diesel locomotive technology was rapidly advancing, but the emphasis rested on those employed in freight service. Little change occurred in the passenger power employed by the two roads in the Tehachapi. From the time they were dieselized until the passenger trains themselves disappeared from the district, Santa Fe schedules remained firmly under the command of the passenger geared F units and ALCO PA's. The ALCO PA's were the first to be retired. On the SP, ALCO PA's and freight F units gave way to passenger geared F units on all schedules. This situation remained until the final three years of passenger service when a single high-horsepower six-axle EMD SDP45 was substituted.

In freight service, the Santa Fe remained content for some time with the four-axle power that had first dieselized the district. The 100 class FT's were being seen less frequently. Some of them, split up and renumbered in the 400 series for helper duties, remained longer. The road's F7's and GP7's were regular features in freight service between Bakersfield and Barstow as was a newcomer, the 700 class GP9. The SP, however, was searching for a better mountain engine than the F7. The ALCO RSD5's had proved successful in a large part due to their six-axle design. When Electro-Motive announced a

six-axle design of their own, the SP took a closer look and liked what they saw.

Early orders of the 1,500 horsepower SD7 and later the 1,750 horsepower SD9 road switchers were tested in the Tehachapi en route to assignments in Oregon. A string of successes on the punishing mountain grades of the Portland and Shasta divisions followed. Convinced of the reliability and suitability of the SD9 for Tehachapi service, the Southern Pacific ordered a stable of these engines specifically for the San Joaquin Mountain District. Forty-four of the units were received from EMD in 1956 displacing F7's which were for the most part transferred to the Coast Division. Delivered in two batches, Class DF 124, Nos. 5449 through 5463 were equipped with a duel-fuel feature and steam generators. Class DF 125, Nos. 5464 through 5493 had neither. All Tehachapi assigned SD9's were heavily ballasted (additional weight added for more tractive effort) to approximately 359,000 pounds. They could generate full power at a minimum continuous speed of eight miles per hour, and were conspicuous by their lack of pilot snow plows. Each engine was stenciled BTF or BAK-TF for the Bakersfield-Tehachapi freight pool.

By the end of the 1950's, the builders were making great steps forward in locomotive design. Responding to the need for increased horsepower per unit, as well as, more sophisticated electrical gear, EMD introduced the 2,400 horsepower, six-axle turbo-charged SD24 in 1959. ALCO's competitive model was the 2,400 horsepower, six-axle DL-600B. The Santa Fe, the first to dieselize the district and possessing a fleet of FT's approaching 15 years old, was quick to embrace these "second generation" units. Orders were placed for 80 SD24's and 50 DL-600B's with deliveries beginning in April, and continuing through September 1960. These engines in the 800 class for the ALCO's and 900 class for the EMD's, began showing up in the Tehachapi soon after they arrived from the builder. Always used in isolated sets of either model, these distinctive engines were turned at Bakersfield and quickly sent east, as they were used system wide.

The SP was not as enthusiastic as the Santa Fe about these new motive power developments. EMD was confident the SP, being the mountain railroad that it was, would order the SD24 in quantity. So assured was EMD that the demonstrators they tested in the Tehachapi, and elsewhere on the SP system, were painted in the road's new grey and scarlet scheme. The anticipated orders never materialized. The fact that the road had fitted out its mountain districts with SD9's, just three years previous to the introduction of the SD24, probably had a great deal to do with the rebuff. Southern Pacific did buy the DL-600B — three to be exact —

and numbered them Nos. 4816 through 4818, class DF 502. In September 1959, the trio made test runs in the Tehachapi with less than satisfactory results. Within the year, they were banished to Texas.

The SP upgraded some of their Tehachapi power not too long after this episode. Twenty 179 ton RSD-5's regularly assigned to the BAK-TF pool were shipped east to the ALCO plant at Schenectady, New York, and upgraded in February and March 1961 to 1,800 horsepower DL-702's. The DL-702's, numbered in the 7000's, were sent back to Bakersfield and performed as both through freight and helper locomotives.

In the next several years a wide assortment of new power paraded across the district. On the SP, most of this power was test-run-only and the bulk of the work fell to the capable SD9's. In November 1961, three new German-built Kraus-Maffei ML4000 diesel hydraulic units worked north over the district with dynamometer car No. 137 en route to Roseville. Although intended for mountain service initially (the Sierra, not the Tehachapi), the hydraulics wound up in the San Joaquin Valley and were frequent visitors at the Bakersfield engine facility. In the years 1962 through 1965, both the SP and the Santa Fe were busy buying new high-horsepower four-axle power. SP's were intended for the comparatively flat Sunset Route and virtually none of this power was seen in the Tehachapi, at least not with any regularity. The Santa Fe, on the other hand, replaced their aging fleet of FT's by trading them in on 2,250 horsepower GP30's from EMD. These were delivered during the first six months of 1963 and assigned to the 1200 class. The following year, in much the same manner, GP35's rated at 2,500 horsepower, were delivered and assigned to the 1300 series. These units were seen frequently in the Tehachapi and displaced the F units which were gradually assigned to the road's Texas lines. At first the two classes were kept separate, but soon the 1200's and 1300's were freely intermixed. By mid-1965 all high horsepower hood units on the Santa Fe were being lashed together at will. It was found, however, that it was best if the 800 class ALCO's did not lead as the controlling unit.

The year 1964 was fascinating as far as new and different motive power was concerned. Fifteen more German hydraulic units, in a new low-nose configuration were ordered by the SP, starting in March and continuing through May they passed over the Tehachapi en route to Roseville. Also in May, four gold ALCO Century series 628 demonstrators were purchased by the SP and given Nos. 4870 through 4873. These were temporarily assigned to the BAK-TF pool and were seen frequently on the mountain that year. Later, when orders for the Century 628's began arriving in the fall of 1964,

they were assigned to Roseville and the gold quartet was eventually sent to join them. Aside from the gold quartet, Century series ALCO's were rare in the Tehachapi. On October 2, 1964, three new ALCO Century 643H hydraulic units were sent north over the Tehachapi. They were tested as helpers while entrained with dynamometer car No. 137 trailing the ponderous machines. Adding to the unique motive power appearing in the mountains during 1964 was the blue and yellow (quasi Santa Fe) painted SD40X demonstrator unit 434 being tested by EMD and its glossy black contemporaries, 434A, 434B, and 434D — the forerunners of yet another advancement in locomotive design. Finally, in December 1964, the SP began taking delivery of EMD SD35's. These six-axle 2,500 horsepower mountain engines Nos. 4816 through 4844, continued to be delivered through March 1965. All were assigned to the BAK-TF pool relegating the 7000's almost exclusively to helper assignments between Bakersfield and Summit. The SD35's sophisticated extended range dynamic braking created a problem with existing units in the pool. Until these were rewired, the 4800's were seen sandwiched between SD9's so as to avoid "frying" the latter's resistance grids. Through the courtesy of train watcher T. G. Schmid, we are favored with a glimpse into this fascinating period in the history of Tehachapi Pass.

AN INTERESTING 12 HOURS IN THE TEHACHAPI
JANUARY 29/30, 1965

—KEY—

SANTA FE POWER

Class	Numbers	Wheel Arr.	Service	Make/Model	Horsepower
52	52-63,64-78	A1A-A1A	PSGR	ALCO PA/PB	2,000
200	200-280	B-B	FRT	EMD F7A/B	1,500
281	281-289	B-B	FRT	EMD F9A/B	1,750
700	700-751	B-B	FRT	EMD GP9	1,750
800	800-849	C-C	FRT	ALCO DL-600B	2,400
900	900-979	C-C	FRT	EMD SD24	2,400
1200	1200-1284	B-B	FRT	EMD GP30	2,250
1300	1300-1349	B-B	FRT	EMD GP35	2,500
2650	2650-2893	B-B	FRT	EMD GP7	1,500

SOUTHERN PACIFIC POWER

Class	Numbers	Wheel Arr.	Service	Make/Model	Horsepower
DF-4	351,352	B-B	PSGR	EMD F7	1,500
DF-503	4816-4844	C-C	FRT	EMD SD35	2,500
DF-120	5339-5371	C-C	FRT	EMD SD9	1,750
DF-121	5372-5386	C-C	FRT	EMD SD9	1,750
DF-122	5387-5444	C-C	FRT	EMD SD9	1,750
DF-124	5449-5463	C-C	FRT	EMD SD9	1,750
DF-125	5464-5493	C-C	FRT	EMD SD9	1,750
DF-8	6388-6391	B-B	PSGR	EMD F7	1,500
DF-12	6446-6461	B-B	PSGR	EMD F7	1,500
DF-127	7000-7020	C-C	FRT	ALCO DL-701	1,800
DF-4	8091	B-B	PSGR	EMD F7B	1,500
DF-11	8290-8303	B-B	PSGR	EMD F7B	1,500

En route to the Tehachapi and Walong siding January 29, 1965.

10:28 P.M. Lancaster SP Eastbound freight 1-808
    5480 4819 4829 5478—83 cars
11:05 P.M. Ansel SP Eastbound freight 2-808
    5450 4818 4817 5491—63 cars
    — note SD35s buried, a common
      arrangement.
11:25 P.M. Mojave SP Eastbound freight 3-808
    5459 7006 5360 5476 5484—80 cars
11:27 P.M. Mojave SP Westbound passenger
    1-57 the *Owl*
    351 6454 8297 6 cars (3 headend)
    — consist of *Owl* had shrunk considerably
      prior to its being pulled off in April.
11:39 P.M. Mojave Santa Fe Eastbound
    freight X1256 East
    1256 1203 1304 1230—86 cars
At Walong Saturday January 30, 1965
Weather: Intermittant snow
12:13 A.M. Santa Fe Eastbound freight X951 East
    951 926 918 925 — 53 cars — 2688 281A 2727
    — 25 cars — 945 972 941 932 — caboose
    — a heavy train, primarily reefers.
12:40 A.M. Santa Fe lite engine west X2727 West
    2727 281A 2688 932 941 972 945
    — two crews. Santa Fe never wired together
      early and later units.
1:12 A.M. Santa Fe Eastbound freight X285C East
    285C 285B 289B 238L 239A 279L —
    88 cars — 2687 2681
1:39 A.M. SP Eastbound freight 1-802 Mojave Shorts
    7011 7018 7016 7000 — 10 cars
    — although SP trains were technically
      extras on the C.T.C. between Bena and
      Tehachapi, special instructions required
      trains to display indication in the
      territory for their schedule east of Mojave
      — for identification purposes.
2:18 A.M. Santa Fe lite engine west X2681 West
    2681 2687
2:25 A.M. SP Eastbound freight 2-802
    5456 7004 5341 5467 — 55 cars —
    5472 5458 5464 5460 — caboose
2:57 A.M. Santa Fe Eastbound passenger
    8 — *Fast Mail & Express*
    70L 61A 68L 8 headend cars and
    one streamlined coach
3:11 A.M. SP Westbound freight 2-57
    Advance Starpacer
    5493 5474 5443 5479 5489 7002 — 45 cars
    mostly pigs
    — just inaugurated, later known as 365.

3:57 A.M. SP Eastbound freight 3-802
    5351 7007 5468 5490 — 61 cars —
    5454 5466 — caboose
4:40 A.M. SP Westbound freight 1-375 *Starpacer*
    4816 4824 4820 4825 — 44 cars pigs
    and auto racks
    — premier train warrants latest power.
4:48 A.M. Santa Fe Westbound freight X844 West
    844 813 845 807 — 51 cars
    — at this point solid sets of ALCOs,
      not intermixed.
5:35 A.M. SP Lite engine west X5466 West
    5466 5454
6:30 A.M. SP Eastbound passenger 58 the *Owl*
    351 6450 8091 3 baggage 3 coach 1 Pullman
    — 351 had been cut at Bakersfield off of 1-57
      and added to the point of 58 — a usual
      procedure.
6:42 A.M. SP lite engine west X5470 West
    5470 5477 5455 5475
7:23 A.M. Santa Fe Westbound passenger
    1 — *San Francisco Chief*
    58L 61L 60L 78L 13 cars (2 flexivans,
    1 baggage, 1 dome, and 2 highlevels.)
7:37 A.M. SP Westbound freight 2-375 2nd *Starpacer*
    5340 5463 5362 5486 5365 — 39 cars
    — 2nd *Starpacer* common occurrence out of
      LA on Friday night
8:21 A.M. Santa Fe Westbound freight X905 West
    905 947 916 946
8:22 A.M. SP Eastbound freight 1-804
    4821 4822 5487 5342 — 72 cars —
    7009 7017 — caboose
8:46 A.M. SP Eastbound freight 2-804
    4873 4870 4872 4871 — 68 cars —
    7008 7001 — 6 cars
    — solid set of gold Century 628
      demonstrators.
9:30 A.M. SP lite engine west X7017 West
    7017 7009
10:06 A.M. SP lite engine west X7001 West
    7001 7008
10:17 A.M. Santa Fe Westbound freight X901
    West *Expediter*
    901 906 915 952 — caboose — 55 cars mostly
    pigs — caboose — caboose at each end
    facilitated rapid turn at Barstow.
10:22 A.M. SP Westbound passenger
    51 — *San Joaquin Daylight*
    6388 8291 8303 — 6 cars
11:18 A.M. SP Westbound freight 1-801 XMUG
    5449 5492 5452 — 94 cars
11:50 A.M. Santa Fe Westbound freight X1308 West
    1308 1240 1305 1208 — 93 cars

One can almost feel the heat as a set of SD9's top the hill at Vincent with 2nd 803 during the summer of 1964.
— RICHARD STEINHEIMER

A westbound train moves cautiously over flood damaged track near Vincent. Coming from Los Angeles, the last few miles to the summit are the most difficult to overcome. — DON SIMS

Each spring, wild flower specials were operated over the Tehachapi Mountains organized by the Pacific Railroad Society. Los Angeles based passenger power was used and the trains were run over the district, in each direction, as the second section of the *San Joaquin Daylight*. (ABOVE) A particularly heavy version of the excursion which required the services of seven F's, snakes through Rowen. — ROD R. ASZMAN COLLECTION (RIGHT) Passengers detrain at Russ in 1964 to set up for a photo run-by, a tradition with these special trains. —BRIAN BLACK

203

Late afternoon shadows fall across train No. 52, the *San Joaquin Daylight*, as it makes a station stop at Bakersfield during 1969. A single unit has brought the train, swollen by summer crowds and deadhead equipment, all the way from Oakland. Ahead lay the formidable Tehachapi, however, and, out of deference to them the head brakeman eases helper No. 9002 to a joint against the train. Its services will be required all the way to Los Angeles. — DICK DORN

Extra No. 7016 east prepares to depart Bakersfield for the mountains. — DON SIMS

Relatively new power and weathered veterans alike bake in the summer heat at Bakersfield during 1969. — DICK DORN (BELOW) A pair of gold ex-demonstrator ALCO Century 628's head for the yard and a Tehachapi helper assignment. In the background stands the imposing brick buildings comprising the Bakersfield back shop. — BRIAN BLACK

Cluttered, dusty, and cursed with temperatures frequently soaring to 115 degrees, Bakersfield is a place to avoid during the long hot summer. Still, in the cool of the evening, with the more sordid aspects of the city masked by a veil of darkness, the place holds a particular fascination. In the 1960's, this was the time to photograph the more exotic Roseville assigned "Valley" power which tended to accumulate here. Two such examples, F-unit No. 6164 and Krause-Maffei No. 9010 decorate the "whiskers" in this 1964 view. — RICHARD STEINHEIMER

Displaced from passenger assignments, former Los Angeles maintained F units, No. 6190 and boiler-equipped booster No. 8118, await a call to Fresno in the summer of 1969. — DICK DORN

A swing helper gets underway at Quantico. Named for a nearby city street, the Quantico herder handles switches leading into SP's Bakersfield yards from the mountains. — TED BENSON

By examining the photos on this and the adjoining page, one can get some idea of the Santa Fe's facilities at Bakersfield in the early 1960's. (ABOVE) A westbound double-headed freight moves onto Santa Fe rails at Kern Junction. — BRIAN BLACK (OPPOSITE PAGE - TOP) A view of the yards looking north. The ice deck appears to the left with the roundhouse in the distance. (OPPOSITE PAGE - LOWER) Valley power predominates on the whisker tracks. — BOTH DON ERB - SANTA FE RAILWAY

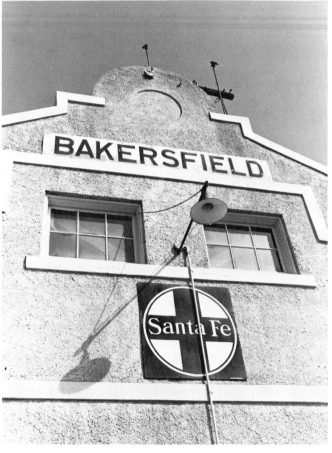

TED BENSON

Santa Fe train No. 1, the *San Francisco Chief*, running slightly off the advertised, is completely encircled by Santa Fe freight Extra 811 east at Walong on July 26, 1960. — STAN KISTLER

On the joint track over the Tehachapi
Mountains there are few places where
grade and curvature will permit trains
to operate at speed. The comparatively flat stretch across the Tehachapi Valley is one, and the long tangent
from Bena down to Bakersfield is
another. (ABOVE) On the latter,
Santa Fe extra No. 343 west races
through Sandcut in 1965. (RIGHT)
Trailing in the double-headed consist
is SD24 No. 908 — a Tehachapi
regular. —BOTH BRIAN BLACK

Returning helpers crest Sandcut hill in 1964 on their way back to Bakersfield. Valley power used in Tehachapi helper service was a frequent occurrence during the summer months. —BRIAN BLACK

During May 1964, the SP acquired four Gold Century 628 demonstrators from ALCO. Hard pressed for motive power at the time, the four were immediately assigned to the Tehachapi run with little more than a strategically placed number here and there to indicate the change in ownership. Here are two of the gold quartet boosting eastbound tonnage at Sandcut. —BRIAN BLACK

At the left, amply powered to maintain its 5 hour 14 minute schedule over the Mountain District, Los Angeles-Portland train No. 375, the *Starpacer,* rolls down off the Tehachapi near Ilmon in 1965. Strings of auto rack cars carrying new automobiles trail the power which includes recently delivered SD35's. (BELOW) Santa Fe No. 343 west leaves Bena for Sandcut the same year. — BOTH BRIAN BLACK

Yet another Oregon lumber drag, running as 3rd 806 reverses itself on the horseshoe at Caliente in 1966. Although the Tehachapi line is C.T.C. and the train technically an extra, special instructions printed in the San Joaquin Division Employees Timetable required that trains display a train number indication over the mountain for their schedule number in the territory east of Mojave. This was done for identification purposes.
— JAMES H. HARRISON COLLECTION

Although it had been some time
since brakemen had been required
to ride the tops of trains on the grade,
tell-tales — devices to warn those
riding the tops of cars of overhead
clearance restrictions — still remained
in place in the 1960's. (ABOVE)
Westbound tonnage passes under
the tell-tales at the east end of tunnel
No. 2 — DON SIMS (RIGHT) Santa Fe
No. 920 glides under the tell-tale as it
emerges from tunnel No. 2. — BRIAN
BLACK

Santa Fe GP7's shove an eastbound tonnage train out of tunnel No. 5. — BRIAN BLACK

In an oft reproduced but classic photograph, SD9's lead a westbound train through Bealville in the late 1950's. A set of Santa Fe light engines follow in the distance near tunnel No. 5. — DON SIMS

Although by no means restricted to Bakersfield-Barstow service, the six-axle 800 and 900 class locomotives of the Santa Fe were ideally suited to the Tehachapi and were frequently seen in the territory throughout the 1960's and early 1970's. (ABOVE) A string of 800's power this westbound at the 4th crossing of Tehachapi Creek. —BRIAN BLACK (RIGHT) A set of 900's emerge from the fog near Walong. — RICHARD STEINHEIMER

Santa Fe SD45's began showing up on the mountain in 1966. — BRIAN BLACK

An interesting helper set assists an eastbound lumber drag out of Woodford in August 1960. Knowing of the ALCO's propensity to smoke, it is surprising that the rear end crew allowed them to be placed so near the caboose. — SOUTHERN PACIFIC COLLECTION

No. 52 departs Walong on a rainy day in the 1960's. Unit No. 6389 has been added at Bakersfield. — DAVE STANLEY COLLECTION

Extra No. 5483 east encircles the loop during October 1964. Shoving hard near the rear are a pair of 7000's. — RICHARD STEINHEIMER

Santa Fe's *Expediter* — easily identified by the caboose trailing the road power — gets runaround by the *San Joaquin Daylight* at Walong on January 30, 1965. Operated in direct competition with SP's *Starpacer* on the Los Angeles-Pacific Northwest run, the *Expediter* had a caboose at either end to facilitate a quick reversal at Barstow. — BRIAN BLACK

Santa Fe extra No. 264-C approaches tunnel No. 9 at Walong, in 1964. — BRIAN BLACK

Eight RSD-15's get underway at Summit Switch on Christmas day in 1972, after having cut out a helper from their 80-car train. — TIM ZUKAS

For a number of years after the installation of C.T.C., Tehachapi continued to issue orders to eastward trains entering the double-track allowing them to run ahead of late first class trains. This explains the single-bladed train order semaphore in this view from the 1950's. — DON SIMS

The headlight of Santa Fe extra No. 264-C, shown above, is out as courtesy to the head end crew of SP train 2-804 (LEFT) as they meet near Summit Switch during 1964. — BOTH BRIAN BLACK

Recently delivered SD40 No. 8402 signals the arrival of a second generation of high-horsepower diesels at milepost 377 in 1966. — JAMES H. HARRISON COLLECTION

A solitary passenger occupies the observation car of No. 52 as it leans into a sweeping curve near Warren in the view below on September 14, 1966. (OPPOSITE PAGE) Earlier in the day, a rather lengthy No. 51 works upgrade in the same vicinity. The large "G" plate on the westward signal allows uphill trains to pass it at restricted speed even if displaying red. In this view, and the one below of the Mountain Local in the Cache Creek narrows near Cameron, the bi-directional signaling of the eastbound track in this section is evident. — ALL T. M. HOTCHKISS

Fresh off the boat from Germany, a trio of diesel-hydraulics cross the Tehachapi near Bealville en route to Roseville during November 1961. Dynomometer car No. 137 trails the power on this test run in the scene above. — DON SIMS - SOUTHERN PACIFIC COLLECTION Although the German engines were never assigned to the Mountain District, these units congregated at Bakersfield while holding down valley district assignments. Because of this, they were subject to occasional off-district trips in helper service. (RIGHT) Two of these "Krauts" returning from the summit, a cab and hood version, move through the westward siding at Caliente in 1966. — BRIAN BLACK

At the left, another trio of unique power, ALCO 643H diesel-hydraulics, pause at Vincent on October 2, 1964. — ROD R. ASZMAN COLLECTION (BELOW) Five years previous, during September 1959, another trio of ALCO's — this time RSD-15's — take a test train through Soledad Canyon east of Ravenna. Neither type of ALCO's saw anything but test runs in the Tehachapi on the SP. — DON SIMS - SOUTHERN PACIFIC COLLECTION

Along with all the motive power experimentation occurring in the mid-1960's, an even more novel idea was considered. At this period of time the subject of electrification of the Tehachapi line — a dead issue since 1921 or so — was revived. In addition to the Tehachapi, studies were made for the Sierra (Roseville to Sparks), Klamath Falls to Portland and Colton to St. Louis via the Golden State Route runs. The proposed locomotives were of a more radically different design than those used elsewhere in the United States. Power would be obtained from a single phase, high voltage overhead system. Following a Swedish prototype, specifications called for 16,000 horsepower two-unit semi-permanently coupled locomotives. Each unit would have four axles with large drivers.

The electrification idea was studied then shelved once again for several important reasons. First off, it was estimated that a period of 8 to 10 years would be required before there would be a substantial return on investment. The fact that the entire signal system would have to be rewired certainly didn't help the cause. At the time of the study, fuel costs of 8.5 cents a gallon loosely paralleled electric rates. Finally, the power companies were not cooperative. They had a considerable lack of knowledge regarding single phase operations and disagreements about this and a refusal to accept regenerated power certainly curtailed efforts to pursue the idea.

In the Tehachapi, the project was postponed because of yet another reason, the uncrystalized Palmdale-Colton cutoff which was in the planning stages to link these two points via Cajon Pass as a Los Angeles bypass.

Cajon Pass, a strategic defile separating the San Gabriel and San Gorgonio Mountains, which ring the Los Angeles coastal plain, has long been utilized by railroads entering the area from the East. The first railroad to penetrate the gap was the California Southern (Santa Fe) in 1885, joined by the San Pedro, Los Angeles & Salt Lake (Union Pacific) in 1905 through the lease of Santa Fe's Dagget to San Bernardino line. It is interesting to note, however, that it was the SP that first entertained the idea. Indeed as early as 1869-70, preliminary lines were run through the pass by SP surveyors pursuing the original Southern Pacific idea of building from Mojave to Yuma over Cajon, and San Gorgonio passes, with a branch line from present Colton to Los Angeles. It will be remembered, however, that the residents of Los Angeles anted up considerable subsidies to place their town on the mainline of the SP. So it was for this reason that Cajon Pass was abandoned for the more lengthy and costly Soledad Canyon entrance into the area.

The SP remained vitally interested in Cajon Pass, however, with the intention of warding off competitors. The fledgling Los Angeles & Independence Railroad was the first to catch the wrath of the SP. The L.A.& I., of which articles of incorporation had been filed January 8, 1875, planned to build through the pass en route to Independence in Inyo County, California, from Los Angeles with a branch to the coast at Santa Monica. Aware of SP's position, L.A.& I. Chief Engineer J. U. Crawford, in a veil of secrecy, broke ground in Cajon Pass the day following incorporation and about 100 feet of tunnel at what is now Pine Lodge was accomplished. It was not too long before a skirmish broke out between the L.A.& I. party and a band of SP men in the crucial Blue Cut area discouraging further activity on the part of the Independence road. Financial setbacks plagued the line and, on June 4, 1877, the property was leased to the SP. The Santa Monica line was the only railroad actually built by the L.A.& I. and became SP's Santa Monica Branch. Later in 1885, the SP challenged the California Southern, then building up from San Diego, at Colton where it would have to cross the SP at grade rather than in Cajon Pass.

The Santa Fe ultimately prevailed in Cajon Pass and slightly over forty years passed with the SP resigned to the situation. During this period, in 1905, the Salt Lake Route gained trackage rights through the pass from the Santa Fe. Then in the exceedingly busy period of the middle-1920's, the SP turned once again to the idea of using Cajon Pass as a way to link Colton with the heavily trafficked San Joaquin Mountain District as a bypass to avoid the congestion of Los Angeles.

A Kramer-Oro Grande cutoff was proposed. As envisioned by the SP, the Santa Fe trackage between Mojave and Kramer would be jointly operated by virtue of a clause in a lease which the two roads had signed in 1884. Santa Fe's line over Cajon Pass from Oro Grande to Colton would be opened up to accept SP's traffic. The gap between the two sections would be bridged by the cutoff to be built at SP's expense. In this 1928 scheme, the Santa Fe stood to gain little. Perhaps 25 miles might be shaved from their route between Los Angeles and northern California via Barstow. The SP was to gain a considerable advantage by shortening their southern transcontinental route over 64 miles and eliminating much of its heavy grades, slow running in Soledad Canyon and Los Angeles terminal congestion. The Santa Fe held all the cards in the deal. Cajon Pass already had all the traffic it could handle — so much so that double track had recently been installed to ease the congestion in the Barstow-San Bernardino corridor. The

Santa Fe was in no mood to accommodate its long time rival unless it was willing to pay for a third track and reverse signals. The matter was dropped by the SP.

The slow period of the depression followed and the hectic war years in which little money or time was available for such projects. In the post war era, the Southern Pacific once again pushed for a cutoff. In the fall of 1956, a Palmdale-Summit cutoff of 48 miles was estimated to cost $9,500,000. The Santa Fe was offered joint use of the line in exchange for the use of their tracks in Cajon Pass from Summit to Colton. Although the Santa Fe stood to shave 44 miles off their run from LA to northern California via Barstow, the Santa Fe still wanted a third track built at SP expense. Disgruntled SP officials, frustrated in their attempts to put together a line piecemeal fashion, set about developing a railroad entirely of their own con-

struction between Colton and Palmdale.

Ground was finally broken on the project April 5, 1966. The contractors, the Vinnell Corporation, handled the grading, culvert and bridge work, using three spreads of equipment. Experienced freeway builders, Vinnell used modern machinery and methods and by February 1967 grading was far enough along to allow SP crews to start laying track from the Palmdale end. Chief engineer on the project was Harry M. Williamson, with Assistant to the Chief, G. J. Lyon in direct charge. Towards the end of the project, track laying was started from the Colton end of the cutoff and the railheads met June 29, 1967, just north of Baseline Road near San Bernardino.

It had taken just 15 months from ground breaking to the driving of the final spike. The new 78.30 mile Palmdale-Colton cutoff cost 22 million dollars and was built to a maximum curvature of six degrees,

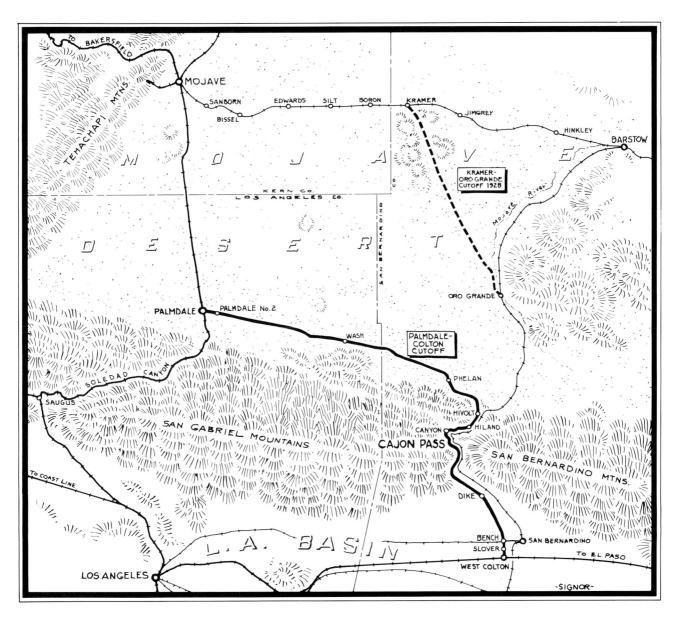

The north section of train No. 7 shown at the left, the *Fast Mail & Express,* pauses at Mojave in 1965. Santa Fe lost the mail contract for No. 7 during the spring of 1967 when the United States Post Office decided mail should move by air and truck. The Santa Fe discontinued the train that November. Another victim of the rash of train-off's occurring in the 1960's was Southern Pacific's celebrated *Owl.* (BELOW) Nearing the end, an eastbound version of this train streaks across the floor of the Antelope Valley at Denis in 1964. The *Owl,* the longest continually operated passenger train on the Tehachapi run, ended its 66 year career on April 11, 1965. — BOTH BRIAN BLACK

with a maximum gradient of 2.2 percent. The line was laid with continuously welded rail and initially equipped with six 8,000 foot sidings. These were identified east out of Palmdale as follows: Palmdale No. 2, Wash, Phelan (station sign only until 1977), Hiland; (at the summit of the grade), Canyon, Dike, Bench (no siding — junction of the Baldwin Park Branch which was the former Pacific Electric San Bernardino line), and Slover. The line's principal engineering feature was at the eastern end where a 963 foot pre-stressed concrete bridge spanned Lytle Creek wash near San Bernardino.

At a dedication of the cutoff held by the SP at Palmdale on July 11, 1967, SP President B. F. Biaginni and California's Lt. Governor Robert H. Finch drove the customary gold spike.

Regular operation of the cutoff commenced shortly thereafter. Soon many changes were being made in the traditional way of doing things on the San Joaquin Division Mountain District. Since a signal system was not provided, operations on the cutoff were carried out by timetable and train order, with operators located at each end of the line. In addition to copying train orders, the operator at Palmdale also operated the interlocking plant controlling the junction between the Saugus and cutoff lines. A series of second class schedules were listed in the timetable. Eastward on the cutoff, train Nos. 516, 518 and 520 were listed. Westward, train Nos. 515, 517 and 519 were used.

Taking advantage of the shorter route to the east, SP created new trains that used the cutoff. The *CLM* (Coast Line Manifest) originated in the San Francisco Bay area, operated via the valley line, and the cutoff, terminating at Tucson where it connected with the *SSE's*. Westbound Bay Area traffic was marshalled at Indio and placed in the consist of the *OCM* (Oakland Coast Manifest) which departed the desert terminal at 10:00 A.M. for Oakland by way of the cutoff. Indio, a desert crew change on the Los Angeles Division 71 miles east of Colton, and traditionally a gathering point for the agricultural products of the Imperial Valley, was now building trains for the cutoff. In addition to the *OCM*, Indio assembled the *IV-NCP* which handled the perishable and manifest traffic from the Imperial Valley destined to the Pacific Northwest and the *IV-VXW* for San Joaquin Valley points.

A new crew district was created when the cutoff became fully operational. Crews continued to run between Bakersfield and Los Angeles, although some crews terminated at Palmdale, if aboard trains routed via the cutoff. Palmdale was set up as a terminal and crews ran between there and Indio, a distance of 156 miles. In as much as the cutoff was split at Hiland, between the Los Angeles and

Westbound tonnage crests Cajon Pass at Hiland. The train order office here, set up in 1974, was discontinued in December 1979 when C.T.C. was installed on the Palmdale-Colton cutoff. — TED BENSON

San Joaquin divisions, crews of both divisions ran through with the LA crews based at Indio, and the San Joaquin crews based at Palmdale. All crew change work, cutting in and out of helpers, and other chores were done at Palmdale No. 2.

The run between Palmdale and Indio was one tough Mountain District in itself. Not only was there the Cajon grade, but the difficult and lengthy Beaumont Hill east of Colton as well. Short helpers were added in the desert on the westbound run between Myoma and Garnet, then cut at Apex. Out of Colton, more short helpers were added at Slover or Dike, and then cut at Hiland. On most trains, in addition to the short helpers, swing helpers worked through between Indio and Bakersfield. So demanding was the run, that additional power was needed in the Bakersfield-Tehachapi Freight Pool soon after the cutoff was completed. Special heavy locomotives were ordered, among them the heaviest single-engine locomotives on the system. Delivered between February and June 1968, General Electric U30C's, Nos. 7900 through 7929, were specially fitted with metal ballast providing them a total of 419,000 pounds on drivers. These engines along with seven more delivered in the fall of 1969 were assigned to the BAK-TF pool. EMD SD39's, six-axle 2,300 horsepower road switchers totaling out to 417,000 pounds, were also ordered for the Tehachapi. Numbered in the 5300 series, 18 were delivered in the fall of 1968 and eight more in 1970. Also in 1968, ten SD40's, Nos. 8479 through 8488, were assigned to the pool. These engines also weighed a great deal more than those assigned elsewhere — 411,000 pounds — or more than 17,000 pounds more than earlier versions of the same model assigned to Roseville. As of January 18, 1970, there were 110 units assigned to the Bakersfield-Tehachapi Freight Pool; 31 SD9's, 18 SD39's, 22 SD35's, 9 SD40's, and 30 U30C's.

Southern Pacific's only valley line passenger schedule received new power in the form of 3,600 horsepower SDP45's in the fall of 1967. Numbered in the 3200 series, only one of these units was required on the shrinking San Joaquin Daylight and when assigned to the train, they released the passenger F7's which then began turning up on the hotshots like the Starpacer.

While the Palmdale-Colton Cutoff was being relied on more heavily, it was at the expense of the railroad line from Palmdale to Burbank Junction via Saugus. The long eastbound Sunset Route trains from the north and the Imperial Valley traffic had been the first to desert the historic line, but as time went on, these were joined by others. In light of the decreased dependence on the Saugus Line, various changes to reduce the grade and curvature under consideration for the district were now shelved. Some of the proposed changes were of a minor nature around Paris, and Ravenna, but six miles of line change had been under consideration between Lang and Humphreys. Between Palmdale and Vincent it had even been suggested that double-track should be created by connecting the sidings of Palmdale and Harold, then develop a one percent grade from there up to Vincent leaving the present main line in place for westward trains.

Over the years, train order offices along the line were steadily reduced in rank with Palmdale being closed in 1958, and Ravenna in 1960. In 1967, following the opening of the cutoff, Vincent and Lang were closed. Lancaster was closed at this time, but Palmdale by reason of its importance in the operation of the cutoff, was reopened. Later, in 1974, the SP found it necessary to open train order offices at Ansel, Hiland and Dike on the Palmdale-Colton cutoff to keep traffic moving.

Railroad-wise, it was becoming rather quiet in Soledad Canyon. For several days in February 1971, the Saugus Line was even more quiet than usual. On the ninth of February at 6:01 A.M., an earthquake with the intensity of 6.6 on the Richter scale closed down the line. The epicenter of the quake was at Newhall, 40 miles from downtown Los Angeles, on the Saugus Line. The quake caused damage in Bakersfield and was felt in Las Vegas over 300 miles to the east, but was most destructive in the vicinity of Sylmar. During the epic shake, five concrete freeway overpasses at the junction of the Foothill and Golden State freeways collapsed, two of which took out the mainline and siding at Sylmar. A third blocked the mainline just east of the tunnel portal. Just beyond, the 6,966 foot San Fernando tunnel miraculously escaped disaster even through its sides had bulged menacingly near the center. Number 51, the San Joaquin Daylight, due to depart Los Angeles Union Passenger Terminal at 7:00 A.M., was annulled as was its counterpart below Bakersfield. Until the damage was repaired and the debris cleared, all traffic routed via Saugus was diverted to the Coast Line or the Palmdale Cutoff. Trains resumed operations over the line February 12th.

In June 1973, the Southern Pacific formally opened a new computerized freight yard at West Colton. Located at the junction of the Los Angeles-Yuma mainline and the Palmdale-Colton Cutoff, at the former station of Bloomington. West Colton Yard cost $39 million to construct and featured a capacity of 7,100 cars and a 48 track classification yard. The Santa Fe unveiled their new $50 million computerized freight yard at Barstow in 1976. Located west of the old yard, the new Barstow yard had much the same capacity as West Colton.

The emergence of these new "Super Yards" had considerable effect on operations over the Tehachapi Mountains. West Colton was designed to originate or terminate most north-south traffic moving over the Valley Line, and in so doing, began to draw more trains from the Saugus Line to the Cutoff. By the end of the decade only the Los Angeles-Portland piggyback forwarders were regularly run through Soledad Canyon. At Barstow, the Santa Fe's philosophy was to create a major regional classification yard. Traffic originating in northern California on their valley lines, excluding container and TOFC en route to points east of Kansas City, was to be forwarded to Barstow on four-hour headways in trains of random consist. The net result was the phenomenon of more and shorter Santa Fe trains in the Tehachapi.

Coincidental with the development of the new yards was the advent of the computer age in train planning, scheduling and identification. The old familiar "symbol" trains of both roads gave way to more functional codes. The SP adopted a letter code. Trains like the PNL now became the PTLAY (Portland Los Angeles), the VXE became the RVLAY (Roseville Los Angeles), the PSSE became the EUASY (Eugene Alton Southern) — Alton Southern being the terminal road at East St. Louis.

The *Starpacer* became the *LABRT* (Los Angeles Brooklyn Trailers) — Brooklyn being the principal yard at Portland.

On the Santa Fe, a number of new codes were utilized. The *OAF* became the 901 train, the *GWS* the 968 train, the *BTX* the 975 train, *SF 59* the 199 train, the *QSF* the 579 train, the *NCX* the 809 train and so on. With the advent of the new super yards, many new trains were created which had no parallel in past operations.

Perhaps the last holdover from steam operations in the Tehachapi Mountains was the makeup of the trains themselves. The types and sizes of equipment had evolved considerably over the years, but as late as 1966, the two roads were operating trains over the mountain differing little in tonnage from those pulled by the Mallets and 2-10-2's in the post-war era. Eastbound out of Bakersfield, Southern Pacific liked to run five units on 5,000 tons with a two-unit helper to Summit. The Santa Fe generally pursued a similar course, although both roads could and would run bigger trains. A westbound SP consisting of primarily Oregon lumber empties might reach 100 cars in length. The Santa Fe might occasionally run an eastbound out of Bakersfield requiring the use of a half dozen or more units cut in.

Operating policies changed, however, and the advent of high horsepower "second generation" mountain locomotives in the late 1960's allowed the SP to experiment with train length. These engines, the SD40 and SD45, introduced in 1966 from General Motors, and the U36C's from General Electric, were congregated at Roseville and Los Angeles, respectively, leaving the BTF pool units to work the San Joaquin Mountain District. But with the West Colton Yard in operation, power began running all the way through between Roseville and Colton, using BAK-TF pool units primarily as helpers. The run through of power became so commonplace that today there remains no trace of the old Bakersfield-Tehachapi Freight Pool.

The Santa Fe tried a short-lived experiment by running unmanned radio-controlled helpers through from Barstow to Bakersfield in 1969-1970. The first railroad to do so in the area, Santa Fe crews experienced troubles with the "remotes" as they were called. In one spectacular incident, an eastward train working up grade developed problems within the confines of tunnel No. 5. Continuity with the "remotes" was disrupted and the crewless helpers, now without any control, went into reverse, breaking the train in five separate pieces. Soon after, the Santa Fe abandoned the experiment preferring to use the remotes on unit mineral trains over its mainlines in Arizona, New Mexico, and Texas. It was obvious that in order to run the unmanned engines in the Tehachapi, it would be necessary to wire the many tunnels on the district to allow clear undisturbed radio reception. This work was carried out during 1973 in advance of SP's own remote trials.

In 1974, SP received 14 radio controlled SD40's which were tested at various places throughout the system. Testing in the Tehachapi began in the spring of 1975 and operations continued steadily for several years thereafter. In January 1976, the SP units were joined by two master SD40's and two remote received units from the Burlington Northern Railroad equipped with Locotrol. At first the remote operation was confined to runs between Bakersfield and West Colton. Extensive testing was also being carried out east of West Colton and was showing favorable results on long runs of heavy trains across the Sunset Route. Soon the two runs were combined. A popular train for remote operation was the *EUASY*. This train, often totalling out to 10,000 tons or better, and blocked to bypass Colton, would run a remote swing helper from Bakersfield to points east of Tucson. If tonnage warranted, additional short helpers were utilized up to Summit.

In the fall of 1976, up to four remote trains a day were operating over the district. Forty more radio equipped SD40's were delivered in 1978, but remote operations were not increased in the Tehachapi. The SP had come to the conclusion, much as the Santa Fe had earlier, that remote operations were better suited to keeping speeds up on tonnage trains over the long haul east. There was a nasty wreck at Palmdale No. 2 siding in 1977 involving remotes acting up. The following year the use of unmanned helpers over the Mountain District was dispensed with entirely. The idea of through swing helpers operating across the Tehachapi district was not abandoned, however, nor the long trains that swing helpers made possible.

With the consistent use of big six-axle locomotives, and the knowledge and experience gained from remote operation, the SP continued to tack more and more tonnage behind the drawbar. Train length was a problem. Across the Mountain District, sidings had been lengthened periodically as train length advanced — some old timers contend that it was done every time one went in the ditch. In the years following World War II a number of other modifications were made to increase the capacity of the railroad. Crossovers had been installed at Sandcut and the track from there to Bena was made double-track with reverse signal C.T.C. for operation in either direction on either track. The east end of Ilmon had been extended, Bealville and Allard connected with a crossover in the middle, and double-track reverse signal C.T.C. created between Cable and Tehachapi. The Mojave operator was given control to allow bi-directional movement on the eastward main track between the crossover at Cameron and Mojave. With the quantum leap in train length made possible by big units and swing helpers — not to mention skilled crews — even more modifications were necessary. In 1975 the sidings of Woodford and Cliff were both extended and the grading was completed to extend the Caliente siding westward, although to date nothing has been done to extend the track there.

Recent developments

The SP, always a firm believer in the use of helper power in the Tehachapi, continues today to utilize the lion's share in the area. Virtually every train east out of Bakersfield gets a helper of one form or another. Swing helpers routinely operate through between Bakersfield and Colton on many trains. Twice a day of late, the SP can be counted on to run east out of Bakersfield with lumber trains approaching 12,000 tons. This requires the services of three and occasionally four helper crews and 15 or 16 locomotives to get the train up the hill and across the district. Remarking recently in the *SP Bulletin,* San Joaquin Division Superintendent L.

H. Nations said of this remarkable feat, "I don't know any other place in the railroad industry where such heavy tonnages have been moved over such steep grades consistently day in and day out."

It is interesting to note that the Santa Fe and SP have traditionally handled equal tonnage annually over the joint track and continue to do so today. There are many contrasts in the way it is done. In this survey completed for the month of February 1982, the Santa Fe operated 89 trains more than the Southern Pacific between Kern Junction and Mojave, yet amazingly enough required 544 less locomotives to do it.

The Santa Fe, aside from their brief fling at remote operation, has continued a policy of running their system power up from Barstow which has gradually been upgraded as new power is delivered. A variety of locomotives can be seen in the mountains, but the SD40's, SD45's and several models of big General Electric units dominate. The SD24's have been rebuilt into SD26's and are still seen, but the ALCO DL-600B's have now vanished. Displacing the older GP7 and GP9 units, the GP30's and GP35's have found a home as "valley engines" north of Bakersfield, but are seen in the Tehachapi with regularity, usually in large sets. Although today the Santa Fe is every bit as capable of running heavy trains, just as the Southern Pacific, it has in general pursued a policy of running shorter and faster trains. In so doing, the road has attracted considerable trailer and container traffic. At present the road is operating six of these trailer trains over the Tehachapi daily.

The Tehachapi line's standing as one of the principal rail arteries in the west was dramatically underscored during the exceedingly wet spring of 1983. For nine and one-half days in March the Mountain District, battered by record storms, lay disjointed and out of service necessitating reroutes and detours which affected virtually every rail line into and out of California.

The stage was set for disaster in the last half of January as record amounts of rainfall fell over virtually the entire state. This pattern continued through February. In a week of storms ending March 2nd, almost five inches of rain fell over southern California — nearly twice normal — causing wide spread destruction. The deeply eroded slopes of the Tehachapi, already soaked from weeks of rain, could absorb no more and Caliente, Tehachapi and Cache creeks swelled to flood stage. The railroad yielded in their tempestuous wakes.

The damage came so quickly that several trains were caught on the mountain and stranded until repairs were made. A westbound SP freight, the 01-WCRVY-27, with four units, 98 cars and 4,019 tons, arrived at Bealville at 6:05 that morning and

---

NUMBER OF TRAINS OPERATED OVER THE TEHACHAPI FOR MONTH OF FEBRUARY 1982

Santa Fe	East	215	Southern Pacific	East	181
	West	224		West	169
		439			350

NUMBER OF UNITS USED IN ROAD AND HELPER SERVICE

Santa Fe			Southern Pacific		
Model	Road	Helper	Model	Road	Helper
CF7	4		GP9	1	
GP30	47	4	SD9	2	13
GP35	117	21	SD39	1	
GP40X	7		GP40	4	1
GP50	37	2	SD40	296	170
SD26	87	2	B30	79	33
SD40	415	29	SD40(8300)	167	95
SD45	322	27	U33C	35	6
SD45(5300)	87	4	SD45	309	201
SD45(5400)	11		SD45T	448	308
SD45(5490)	7		SD40(UP)	203	76
F45	89	1	C30(UP)	24	7
FP45	4			1,569	914
U23B	2				
B36	84	8	Total— 2,483		
C30	388	28			
U36C	102	3			
	1,810	129			

Total— 1,939

In this colorful painting by John R. Signor, five EMD SD9s drop down off the Tehachapi at milepost 377. Running as the third section of No. 802, the train is a few minutes outside of Mojave on a cold winter morning.

Looking much as it did when new, train No. 1, the *San Francisco Chief,* is about to enter tunnel No. 2 near Allard in 1967.

— GORDON GLATTENBERG

was tied down. Eastbound Santa Fe train 918-BH-2, with three units, 51 cars and 1,930 tons, parked at Summit Switch at 5:30 AM. An eastbound SP, the 11-SELAK-25, with four units, 96 cars and 9,333 tons, arrived there about five hours later after pausing at Walong and Marcel for crews to check the track. It too was tied town. With many sections impassible, it was not until the morning of March 2nd that officials, with the aid of a helicopter, were able to fully assess the damages.

The report they filed read like a battlefield casualty list. On the north slope, the narrows of Caliente Creek between the loop at Caliente and Sandcut — historically vulnerable to high water — were particularly hard hit. So swift were the waters that Caliente Creek jumped its banks in the vicinity of the first crossing cutting a new channel through Bena to Walker Basin Creek. At the Walker Basin Creek bridge the west subgrade was washed out for 250 feet taking out the helper spur. The No. 1 (north) track was left swinging in mid-air from the bridge to the road crossing at Bena. Track and fill were completely gone from the east switch at Bena to the first crossing of Caliente Creek and from the first crossing all the way to the west switch at Caliente, ten other major washouts had occurred. Caliente was out of service with all three tracks undermined at the west end by a washout 200 feet long by 15 feet deep. The loop and third crossing bridge at Caliente had suffered at the hands of the flood and the west end of the bridge had sunk two feet and was 1.5 feet out of line. Further up the line, the short siding at Woodford was washed out for 300 feet and a culvert had plugged cascading water and debris over the tracks for a quarter of a mile. The west end of tunnel No. 17 was obscured by a slide 40 feet long and four feet deep. On the south slope Cache Creek overflowed depositing from one to three feet of mud and rocks on the tracks between Cameron Canyon Road and the

Twenty-six days after the 1983 flood,
Caliente Creek is still muddy and swollen.
— TIM ZUKAS

crossover at Cameron. Further down the hill, in the narrows at mile post 371.4, both mainlines were washed out for 250 feet. On the big curve below Warren a long running side-wash had occurred with the westbound main track being left undermined and swinging in mid-air at mile post 375.7. In addition, the Saugus line was out of service with most of the damage confined to the section between Ravenna and Lang. The Palmdale-Colton cutoff was relatively undamaged.

Simultaneously with the closing of the Tehachapi line, SP's Coast line was taken out of service with a major washout at Moorpark. The principal problem, however, was the loss of the 549 foot bridge spanning Santa Ynez River at Surf. The Coast line would be out for seven days preventing its use as a detour for Tehachapi traffic. By midnight on March 3rd, Santa Fe was detouring its northern California traffic east over the Western Pacific to Salt Lake City where another diversion was made via the

Union Pacific to Denver or to southern California. March 7th was the peak of this operation when 26 trains passed over Western Pacific's Feather River Canyon line in 24 hours.

The SP diverted much of its traffic east over the Overland Route — which surprisingly remained open over Donner Summit throughout the ordeal — and some trains traveled north out of Los Angeles over the Union Pacific. Many trains, however, were simply parked awaiting the reopening of the Coast line which occurred at 12:01 A.M. March 8th. In the next three days 54 through trains moved over the Coast line. To handle the surge, temporary train order offices were set up at Santa Susana and Gaviota.

In the early morning hours of March 7th the westbound main was restored to service between Cameron and Mojave but it was not until nearly ten days of intensive effort had passed that a through route was pieced together over the

For ten days in early March 1983, the Tehachapi line lay out of service due to storms. As in previous episodes, the Caliente Creek narrows sustained the heaviest damage. This view, looking down through Ilmon 16 days after the line was reopened, clearly illustrates the magnitude of the problem. — TIM ZUKAS

Tehachapi. The switch at Bena was spiked for the No. 2 main (south side) making it single track east of Sandcut. Between Sandcut and Ilmon all signals and CTC were out. At Caliente, the only route open was by way of the westward siding. The siding at Cliff was out of service as was the short siding at Woodford. Slow orders blanketed the district.

The first through westbound train — not including those stranded on the mountain — departed Mojave at 11:05 A.M. March 10th. This train, the SP 01-WCRVY-28, with four units, 122 cars and 5,086 tons, had been parked at Ansel since March 1st. The first eastbound, Santa Fe 981-I-1, with five units, 51 cars and 3,565 tons, departed Bakersfield at 6:22 P.M. the same day. Operations through Soledad Canyon did not resume until March 13th.

The Santa Fe is expected to shoulder 45% of an estimated $5.4 million poured into the reconstruction of the flood-ravaged Tehachapi line. As this volume goes to press work continues on restoring the railroad to normal operation. The roadbed in the section between Bena and Caliente is being rebuilt to accept a second track. The extra width is being accomplished by removing material from above tunnel No. ½. This has given rise to the persistant, but as yet unconfirmed, rumor that the tunnel will be daylighted and double track extended from Bena to Caliente.

The quick profits made over a century ago from the station site on flat ground at Caliente with its necessary requirement that the road be built up through the trecherous lower Caliente Creek narrows, have long been swept away by a rising tide of maintenance costs. Given the events of March 1983, and similar costly episodes in February 1938, September 1932 and 1890, 1886 and 1884, it seems to this writer that the Southern Pacific has paid a large price for taking the advice of David Colton over the objections of its Chief Engineer William Hood.

Following completion of the Palmdale-Colton cutoff in 1967, the Saugus line experienced a sharp downturn in traffic. By the mid-1970s only a handful of trains regularly threaded Soledad Canyon. The *BRLAT*, seen near Acton, was one of them. The train, handling merchandise and piggyback cars from Portland to Los Angeles, is running as No. 340 across the district. — DONALD DUKE

The three-times-a-week Lone Pine local, at the left, shoves two cars toward the west leg of the wye at Lone Pine. — RICHARD STEINHEIMER While the SP sought abandonment in later years of the greater part of the "Jawbone," the lower end of the branch was not threatened. Major shipper Kerr-McGee Chemical Company at Trona can ship upwards of 200 cars a week and the SP has catered to the business. (BELOW) A unit coal train destined for Kerr-McGee moves through the desert near Cantil en route to Searles during April 1982. — DICK DORN

Trona Railway Baldwins switch the interchange with the Southern Pacific at Searles a decade earlier. — TED BENSON

Sunset near Ansel. — DICK DORN

Norfolk & Western units used in helper service drop down through Warren in 1978. The use of off-line power has increased in recent years. — GARY ALLEN

Conforming to Cache Creek, the railroad makes an "S" curve near Warren. — TED BENSON

Blasting out of the Mojave sink, an amply powered westbound assaults the Tehachapi grade. — RICHARD STEINHEIMER

Adding power for the hill is one of the more frequent switching moves performed at Mojave. — RICHARD STEINHEIMER

The Searles tunnel caught fire on February 22, 1981, resulting in a partial collapse of the 4,340 foot bore. With key shipper Kerr-McGee isolated by the incident, crews moved quickly to restore service. While the tunnel was still smoldering, Caterpillar tractors went to work clearing brush from a surprisingly well preserved shoofly grade used 73 years previous while the tunnel was originally being built. Dubbed "Kelly's Kink," for Mojave Trainmaster W. S. Kelly, the extreme curvature and 3.5 percent grades found on the shoofly prevented normal heavy unit train operation. While small four-axle power, imported for the occasion, routinely tripled the hill, engineers scoured the area for alternatives to rebuilding the tunnel. A five mile 1.5 percent grade was surveyed to the east but environmentalists argued to save the tunnel — the top served as the only migratory path for the endangered desert tortoise. (ABOVE AND BELOW) An eight-unit westbound Searles Turn makes a run for El Paso Summit then drops down through the horseshoe on the other side in February 1982. — BOTH TOM TAYLOR (LEFT) The vertical curve at the summit was remarkably abrupt. — RICHARD STEINHEIMER Seventeen months later the tunnel was restored to service and the shoofly abandoned and left to bleach in the desert once again.

In the above scene, the KI (Tehachapi) Local switches Monolith during March 1974. (LEFT) Monolith Portland Cement operated a narrow gauge industrial line from this point out to a quarry several miles to the northeast for many years. Motor No. 12 switches the quarry in December 1972. The operation was abandoned in favor of trucks the following year. — BOTH GARY ALLEN

Santa Fe No. 5938 rolls eastbound at milepost 366.5. The Monolith Portland Cement company may be seen in the background. — DAVE STANLEY

Bathed in early morning light, the Tehachapi Mountains rise dramatically from the valley floor at Sandcut. — TIM ZUKAS

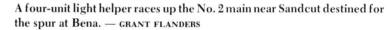

A four-unit light helper races up the No. 2 main near Sandcut destined for the spur at Bena. — GRANT FLANDERS

244

Santa Fe extra No. 5614 west rolls through Sandcut on May 8, 1970. Tucked away toward the rear is a four-unit remote helper. Santa Fe was the first to experiment with un-manned radio-controlled helpers in the Tehachapi. — BOTH TOM TAYLOR

245

Two units mark time on the spur at Bena ready to cut into extra No. 3965 east. The spur, laid in the spring of 1971, allows helpers to await assignments without fouling the No. 2 main. — TED BENSON

With its train wrapped around the great Caliente horseshoe, a westbound SP train fills the narrow canyon with dynamic brake howl and flange squeal. — GRANT FLANDERS

The rolling oak-studded hills through which Bealville siding meanders reflects the Tehachapi in its most pastoral state. In the spring, wild flowers carpet the rich green slopes creating a country club or park-like setting. (LEFT) No. 340 works through "Railroad Park" near tunnel No. 2. — DAVE STANLEY (ABOVE) Allard and Bealville were joined in the 1960's creating one 13,270 foot siding. Freshly silvered signals protect the crossover between the two. — BRIAN BLACK (BELOW) Eastbound tonnage negotiates the great horseshoe near the crossover. — DICK DORN

At Cliff, one of the more remote sections of the Tehachapi grade, the railroad clings to a shelf cut in the mountainside high above Tehachapi Creek. At the west end Caliente is only a mile away as-the-crow-flies yet 700 feet lower and six miles distant by rail. — TIM ZUKAS

Yet another momento of maximum mountain railroading — a drawbar — lies beside the tracks at Cliff. — TED BENSON

Toward the east end of Cliff, Tehachapi Creek begins to rise rapidly. At Rowen, the creek is just a few feet below grade. — TIM ZUKAS

The Mountain Local gets the signal while the Santa Fe waits in a three-way meet at Woodford as photographed by Dave Stanley in 1974. Such incidents gave rise to the following tome found scrawled in a phone booth some years ago on the grade . . .

May God have pity
   on this damned dispatchers soul.
He's stabbing us to death,
   he's always go us in the hole.
When we go up the hill,
   he's always bring the SP's down.
When we go down the hill
   it's the other way 'round.

An eastbound Southern Pacific train holes through 262 foot tunnel No. 16, one of four remaining short tunnels between Marcel and Cable. — RICH-ARD STEINHEIMER

Silver trailers of SP's *BRLAT* clearly deliniated the arrangement of tracks at Marcel in April 1982. — DICK DORN

Unit export coal train *RGLRL* rolls toward Tehachapi on January 8, 1983. Twelve heavy locomotives — a four-unit road engine and two four-unit swing helpers — power the 10,972 ton train destined for Los Angeles harbor. — TIM ZUKAS

Train No. 52, the *San Joaquin Day-light,* snakes through a double reverse curve above Cable. In the final years of its operation, a single SDP45 handled the skimpy consist. — RIC-HARD STEINHEIMER

Running for the switch, the No. 8000 east meets a Santa Fe at Tehachapi Summit in the rain.
— GRANT FLANDERS

A snowfall overtakes the engine for the KI
local on its rest day at Tehachapi in 1974.
—GARY ALLEN

A sign on the highway reminds travelers that Tehachapi is "the land of four seasons," a fact well known by railroaders. Snow regularly falls at Woodford and, driven by high winds, can make the brakeman's life miserable at Mojave. The mood of the mountain changes under a mantle of snow and impressions of the grade in this condition are herewith presented. — (Left and Below) TED BENSON — (Bottom) RICHARD STEINHEIMER

253

A midwinter sunset backlights train No. 52, the *San Joaquin Daylight,* at Monolith in February 1070. By this time the train was down to 9 cars. — DONALD DUKE

Making a run for the hill, train No. 1-521, consisting entirely of 9,800 tons of "beets," powers out of the Mojave sink in July 1978. The swing helper, cut deep into the train, has come all the way from Colton. — JAMIE SCHMID

A swing helper cut into Southern Pacific lumber drag 11-*SECIK*-15 moves through Bealville on April 18, 1983. An unusually wet spring has left a rich carpet of green in its wake. — JAMIE SCHMID (RIGHT) Santa Fe eastbound train led by General Electric locomotive No. 8728 rounds the loop at Walong as it moves toward Tehachapi. — DONALD DUKE

256

Epilogue

During the last century, an incredible tide of commerce has passed over the railroad in the Tehachapi Mountains. The biggest and most durable men and machines of each generation have been thrown at the district's formidable grades. Historians might argue that it was in the 1920's that operations in the Tehachapi reached their zenith, or perhaps it was during World War II. It is true that certain aspects of the "romance of the rails" departed with the steam locomotive and the passenger train. With the business of railroading in the Tehachapi, there is always change. Yet the basics have remained fundamentally the same.

The trains of the Santa Fe and Southern Pacific must still thread the narrow defile that is the Tehachapi crossing, much as they always have. The line of track has deviated little from that which was located by William Hood in the 1870's. With the main flow of highway traffic funneling over Tejon Pass to the west, Tehachapi Pass has seen little of the despoiling and development which is the hallmark of our modern culture. The trains of today pass through a country of remarkable beauty, not unlike that which Hood gazed upon in those

hectic months of 1875.

The Tehachapi grade has traditionally soaked up horsepower like a sponge and today a wider variety of locomotives routinely work the grade than at any time in history. The previously unthinkable spectacle of 12 to 16 locomotives, and three or four engine crews, boosting 11,000 ton trains over the pass can be witnessed daily.

A careful look at operating department figures demonstrates there is more tonnage being handled now than in virtually any period in the past — in heavier trains with larger capacity cars. During the spring of 1982, better than 50 train movements were being logged in some 24 hour periods on the mountain — a respectable figure for a recession year.

Rail enthusiasts are likely to find other locations in this country through which more trains will run. But few can rival the Tehachapi as a place to take in the drama of big-time mountain railroading at its gut-wrenching best. Be it from the vantage point of a poppy-strewn hillside overlooking the Caliente gorge, the famous loop or the great horse-shoe below Bealville, the railroad buff will find much to see and do in the heart of California's Tehachapi Pass.

Warren telegraph as sketched on
January 17, 1908 by Ross Green, the
day operator. — OLA MAE FORCE
COLLECTION

Selected Mountain District Timetables

MOJAVE DIVISION: Bakersfield and Mojave.

FROM SAN FRANCISCO — **TOWARD SAN FRANCISCO**

TIME TABLE No. 3, Nov. 1, 1892.

Third Class 25 Way Freight Daily	Second Class 23 Freight Daily	Second Class 21 Sunset Frt. Limited Daily	First Class 19 Atlantic Express Daily	First Class 17 Los Angeles Express Daily	DISTANCE FROM SAN FRANCISCO	STATIONS	DISTANCE FROM LOS ANGELES	First Class 18 Los Angeles Express Daily	First Class 20 Pacific Express Daily	Second Class 22 Steamer Frt. Limited Daily	Third Class 24 Freight Daily	Third Class 26 Way Freight Daily
A M LV	A M LV	P M LV	A M LV	P M LV				A M AR	AR	A M AR	P M AR	P M AR
			9.00	5.30	0.00	SAN FRANCISCO	482.26	9.15	8.45			
4.10	7.40	P M 11.15	P M 10.20	A M 4.00	314.04	dn. BAKERSFIELD 7.25	168.22	P M 11.15	P M 7.40	A M 11.55	P M 2.00	P M 9.15
4.35	8.02	11.37	10.37	f 4.15	321.29	Wade 4.88	160.97	10.59	f 7.22	11.30	1.35	9.15
4.54	8.20	11.53	f 10.50	f 4.26	326.17	Sand Cut. 2.83	156.09	f 10.50	f 7.11	11.12	1.17	8.55
5.05	8.30	A M 12.04	s 11.00	f 4.32	329.00	d. Pampa W 7.35	153.26	f 10.43	f 7.04	11.00	1.05	8.40
5.40	9.05	12.34	s 11.27	s 4.50	336.35	dn. Caliente W 5.30	145.91	s 10.20	s 6.45	10.20	12.25	8.00
6.26	**9.45**	1.07	f 11.52	f 5.13	341.65	d. Bealville W 4.80	140.61	f 10.00	f **6.26**	**9.45**	P M 11.55	7.28
7.10	10.30	1.35	A M 12.14	f 5.32	346.45	Rowan 3.50	135.81	f 9.41	f 6.04	9.10	11.30	7.05
7.35	**11.05**	1.55	s 12.30	s **5.50**	349.95	dn. Keene W 5.37	132.31	s 9.26	s **5.50**	8.50	**11.05**	6.45
8.20	11.45	2.30	f 12.55	6.12	355.32	d. Girard W 6.38	126.94	f 9.05	s 5.26	**8.20**	10.35	6.15
9.10 / 9.30	P M 12.35	3.10	s 1.25	s 6.40	361.70	dn. Tehachapi W 1.82	120.56	s 8.40	s 5.05	7.50	9.55	5.45
9.45	12.45	3.18	1.32	6.45	363.52	Summit Switch 7.46	118.74	8.34	5.00	7.40	**9.45**	5.35
10.10	1.20	3.50	f 1.52	f **7.05**	370.98	d. Cameron W 5.19	111.28	f 8.13	f 4.42	**7.05**	9.15	5.00
10.37	1.47	**4.24**	2.07	7.20	376.17	Warren 5.60	106.09	f 7.54	**4.24**	6.20	8.45	4.33
11.10	2.15	4.55	2.25	7.35	381.77	dn. MOJAVE W	100.49	7.35	4.00	5.45	**8.10**	4.00
A M AR	A M AR	A M AR	A M AR	P M AR				P M LV	P M LV	A M LV	A M LV	P M LV
Daily.	Daily.	Daily.	Daily.	Daily.				Daily.	Daily.	Daily.	Daily.	Daily.

2

SAN JOAQUIN DIVISION: Bakersfield and Mojave.

TIME TABLE No. 55, Mar. 14, 1901.

FROM SAN FRANCISCO (westbound, read top → bottom) — Second Class: 134 (Santa Fe), 244 (Sunset Fri. Limited), 242 (Way Freight); First Class: 104 (Santa Fe Limited), 108 (Santa Fe Overland), 26 (The Owl), 10 (Atlantic Express), 8 (Los Angeles Express). All Daily.

TOWARD SAN FRANCISCO — First Class: 7 (Los Angeles Express), 9 (Pacific Express), 25 (The Owl), 103 (Santa Fe Limited), 107 (Santa Fe Overland); Second Class: 241 (Way Freight), 243 (Steamer Fri. Limited), 133 (Santa Fe). All Daily.

134	244	242	104	108	26	10	8	Pass. min.	Dist. from S.F.	STATIONS	Dist. from L.A.	Frt. min.	7	9	25	103	107	241	243	133
11.05	9.00	4.40	5.40	7.50	1.10	4.40	9.20		314.04	dn..BAKERSFIELD .72	168.22		¶7.00	7.50	2.05	8.50	5.45	7.00	8.30	
11.25	9.03	4.42	5.50	8.05	1.11	4.41	9.22	10	314.76	dn..KERN JUNC 5.53	167.50	19	6.57	7.48	2.03	8.38	5.30	6.57	8.25	2.45
11.39	9.22	5.02	5.56	8.15	1.22	f4.54	9.36	7	321.29	Wade 4.88	160.97	14	f6.44	f7.35	1.53	8.27	5.20	6.40	8.05	2.25
11.49	9.36	5.20	6.01	8.22	1.32	f5.04	9.51	4	326.17	Sand Cut 2.83	156.09	8	f6.32	f7.23	1.43	8.22	5.12	6.20	7.41	2.11
12.03	9.46	5.30	6.07	8.30	1.38	f5.12	9.58	5½	329.00	n..Pampa...W 3.40	153.26	10	f6.27	f7.16	1.38	8.15	5.06	6.01	7.33	2.00
12.23	9.58	5.41	6.17	8.41	1.44	5.19	10.12	9	332.40	Ilmon 3.95	149.86	15	6.18	7.10	1.28	8.05	4.56	5.45	7.22	1.44
1.00	10.25	6.08	6.42	9.02	1.54	s5.30	s10.25	13	336.35	dn..Caliente...W 5.30	145.91	21	s6.08	s6.57	1.15	7.47	4.41	5.25	7.05	1.25
1.30	11.05	6.43	6.58	9.19	2.11	f5.53	10.50	12	341.65	n..Bealville...W 4.80	140.61	20	f5.53	s6.42	1.00	7.32	4.23	4.55	6.43	1.00
2.07	11.45	7.32	7.12	9.35	2.27	f6.10	11.20	9	346.45	Rowen 3.50	135.81	15	5.37	6.23	12.46	7.21	4.12	4.25	6.10	11.45
2.45	12.36	7.50	7.33	9.52	2.43	s6.35	s11.44	13	349.95	dn..Keene...W 5.37	132.31	21	s5.25	s6.10	12.36	7.05	3.55	4.10	5.52	11.20
3.00	1.10	8.20	7.43	10.05	3.05	f7.05	f12.20	6	355.32	n..Girard...W 2.50	126.94	10	s5.12	f5.52	12.20	6.55	3.45	3.40	5.30	10.55
3.30	1.32	8.40	7.56	10.19	3.16	f7.17	12.35	9	357.82	Cable 3.88	124.44	15	f5.01	f5.44	12.13	6.45	3.30	3.30	5.19	10.30
3.40	2.00	9.30	8.00	10.22	3.30	s7.35	s12.57	2	361.70	dn..Tehachapi...W 1.82	120.56	5	s4.46	s5.33	12.04	6.43	3.26	3.10	5.05	10.14
	2.05	9.40			3.32	7.42	1.03	} 11	363.52	Summit Switch (Spur) 2.03	118.74	} 25	4.40	5.26	12.02			2.45	5.00	9.55
......	......	......	......	......	......	......	......		365.55	Sullivan (Spur) 2.95	116.71		......	......	......	......	......	......	......	9.40
......	......	......	......	......	......	......	......		368.50	Eric (Spur) 2.48	113.76		......	......	......	......	......	......	......	......
{4.17 4.30}	2.30	10.10	8.15	10.39	3.46	f7.59	1.22	11	370.98	dn..Cameron...W 5.19	111.28	20	f4.17	f5.08	11.52	6.26	3.10	2.15	4.30	9.00
5.05	2.54	10.34	8.26	10.50	3.58	f8.14	1.41	6	376.17	Warren 2.80	106.09	10	3.58	f4.50	11.34	6.07	2.54	1.45	3.58	8.26
5.27	3.15	10.48	8.32	10.58	4.06	f8.21	1.50	6	378.97	Fram...W 2.80	103.29	10	3.40	f4.40	11.24	5.54	2.40	1.30	3.15	7.50
5.45	3.30	11.00	8.40	11.05	4.13	¶8.30	1.59		381.77	dn..MOJAVE...W	100.49		3.30	4.30	11.15	5.45	2.30	1.15	3.00	7.30

Nos. 241 and 242 will carry passengers.

All west-bound trains have absolute right of track over all east-bound trains of the same or inferior class. See Rule 384.

SAN JOAQUIN DIVISION: Mojave, Saugus and Los Angeles.

TIME TABLE No. 84. July 6, 1904.

TOWARD SAN FRANCISCO.

Station	Dist. from Mojave	Dist. from S.F.	243 Sunset Freight Limited (Daily)	253 Sunset Freight Limited (Daily)	39 Passenger and Freight (Daily Ex. Sun.)	233 Way Freight (Daily)	241 Way Freight (Daily)	7 Los Angeles Passenger (Daily)	25 The Owl (Daily)	99 S. Barbara Passenger (Daily)	9 Sunset Limited (Daily)	21 Coaster (Daily)	97 S. Barbara Passenger (Daily)
DN..MOJAVE..W.	0.00	381.77	1.10 AM AR				12.20 PM AR	4.05 AM AR	8.40 PM AR				
Fleta (Opar.)	6.61	388.38											
Gloster	9.81	391.68	12.45				11.47	3.46	8.26				
Lexis (Opar.)	13.83	395.60											
N..Rosamond..W.	19.43	401.26	12.25				11.25	f3.29	8.13				
Oban	24.83	406.66	12.04 / 11.42				11.04	3.19	8.06				
DN..Lancaster..W.	33.35	415.10	11.15				10.45	f3.10	s7.57				
DN..Palmdale	35.60	417.37	11.05				10.18	s2.52	7.45				
Harold..W.	39.81	421.68	10.45				10.03	f2.44	7.40				
DN..Vincent..W.	46.59	427.36	9.55				9.45	f2.35	7.33				
DN..Actos	48.31	430.08	9.40				9.10	f2.13	7.14				
DN..Ravenna..W.	53.91	435.68	9.07				8.50	s2.07	7.06				
DN..Russ..W.	58.11	439.88	8.40				8.10	f1.44	6.48				
DN..Lang..W.	62.51	444.28	8.26				7.40	s1.30	6.39				
Humphreys	66.31	448.08	8.10		(See page 4)		7.15	f1.18	6.29	(See page 4)		(See page 4)
Mowby	69.88	451.66	7.55				6.50	f1.08	6.20			
DN..SAUGUS..W.	72.38	454.16	7.45			8.55 / 8.45 AM AR	6.30 / 5.30	s12.56	s6.11	PM AR 4.20		AM AR 8.30
D..Newhall	73.10	454.87				8.45	5.20	s12.51	6.06	4.15		s8.25
Elayon	75.95	457.72	7.25			8.25	4.50	12.40	5.57	f4.05		f8.14
DN..Tunnel	78.55	460.39										
Sylmar	81.15	462.92			7.59	7.59 / 7.40	4.15	s12.22	5.46	s3.53		7.59
DN..Fernando..W.	83.81	464.68	6.54 / 6.44				3.40	12.18	5.42	f3.49		7.54
Pacoima	86.59	468.36										
Tejunga	87.23	469.00										
Roscoe	91.00	473.25	6.10			7.20	3.15	12.08	5.34	f3.39		f7.43
DN..BURBANK	91.48	465.71	5.50 PM LV	6.23 PM AR / 5.50	7.15	7.00	2.50	s11.59	5.27	s3.29	2.11	8.27	s7.32
Sepulveda	93.70	465.93		6.13 / 5.37	7.04		2.30	11.54	5.24	3.24	2.06	8.24	7.26
West Glendale..W.	94.40	466.63		6.10 / 5.35	7.02		2.27	11.53	5.23	f3.23	2.04	8.23	f7.25
D..Tropico	96.38	468.61		6.05 / 5.30	6.56	6.35	2.22	11.50	5.20	s3.20	2.00	8.20	f7.21
DN..RIVER STATION (Los Angeles)	100.49	472.72		5.45 / 5.10	6.30	6.15	2.00	11.40	5.10	3.10	1.50	8.10	7.10
DN..LOS ANGELES..W.	102.59	474.62		5.45 PM LV		AM LV	AM LV	11.30 AM LV	5.00 PM LV	3.00 PM LV	1.40 PM LV	8.00 AM LV	7.00 AM LV
Daily totals			(0.38)	(8.00)	(0.45)	(2.85)	(10.50)	(4.55)	(3.40)	(1.20)	(0.51)	(0.27)	(1.30)

FROM SAN FRANCISCO.

Station	Dist. from S.F.	40 (Daily Ex. Sun.)	242 Way Freight (Daily)	234 Way Freight (Daily)	244 Sunset Limited Freight (Daily)	254 Sunset Freight Limited (Daily)	22 Coaster (Daily)	96 S. Barbara Passenger (Daily)	98 S. Barbara Passenger (Daily)	10 Sunset Limited (Daily)	26 The Owl (Daily)	8 Los Angeles Passenger (Daily)
DN..MOJAVE..W.	381.77		1.45 PM LV			5.40 AM LV				10.43 AM LV	5.13 AM LV	2.35 AM LV
Fleta (Opar.)	388.38		2.05			6.00					5.21	f2.48
Gloster	391.68											
Lexis (Opar.)	395.60											
N..Rosamond..W.	401.26		2.25			6.20				10.46	5.31	f3.02
Oban	406.66		2.40			6.38				10.48	5.38	3.19
DN..Lancaster..W.	415.10		3.00			6.55				10.52	5.45	s3.31
DN..Palmdale	417.37		3.50			7.30					6.00	f3.50
Harold..W.	421.68		4.00			7.40					6.04	f3.56
DN..Vincent..W.	427.36		4.40			8.10					6.18	f4.15
DN..Actos	430.08		5.10			8.35					6.31	4.30
DN..Ravenna..W.	435.68		5.30			8.50					6.39	4.37
DN..Russ..W.	439.88		5.50			9.20					6.52	4.53
DN..Lang..W.	444.28		6.06			9.45					7.06	f5.07
Humphreys	448.08		6.43 (See page 4)	1.35 PM LV		10.03					7.15	5.17
Mowby	451.66		7.00			10.22					7.24	f6.26
DN..SAUGUS..W.	454.16		7.45	1.50		10.40		10.55 AM LV (See page 4)	6.11 PM LV	10.41	s7.35	s6.35
D..Newhall	454.87		8.10	2.30		10.55		s10.41	s6.17		7.39	f5.44
Elayon	457.72							f10.52	f6.31	10.52	7.50	f6.00
DN..Tunnel	460.39		8.45			11.18						
Sylmar	462.92		8.55									
DN..Fernando..W.	464.68		8.55	2.50		11.42		s11.04	s6.42	11.04	8.04	f6.15
Pacoima	468.36			3.00		11.48		f11.08	f6.44	11.08		f6.19
Roscoe	473.25		9.10	3.15		12.10		f11.17	f6.53	11.17	8.12	f6.30
DN..BURBANK	465.71	4.55 PM LV	9.35 PM AR	3.29 AR / 3.29 LV	12.40	12.22	10.17 PM LV	s11.25	s7.01	11.25	8.18	s5.43 AR / 6.43 LV
Sepulveda	465.93	5.03		3.38	12.49	12.28	10.21	11.30	7.06	11.30	8.24	6.50
West Glendale..W.	466.63	5.06		3.43	12.51	12.31	10.22	f11.31	f7.08	11.31	8.27	6.51
D..Tropico	468.61	5.15 / 5.30		3.50	1.00	12.40	10.25	s11.35	f7.12	11.35	8.33	f6.51 / s3.56
DN..RIVER STATION (Los Angeles)	472.72	5.45		4.10	1.25	1.05	10.35	11.50	7.25	11.50	8.45	7.10
DN..LOS ANGELES..W.	474.62	5.45 PM AR	PM AR	4.10 PM AR	1.25 PM AR	1.25 PM AR	10.45 PM AR	12.01 PM AR	7.35 PM AR	12.01 PM AR	8.55 AM AR	6.45 AM AR
Daily totals		(0.55)	(8.40)	(2.85)	(0.45)	(7.25)	(0.28)	(1.26)	(1.24)	(0.88)	(3.42)	(4.85)

All west-bound trains have absolute right over all east-bound trains of same or inferior class. See Rule 81. Nos. 241 and 242 will carry passengers between Los Angeles and Mojave.

BAKERSFIELD AND MOJAVE SUBDIVISION

FROM SAN FRANCISCO

Eastward

Time Table No. 135 — November 14, 1920.

Siding / Rule	STATIONS (Automatic Block Signal)	Distance from San Francisco	334 Freight Leave Daily	340 Freight Leave Daily	342 Way Freight Leave Daily	306 Bakersfield Oilg Mixed Leave Daily Ex. Sunday	338 Freight Leave Daily	252 Sunset Manifest Freight Leave Daily	8 San Francisco Los Angeles Passenger Leave Daily	10 Santa Fe Passenger Leave Daily	20 Santa Fe Passenger Leave Daily	86 Oil Fields Passenger Leave Daily	108 Fresno Los Angeles Express Leave Daily	2 Santa Fe Tourist Express Leave Daily	50 San Joaquin Valley Passenger Leave Daily	26 The Owl Leave Daily	60 The Sacramento Leave Daily
WPTYOP Yard	DN-B BAKERSFIELD 0.7	812.9	6.25PM	12.50PM	9.00AM	7.00AM	6.05AM	12.01AM	11.40PM	7.50PM	5.30PM	12.25PM	12.20PM	7.55AM	3.17AM	2.30AM	1.40AM
P I	DN-B KERN JCT.	813.6	6.33	12.58	9.15	7.05AM	6.12	12.09	11.43	7.56	5.35	12.28PM	12.23	8.00	3.20	2.33	1.43
75 P	MAGUNDEN 2.5	817.0	6.40	1.05	9.35		6.18	12.13	11.55PM				12.28		3.25	2.38	1.48
	SOLY 0.6	819.7															
70 P	DN EDISON 4.9	820.1	6.52	1.17	9.50		6.27	12.23	s12.03AM	8.04	5.39		s12.34	8.04	3.29	2.42	1.52
68 P	N SIVERT 2.9	825.0	6.58	1.23	10.00		6.33	12.35	12.13	8.11	5.46		f12.44	8.11	3.36	2.48	1.59
71 PW	D BENA 3.4	827.9	7.06	1.31	10.10		6.41	12.43	12.24	8.16	5.51		f12.49	8.16	3.41	2.53	2.04
66 P	ILMON 3.9	831.3	7.35	2.00	11.00		6.55 / 7.15	1.11	12.32	8.23	5.58		12.56	8.22	3.47	2.59	2.11
East 61 PW / West 78	DN CALIENTE 3.0	835.2	7.47	2.12	11.15		7.27	1.23	s12.43	s8.32	6.07		s1.08	8.32	3.55	3.07	2.20
67 P	ALLARD 3.0	838.2	7.57	2.22	11.35		7.37	1.33	12.52	8.40	6.14		1.18	8.39	4.01	3.13	2.27
West 70 PW / East 61	DN BEALVILLE 2.3	840.5	8.05	2.30	11.45AM		7.45	1.41	1.02	8.46	6.20		f1.26	8.45	4.06	3.18	2.33
25 P	OLIFF 1.8	842.3	8.20	2.45	12.05PM		8.00	2.05	1.12	8.51	6.25		1.32	8.49	4.10	3.22	2.38
East 61 M23 / West 63 P	DN BOWEN 3.2	845.5	8.45	3.07	12.40		8.25	2.30	1.24	8.59	6.33		f1.42	8.57	4.17	3.29	2.46
	TAMAR 2.2 (6pw)	847.7															
68 PW	DN WOODFORD 3.0	848.8	9.00	3.22	12.55		8.40	2.45	1.41	9.16	6.48		2.00	9.13	4.31	3.44	3.01
Houss 84	WALONG 2.3	851.8	9.15	3.40	1.10		8.55	3.00	1.50	9.26	6.56		2.10	9.23	4.41	3.52	3.10
68 P	DN MAROEL 0.8 (6pw)	854.1	9.30	3.55	1.26		9.10	3.15	2.00	9.36	7.05		2.20	9.33	4.49	3.59	3.18
West 74 PW / East 65	SEDWELL 1.8	854.9															
68 P	OABLE 3.9	858.7	9.45	4.10	2.20		9.25	3.37	2.11	9.45	7.13		2.30	9.43	4.56	4.06	3.27
103 PW	DNR TEHACHAPI 1.8	860.6	10.05	4.25	2.50		9.40	3.52	s2.25	s9.57	7.24		s2.45	s9.56	5.08	4.16	3.37
111 PY	SUMMIT 2.6	862.4	10.23	4.35	3.10		9.50	4.02	2.31	10.05	7.31		2.50	10.04	5.15	4.22	3.43
65 P	MONOLITH 2.1	865.0							2.35				2.55				
YP	PROCTOR 0.9	867.1							2.39	10.11	7.38		3.00	10.12	5.22	4.28	3.49
137 PW	ERIO 1.9 (Wp)	868.0															
60 P	D CAMERON 2.8	869.9	10.55	4.45	3.20		10.18	4.20	2.44	10.16	7.43		3.07	10.18	5.27	4.32	3.53
61 P	N LAROSE 2.7	872.7	11.15	5.05	3.40		10.40	4.36	2.49	10.25	7.49		3.13	10.24	5.31	4.36	3.58
63 P	D WARREN 2.4	875.4	11.35	5.25	4.00		11.00	4.56	2.54	10.35	7.55		f3.20	10.30	5.36	4.41	4.03
	N FRAM 1.3	877.8	11.49PM	5.50	4.10		11.20	5.06	2.59	10.39	8.01		3.26	10.36	5.42	4.47	4.08
	RESERVOIR 0.4 (6pw)	879.1															
	SAGE 1.2 (8pw)	879.5															
Yard WPTYOP	DN-B MOJAVE	880.7	12.05AM	6.20AM	4.30PM		11.35AM	5.31AM	s3.05AM	s10.45PM	8.10PM		s3.35PM	s10.45AM	s5.50AM	s4.55AM	4.15AM
			Arrive Daily	Arrive Daily	Arrive Daily	Arrive Ex. Sunday	Arrive Daily	Arrive Daily	Arrive Daily	Arrive Daily	Arrive Daily	Arrive Daily	Arrive Daily	Arrive Daily	Arrive Daily	Arrive Daily	Arrive Daily
Time over District / Average speed per hour			(5.40) 11.82	(5.30) 12.20	(7.30) 8.94	(1.06) 8.40	(5.30) 12.20	(5.30) 12.20	(3.25) 19.84	(2.55) 23.00	(2.40) 25.16	(4 03) 14 00	(3.15) 20.86	(2.50) 23.68	(2.33) 26.58	(2.35) 28.05	(2.35) 26.24

SECOND CLASS	FIRST CLASS

Westward trains are superior to trains of the same class in the opposite direction.

ADDITIONAL STOPS

No. 50 will stop on signal at all stations to receive passengers for Yuma or east.

Westward

BAKERSFIELD AND MOJAVE SUBDIVISION
TOWARD SAN FRANCISCO

Distance from Mojave	STATIONS	FIRST CLASS												THIRD CLASS	
		19	109	9	107	87	21	25	59	49	341	333	307	253	251
		Santa Fe Passenger	Sunset Express	Santa Fe Mail and Express	Los Angeles Fruno Express	Oil Fields Passenger	Santa Fe Passenger	The Owl	The Sacramento	San Joaquin Valley Passenger	Way Freight	Freight	Olig Bakersfield Mixed	Freight	Sunset Manifest Freight
		Arrive Daily	Arrive Daily	Arrive Daily	Arrive Daily	Arrive Daily	Arrive Daily	Arrive Daily	Arrive Daily	Arrive Daily	Arrive Daily	Arrive Daily	Arrive Daily Ex. Sunday	Arrive Daily	Arrive Daily
67.8	DN-R BAKERSFIELD		s 5.55AM		s 4.55PM	s 6.10PM	8.15PM	s 12.04AM	s 12.48AM	s 2.20AM			s 2.40PM	8.10PM	3.00AM
67.1	DN-R KERN JCT.	3.20AM	5.51	7.35AM	4.51	6.07PM	8.09	12.01AM	12.44	2.16	8.50AM	2.10PM	2.37PM	7.56	2.50
63.7	MAGUNDEN	3.14	5.46	7.30	4.45			11.55PM	12.39	2.11	8.36	2.02			
61.2	SOLY														
60.6	DN EDISON	3.09	s 5.41	7.26	s 4.40		8.04	11.51	12.35	2.07	8.23	1.55		7.40	2.42
55.7	N SIVERT	2.59	5.32	7.20	f 4.31		7.55	11.45	12.29	1.59	8.11	1.45		7.25	2.26
52.8	D BENA	2.53	5.27	7.15	f 4.26		7.49	11.40	12.24	1.48	8.01	1.39		7.15	2.20
49.4	ILMON	2.45	5.20	7.09	4.19		7.43	11.34	12.18	1.39	7.53	1.31		7.06	2.11
45.5	DN CALIENTE	2.36	s 5.10	s 7.00	s 4.10		s 7.35	11.26	12.09	1.30	7.39	1.08		6.40	1.40
42.5	ALLARD	2.27	4.57	6.51	4.01		7.28	11.20	12.02AM	1.23	7.27	12.40		6.29	1.23
40.2	DN BEALVILLE	2.19	4.52	6.46	f 3.54		7.22	11.15	11.57PM	1.17	7.00	12.32		6.20	1.02
38.4	CLIFF	2.13	4.48	6.42	3.48		7.17	11.11	11.53	1.12	6.49	12.16		6.00	12.40
35.2	DN ROWEN	2.05	4.40	6.34	f 3.40		7.10	11.04	11.46	1.05	6.34	12.05PM		5.49	12.25
33.0	TAMAR (Spur)														
31.9	DN WOODFORD	1.57	f 4.31	6.26	3.31		7.03	10.57	11.38	12.58	6.15	11.39AM		5.35	12.05AM
28.9	WALONG	1.50	4.10	6.19	3.22		6.56	10.51	11.31	12.52	5.55	11.19		5.15	11.40PM
26.6	DN MAROEL	1.44	3.59	6.13	3.16		6.50	10.46	11.25	12.47	5.36	10.50		5.05	11.25
25.8	SEDWELL (Spur)														
24.0	CABLE	1.38	3.50	6.08	f 3.07		6.44	10.40	11.18	12.41	5.20	10.30		4.45	11.05
20.1	DN-R TEHACHAPI	1.29	s 3.37	s 5.57	s 2.50		s 6.35	10.32	11.09	f 12.33	5.08	10.15		4.30	10.50
18.3	SUMMIT	1.26	3.32	5.53	2.45		6.32	10.29	11.06	12.29	4.50	10.04		4.25	10.45
15.7	MONOLITH	1.20	3.28	5.47	2.41										
13.6	N PROCTOR	1.13	3.24	5.40	f 2.35		6.26	10.23	11.00	12.23	4.28	9.50		4.10	10.28 / 10.06
12.7	ERIO (Wye)														
10.8	D CAMERON	1.03	f 3.16	5.31	2.25		6.19	10.16	10.55	12.16	4.10	9.35		3.55	9.57
8.0	N LAROSE	12.54	3.04	5.17	2.15		6.09	10.07	10.45	12.07AM	3.58	9.21		3.40	9.45
5.3	D WARREN	12.45	2.54	5.06	2.05		5.59	9.58	10.35	11.58PM	3.40	9.05		3.20	9.32
2.9	N FRAM		2.45				5.50	9.49	10.25	11.49	3.25	8.50		3.05	9.20
1.6	RESERVOIR (Spur)														
1.2	SAGE (Spur)														
0.0	DN-R MOJAVE	12.35AM	2.35AM	4.55AM	1.55PM		5.40PM	9.40PM	10.16PM	11.40PM	3.05AM	8.30AM		2.45PM	9.00PM
(67.8)		Leave Daily	Leave Daily	Leave Daily	Leave Daily	Leave Daily	Leave Daily	Leave Daily	Leave Daily	Leave Daily	Leave Daily	Leave Daily	Leave Daily Ex. Sunday	Leave Daily	Leave Daily
	Time over District	(2.45)	(3.20)	(2.40)	(3.00)	(0.03)	(2.35)	(2.24)	(2.32)	(2.40)	(5.45)	(5.40)	(0.03)	(5.25)	(6.00)
	Average speed per hour	24.40	20.34	25.16	22.60	14.00	25.97	28.25	26.76	25.43	11.66	11.52	14.00	12.08	11.18

Automatic Block Signals

Westward trains are superior to trains of the same class in the opposite direction.

TEHACHAPI SUBDIVISION

EASTWARD

Capacity of sidings in car lengths		FIRST CLASS						Mile Post Location	Timetable No. 169 January 23, 1949 STATIONS	Distance from Bakersfield
		56 Passenger (c)	**2** AT&SFRy Passenger	**52** San Joaquin Daylight	**24** AT&SFRy Passenger	**58** Owl	**60** West Coast			
		Leave Daily	Leave Daily	Leave Daily	Leave Daily	Leave Daily	Leave Daily			
BKWOTYP		PM 10.25		PM 3.08		AM 3.25	AM 3.10	312.9	TO-R **BAKERSFIELD**	0.0
KIP		10.27	PM 6.55	3.10	PM 2.28	3.27	3.12	313.6	TO-R **KERN JCT.**	0.7
P								316.6	3.0 **MAGUNDEN**	3.7
M-82 P								327.9	11.3 **BENA**	15.0
89 P								331.3	3.4 **ILMON**	18.4
101 / 101 WP		s 11.07	c 7.28		c 3.00			335.1 / 335.2	3.8 **CALIENTE**	22.2
87 P								338.2	3.0 **ALLARD**	25.2
106 / 106 WP								340.5	2.3 **BEALVILLE**	27.5
112 P								342.3	1.8 **CLIFF**	29.3
78 / 79 P								345.5	3.2 **ROWEN**	32.5
123 / 71 WP		PM s 11.54	c 8.02		c 3.33			348.8	3.3 **WOODFORD**	35.8
102 P								351.8	3.0 **WALONG**	38.8
120 / 106 P								354.5	2.3 **MARCEL**	41.1
85 P								356.6 / 356.7	2.5 **CABLE**	43.6
90 / No. 2-90 IWP		AM s 12.44	c 8.31	s 4.41	c 4.01	f 5.11	4.56	360.6	TO 3.9 **TEHACHAPI**	47.5
E-103 YP		12.46	8.33		4.03	5.13	4.58	362.4	1.8 **SUMMIT**	49.3
M-74 P		s 12.54	8.37		4.07	5.17	5.02	365.0	2.6 **MONOLITH**	51.9
Yard Limits YP		12.59	8.41	4.50	4.11	5.21	5.06	368.0	3.0 **ERIC**	54.9
M-81 P		1.11	8.52	4.59	4.22	5.32	5.17	374.3	6.3 **WARREN**	61.2
Mojave yard BKWOYP		s 1.25 AM	s 9.05 AM	s 5.08 PM	s 4.35 PM	s 5.45 AM	s 5.30 AM	380.7	TO-R 6.4 **MOJAVE**	67.6
		Arrive Daily	Arrive Daily	Arrive Daily	Arrive Daily	Arrive Daily	Arrive Daily		(67.6)	
		(3.00) 22.53	(2.10) 30.87	(2.00) 33.80	(2.07) 31.60	(2.20) 28.97	(2.20) 28.97		Time over District Average Speed per Hour	

Left side notation: Bakersfield yard; Yd Limits; Mojave yard
Right side notation: D.T.; Automatic Block System; Centralized Traffic Control; Double Track

---

Capacity of sidings in car lengths	EAST-WARD Mile Post Location	Timetable No. 169 January 23, 1949 Arvin Branch STATIONS	WEST-WARD Distance from Arvin
Bakersfield yard P	316.6	**MAGUNDEN**	16.5
P	324.6	8.00 **LAMONT**	8.5
	326.8	2.2 **RIBIER**	6.3
YP	328.8	2.0 **DI GIORGIO**	4.3
P	333.1	4.3 **ARVIN**	0.0
		(16.5)	

Left side notation: Yard Limits

ADDITIONAL STATIONS

NAME	Mile Post	Capacity
Algoso	316.9	12 P
Harpertown	321.1	13
Patch (Spur)	325.9	8

No. 56 stop at Edison to exchange U. S. mail.

ADDITIONAL STATIONS

NAME	Mile Post	Capacity
Edison	320.1	P
Cameron (Spur)	369.9	13 P

WESTWARD

Mile Post Location	Timetable No. 169 January 23, 1949 STATIONS	Distance from Mojave	FIRST CLASS							SECOND CLASS			
			55 Passenger (c) Arrive Daily	**23** AT&SFRy Passenger Arrive Daily	**51** San Joaquin Daylight Arrive Daily	**7** AT&SFRy Passenger Arrive Daily	**57** Owl Arrive Daily	**59** West Coast Arrive Daily		**447** V. M. W. Ar. Daily Ex. Sat. Sun. Mon.			
312.9	TO-R **BAKERSFIELD** 0.7	67.6	AM s 4.25		PM s 12.43		PM s 11.35	AM s 1.05		AM 2.30			
313.6	TO-R **KERN JCT.** 3.0	66.9	4.21	AM 10.40	12.40	PM 9.10	11.31	1.01		2.25			
316.6	**MAGUNDEN** 11.3	63.9											
327.9	**BENA** 3.4	52.6	3.50	10.23	12.24 PM	8.53	11.10	12.40 AM		2.00			
331.3	**ILMON** 3.8	49.2											
335.1 335.2	**CALIENTE** 3.0	45.4	s 3.33	c 10.07		c 8.37							
338.2	**ALLARD** 2.3	42.4											
340.5	**BEALVILLE** 1.8	40.1											
342.3	**CLIFF** 3.2	38.3											
345.5	**ROWEN** 3.3	35.1											
348.8	**WOODFORD** 3.0	31.8	s 2.39	c 9.34		c 8.02							
351.8	**WALONG** 2.3	28.8											
354.1	**MARCEL** 2.5	26.5											
356.6 356.7	**CABLE** 3.9	24.0											
360.6	**TEHACHAPI** 1.8	20.1	s 2.05	c 9.01	s 11.10 AM	c 7.33	f 9.55	11.25 PM		12.25			
362.4	**SUMMIT** 2.6	18.3	1.44	8.58		7.30	9.48	11.20		12.21			
365.0	**MONOLITH** 3.0	15.7	s 1.40	8.54		7.26	9.43	11.15		12.16			
368.0	**ERIC** 6.3	12.7	1.32	8.50	10.59	7.22	9.38	11.10		12.10 AM			
374.3	**WARREN** 6.4	6.4	1.22	8.37	10.50	7.13	9.26	10.58		11.57 PM			
380.7	TO-R **MOJAVE** 0.0	0.0	1.10 AM	8.20 AM	10.41 AM	7.00 PM	9.15 PM	10.47 PM		11.45 PM			
	(67.6)		Leave Daily	Leave Daily	Leave Daily	Leave Daily	Leave Daily	Leave Daily		Lv. Daily Ex. Fri. Sat. Sun.			
	Time over District Average Speed per Hour		(3.15) 20.80	(2.20) 28.97	(2.02) 33.25	(2.10) 30.87	(2.20) 28.97	(2.18) 29.39		(2.45) 24.58			

Automatic Block System — D. T. — Centralized Traffic Control — Double Track

No. 55 stop at Edison to exchange U. S. mail.

EASTWARD

Capacity of sidings in car lengths	THIRD CLASS				FIRST CLASS				Mile Post Location	Timetable No. 169 — January 23, 1949 — STATIONS	Distance from Mojave
	808 Freight	806 Freight	804 Freight	802 Freight	52 San Joaquin Daylight	58 Owl	60 West Coast	56 Passenger (c)			
	Leave Daily	Leave Daily	Leave Daily	Leave Daily	Leave Daily	Leave Daily	Leave Daily	Leave Daily			
Mojave Yard BKWOYP	PM 8.25	PM 2.10	AM 8.40	AM 1.05	PM 5.11	AM 5.50	AM 5.35	AM 1.55	380.7	TO-R **MOJAVE**	0.0
P	8.27	2.12	8.42	1.07	5.12	5.51	5.36	1.56	381.3	0.6 **EAST-MOJAVE**	0.6
87 P	8.33	2.18	8.48	1.13		5.55	5.40	2.01	384.8	3.5 **FLETA**	4.1
88 P	8.37	2.22	8.53	1.17		5.59	5.44	2.05	387.3	2.5 **GLOSTER**	6.6
84 P	8.42	2.27	8.58	1.22		6.03	5.48	2.09	390.4	3.1 **ANSEL**	9.7
98 P	**8.48**	2.33	9.04	1.28	5.24	6.08	5.53	s 2.19	394.3	3.9 **ROSAMOND**	13.6
109 P	8.57	2.42	9.14	1.37		6.15	6.00	2.26	399.9	5.6 **OBAN**	19.2
Yard Limits 118 WP	9.06	2.51	9.24	1.46	s 5.35	c 6.23	c 6.08	s **2.47**	405.5	5.6 TO **LANCASTER**	24.8
109 P	**9.13**	**2.58**	**9.31**	1.53		6.29	6.14	2.53	409.8	4.3 **DENIS**	29.1
73 YP	9.19	3.04	9.37	1.59		c 6.34	6.19	s 3.04	413.8	4.0 TO **PALMDALE**	33.1
93 P	9.23	3.08	9.41	2.03	5.46	6.38	6.22	3.08	416.3	2.5 **HAROLD**	35.6
E-97 W-97 Yard Limits IYP	**9.43**	3.19	**9.51**	**2.15**	5.54	6.51	6.35	3.19	420.5	4.2 TO **VINCENT**	39.8
87 P	9.57	3.33	10.06	2.29	6.03	7.00	6.44	3.28	425.0	4.5 **PARIS**	44.3
91 WP	**10.10**	3.43	10.16	2.39	6.11	7.08	6.52	f 3.40	429.0	4.0 TO **RAVENNA**	48.3
81 P	10.24	3.57	10.30	2.53	6.22	7.20	7.04	3.52	434.6	5.6 **RUSS**	53.9
102 P	10.35	4.08	10.41	3.04	6.30	7.28	7.12	f 4.01	438.6 / 438.8	4.0 TO **LANG**	57.9
87 P	**10.45**	4.19	10.52	3.15	6.37	7.35	7.19	4.09	443.0 / 443.1	4.2 **HUMPHREYS**	62.1
84 P	10.55	4.29	11.02	3.25	6.45	7.43	7.27	4.17	446.9	3.8 **HONBY**	65.9
E-103 W-112 Yard Limits WOIYP	11.04	4.38	11.12	3.35	c 6.52	f **7.50**	c 7.35	s 4.38	450.6	3.7 TO-R **SAUGUS**	69.6
173 IP	11.10	4.44	11.18	3.41	**6.56**	7.56	**7.39**	s 4.49	453.0	2.4 **NEWHALL**	72.0
104 P	11.26	5.00	11.35	3.57	**7.06**	8.10	7.52	5.02	459.2	6.2 **SYLMAR**	78.2
Yard Limits 94 WP	11.31	5.08	11.43	4.05	7.11	c 8.14	c 7.58	s 5.23	461.8	2.6 TO **SAN FERNANDO**	80.8
75 P	11.38	5.12	11.47	4.09	7.13	8.17	8.01	s 5.30	463.4	1.6 **PACOIMA**	82.4
87 P	11.49	5.23	AM 11.59	4.20	7.18	**8.31**	8.08	s 5.45	467.9	4.5 **ROSCOE**	86.9
Los Angeles yard 83 IP	11.59 PM	5.35 PM	12.10 PM	4.30 AM	7.23 PM	8.39 AM	8.15 AM	5.55 AM	471.6	3.7 **BURBANK JCT.**	90.6

Time at Glendale, Los Angeles Yard and Los Angeles for information only.
See Los Angeles Division current timetable for train movements between Burbank Jct. and Los Angeles.

	808	806	804	802	52	58	60	56			
					7.33	8.52	8.25	6.07		**GLENDALE**	
	12.25 AM	6.00 PM	12.35 PM	4.55 AM						**LOS ANGELES YARD**	
					7.50 PM	9.10 AM	8.45 AM	6.30 AM		**LOS ANGELES**	
	Arrive Daily	Arrive Daily	Arrive Daily	Arrive Daily	Arrive Daily	Arrive Daily	Arrive Daily	Arrive Daily			
	(3.34) 25.40	(3.25) 26.52	(3.30) 25.89	(3.25) 26.52	(2.12) 41.18	(2.49) 32.16	(2.40) 33.97	(4.00) 22.65		Time over District / Average Speed per Hour	

RULE 5. Schedule time and train-order time at Burbank Jct. apply at the end of double track.

RULE 86. Second- and third-class trains, extra trains and engines must be clear of main track and insulated joints at meeting and passing points for Nos. 51 and 52.

Track on station side next to main track at Ravenna, designated No. 2 track, capacity 36 cars, must be left clear of cars, to be used for meeting or passing trains when instructed by train order.

No. 56 stop at Acton to exchange U. S. Mail.

WESTWARD

Mile Post Location		STATIONS	Distance from Burbank Jct.	FIRST CLASS				SECOND CLASS	THIRD CLASS					
Timetable No. 169 January 23, 1949				51 San Joaquin Daylight	57 Owl	59 West Coast	55 Passenger (c)	447 V. M. W.	801 Freight	803 Freight	805 Freight	807 Freight		
				Arrive Daily	Arrive Daily	Arrive Daily	Arrive Daily	Ar. Daily Ex. Fri. Sat. Sun.	Arrive Daily	Arrive Daily	Arrive Daily	Arrive Daily		
380.7	TO-R MOJAVE	0.6	90.6	AM s 10.37	PM s 9.08	PM s 10.41	AM s 12.45	PM 11.34	AM 3.35	AM 10.20	PM 3.55	PM 10.10		
381.3	EAST-MOJAVE	3.5	90.0	10.35	9.06	10.39	12.43	11.32	3.33	10.17	3.52	10.07		
384.8	FLETA	2.5	86.5		9.02	10.35	12.39	11.28	3.25	10.11	3.44	9.59		
387.3	GLOSTER	3.1	84.0		8.58	10.31	12.35	11.25	3.19	10.07	3.38	9.53		
390.4	ANSEL	3.9	80.9		8.53	10.26	12.31	11.21	3.13	10.02	3.32	9.47		
394.3	ROSAMOND	5.6	77.0	10.22	8.48	10.21	s 12.25	11.16	3.06	9.56	3.24	9.39		
399.9	OBAN	5.6	71.4	10.17	8.41	10.14	12.16	11.09	2.57	9.47	3.15	9.30		
405.5	TO LANCASTER	4.3	65.8	s 10.11	s 8.34	c 10.07	s 12.09 AM	11.02	2.47	9.38	3.06	9.21		
409.8	DENIS	4.0	61.5		8.26	9.59	11.52 PM	10.56	2.40	9.31	2.58	9.13		
413.8	TO PALMDALE	2.5	57.5		c 8.21	9.54	s 11.48	10.51	2.34	9.25	2.51	9.07		
416.3	HAROLD	4.2	55.0	9.59	8.17	9.51	11.38	10.45	2.28	9.19	2.45	9.01		
420.5	TO VINCENT	4.5	50.8	9.51	8.09	9.43	11.30	10.32	2.15	9.06	2.32	8.48		
425.0	PARIS	4.0	46.3	9.43	7.58	9.32	11.22	10.20	2.02	8.54	2.20	8.36		
429.0	TO RAVENNA	5.6	42.3	9.35	7.50	9.24	f 11.14	10.10	1.52	8.44	2.10	8.26		
434.6	RUSS	4.0	36.7		7.37	9.11	11.02	9.56	1.38	8.30	1.56	8.12		
438.6 438.8	TO LANG	4.2	32.7	9.16	7.29	9.03	f 10.54	9.46	1.28	8.20	1.46	8.02		
443.0 443.1	HUMPHREYS	3.8	28.5	9.09	7.21	8.55	f 10.45	9.35	1.17	8.09	1.35	7.51		
446.9	HONBY	3.7	24.7		7.13	8.47	10.37	9.25	1.07	7.59	1.25	7.41		
450.6	TO-R SAUGUS	2.4	21.0	c 8.55	s 7.06	c 8.40	s 10.28	9.16	12.58	7.50	1.16	7.32		
453.0	NEWHALL	6.2	18.6	c 8.51	6.56	8.32	s 10.16	9.10	12.45	7.39	1.05	7.22		
459.2	SYLMAR	2.6	12.4	8.42	6.38	8.21	9.55	8.54	12.29	7.18	12.49	7.06		
461.8	TO SAN FERNANDO	1.6	9.8	c 8.38	c 6.33	c 8.16	s 9.50	8.48	12.23	7.10	12.43	7.00		
463.4	PACOIMA	4.5	8.2	8.36	6.30	8.13	s 9.33	8.45	12.20	7.06	12.40	6.57		
467.9	ROSCOE	3.7	3.7	8.31	6.25	8.08	s 9.25	8.37	12.12	6.56	12.32	6.48		
471.6	TO BURBANK JCT.		0.0	8.27 AM	6.20 PM	8.03 PM	9.10 PM	8.30 PM	12.05 AM	6.45 AM	12.25 PM	6.40 PM		

Time at Glendale, Los Angeles Yard and Los Angeles for information only.
See Los Angeles Division current timetable for train movements between Burbank Jct. and Los Angeles.

			FIRST CLASS				SECOND CLASS	THIRD CLASS				
GLENDALE			8.18	6.10	7.53	8.57						
LOS ANGELES YARD							8.10 PM	11.40 PM	6.20 AM	12.01 PM	6.15 PM	
LOS ANGELES			8.00 AM	5.50 PM	7.30 PM	8.30 PM						
			Leave Daily	Leave Daily	Leave Daily	Leave Daily	Lv. Daily Ex. Fri. Sat. Sun.	Leave Daily	Leave Daily	Leave Daily	Leave Daily	
Time over District Average Speed per Hour			(2.10) 41.82	(2.48) 32.36	(2.38) 34.40	(3.35) 25.28	(3.04) 29.54	(3.30) 25.89	(3.35) 25.28	(3.30) 25.89	(3.30) 25.89	

RULE 5. Schedule time and train-order time at Burbank Jct. apply at end of double track.

RULE 86. Second- and third-class trains, extra trains and engines must be clear of main track and insulated joints at meeting and passing points for Nos. 51 and 52.

Track on station side next to main track at Ravenna, designated No. 2 track, must be left clear of cars, to be used for meeting or passing trains when instructed by train order.

ADDITIONAL STATIONS		
NAME	Mile Post	Capacity
Acton............(Spur)	426.1	11 P
Tunnel............(Spur)	456.6	18 P

No. 55 stop at Acton to exchange U. S. Mail.

MOJAVE SUBDIVISION
LOS ANGELES DIVISION TIMETABLE No. 11, APRIL 27, 1980

Colton Line

Mile Post Location	EASTWARD ↓ — STATIONS / SIDING CAPACITIES AND FACILITIES	Station Number	WESTWARD — Distance from West Colton
312.9	TO-R BAKERSFIELD BKYPQ	28250	181.3
313.6	0.7 TO-R KERN JCT. KIP	28280	180.6
316.6	3.0 MAGUNDEN P	28505	177.6
320.1	3.5 EDISON P	28605	174.1
325.0	4.9 SANDCUT P	28611	169.2
327.9	2.9 BENA P	28615	166.3
331.3	6170 3.4 ILMON P	28619	162.9
335.1 / 335.2	4990 / 4990 3.8 CALIENTE P	28624	159.1
339.5	13270 4.3 BEALVILLE P	28631	154.7
342.3	7530 2.8 CLIFF P	28633	151.9
345.5	8080 3.2 ROWEN P	28638	1.487
348.8	8960 / 3470 3.3 WOODFORD P	28642	145.4
351.8	4800 3.0 WALONG P	28646	142.4
354.1	5300 / 5300 2.3 MARCEL P	28649	140.1
356.6 / 356.7	2.5 CABLE P	28655	137.5
358.5	1.9 CABLE X-OVER P		135.7
360.5	2.0 TEHACHAPI P	29000	133.7
362.4	E-5040 1.9 SUMMIT SWITCH YP	29003	131.8
370.4	8.0 CAMERON IP	29012	123.8
380.7	TO-R 10.3 MOJAVE BKIYP	29030	113.5
381.3	0.6 EAST MOJAVE I	29302	112.9
390.4	8340 9.1 ANSEL P	29312	103.8
399.9	8350 9.5 OBAN P	29324	94.3
409.8	8350 9.9 DENIS P	29338	84.4
413.8	TO 4.0 PALMDALE BKPQ	29345	80.4
420.0	7370 6.2 PALMDALE NO. 2		76.9
435.1	9000 15.1 WASH P	29368	59.1
451.1	9000 16.0 PHELAN P	29384	43.1
463.0	9097 11.9 HILAND P	29396	31.2
470.0	9515 7.0 CANYON P	29403	24.2
481.0	7950 11.0 DIKE P	29415	13.2
489.8	8.8 BENCH P	29422	4.4
491.1	9127 1.3 SLOVER P	29424	3.1
494.2 / 535.7	Yard Limits 3.1 TO-R WEST COLTON KBYIPQ	45500	0.0
	(181.3)		

Line markings (left to right): Yard Limits; No. 2 Trk / No. 1 Trk; Automatic Block Signal System; No. 2 Track / No. 1 Track; Double Track; Centralized Traffic Control.

Saugus Line

Mile Post Location	STATIONS / SIDING CAPACITIES AND FACILITIES	Station Number	Distance from Los Angeles
413.8	TO PALMDALE BKIPQ CTC	29345	68.7
420.5	6.7 VINCENT P DT	29516	62.0
425.0	4160 4.5 PARIS P	29521	57.5
429.0	6090 4.0 RAVENNA P	29527	53.5
434.6	3960 5.6 RUSS P	29534	47.9
438.6 / 438.8	4990 4.0 LANG P	29539	43.9
443.0 / 443.1	4110 4.2 HUMPHREYS P	29544	39.7
450.6	E-5040 7.5 W-5480 Yd. Lmts. SAUGUS P	40000	32.2
459.2	6050 8.6 SYLMAR P	40030	23.6
461.8	4600 2.6 TO SAN FERNANDO P	40040	21.0
463.4	3070 1.6 PACOIMA P	40050	19.4
467.9	4260 4.5 SUN VALLEY P	40060	14.9
472.1	4.3 TO BURBANK JCT. KIPQ	40300	11.2
473.4	1.8 Allen Ave. X-Overs I		9.4
477.1	3.7 GLENDALE P	40300	5.7
478.5	1.4 TO-R LOS ANGELES YD. BKYPQ	40400	4.3
479.4	0.9 Main Line Tower X-Over IQ		3.4
480.7	1.3 Dayton Ave. Tower IQ	40410	2.1
481.9	1.2 EAST BANK JCT. I	40420	0.9
482.8	0.9 Los Angeles (LATC) YPQ	40490	0.0
	(68.7)		

Line markings: Automatic Block Signal System; Yard Limits; No. 2 Tk / No. 1 Tk; D.T.; No. 2 Track / No. 1 Track.

Lone Pine Branch

Mile Post Location	EASTWARD ↓ — STATIONS / SIDING CAPACITIES AND FACILITIES	Station Number	WESTWARD — Distance
380.7 / 379.5	TO-R MOJAVE BKYPQ	29030	139.3
380.8	2350 1.3 CHAFFEE	29205	138.0
402.5	1970 21.7 CANTIL	29215	116.3
428.4	2600 25.9 SEARLES Y	29240	90.4
447.2	2470 18.8 INYOKERN	29250	71.6
461.5	14.3 LINNIE	29260	57.3
493.3	1230 31.8 OLANCHA	29280	25.5
518.8	1320 25.5 LONE PINE BKY	29299	0.0
	(139.3)		

OAK CREEK BRANCH

Mile Post Location	STATIONS / SIDING CAPACITIES AND FACILITIES	Station Number	Distance
380.7 / 379.7	Yd. Lmts. TO-R MOJAVE BKYPQ	29030	10.2
389.9	10.2 CREAL	29120	0.0
	(10.2)		

Bibliography

BOOKS

Barras, Judy. *The Long Road to Tehachapi.* Tehachapi: Judy & Bud Barras, 1976.

Boynton, James E. *Three Barrels of Steam.* Felton: Glenwood Publishers, 1976.

Bradley, Bill. *The Last of the Great Stations.* Glendale: Interurban Press, 1979.

Church, Robert J. *The 4300 4-8-2's.* Wilton: Central Valley Railroad Publications, 1980.

Duke, Donald and Stan Kistler. *Santa Fe Steel Rails Through California.* San Marino: Golden West Books, 1963.

Farrington, Jr., S.Kip. *Railroads at War.* New York: Samuel Curl Inc., 1944.

Glasscock, C.B. *Bandits and the Southern Pacific.* New York; Fredrick A. Stokes Co., 1929.

Griswold, Wesley S. *Trainwreck.* Brattleboro: Stephen Greene Press, 1969.

Kennan, George. *E.H. Harriman — A Biography* Vol. 1. New York: Houghton Mifflin Co., 1922.

Marshall, James. *Santa Fe The Railroad that Built an Empire.* New York: Random House, 1945.

Nordhoff, Charles. *California for Health, Pleasure and Residence.* Berkeley: Ten Speed Press, 1973.

Russell, Charles Edward. *Stories of the Great Railroads.* New York: Charles H. Kerr, 1914.

White, Gerald T. *Standard Oil of California: Formative Years in the Far West.* New York: Appleton, Century, Crofts, 1962.

UNPUBLISHED MATERIALS

Bristow, Barbara M. "Mussel Slough Tragedy: Railroad Struggle or Land Gamble? Masters Thesis—Fresno State College, 1971.

Hood, William. Letters in the Southern Pacific Collection 1909-1923.

Santa Fe Railway History of the Coast Lines. 1940.

PERIODICALS

Babcock, Allen H. "Mountain Railway Electrification." *Railway Age Gazette,* Vol. 55. (September 1913): pp. 447-449.

"Kern County Long White Potato Is King." *California Fruit & Vegetable Review,* Vol. 2 No. 1 (April 1946).

Kimball, Ward, "A Day In The Life Of An Engineer." *Trains Magazine,* Vol. 8 No. 12. (October 1948): pp. 44-51.

Morgan, David P., "Earthquake." *Trains Magazine,* Vol. 13 No. 1. (November 1952): pp. 14-20.

"Operation Spud Santa Fe Style." *Modern Railroads,* Vol. 8. (July 1953).

Railway Age Gazette. New York, 1875-1925.

Santa Fe Magazine. Chicago, 1908-1953.

Southern Pacific Bulletin. San Francisco, 1913-1983.

Stagner, Lloyd. "The Ultimate Development." *Trains Magazine,* Vol. 35 No. 10. (August 1975): pp. 18-55.

Steinheimer, Richard. "Tehachapi." *Trains Magazine,* Vol. 37 No. 3. (January 1977): pp. 24-41.

Sunset Magazine. San Francisco, 1895-1910.

Tyler, Charles W., and E.M. Kennedy. "Tehachapi." *Railroad,* Vol. 48 No. 1. (February 1949): pp. 12-39.

NEWSPAPERS

Bakersfield Californian, Bakersfield, California.

Kern Weekly Record, Bakersfield, California.

Los Angeles Examiner, Los Angeles, California.

PAMPHLETS

Kern County Historical Society Almanac. 1961.

The Story of Kern County. Title Insurance & Trust Co., 1961.

The San Joaquin Valley of California. Southern Pacific Co., 1908.

DOCUMENTS

Agreement between Southern Pacific Railroad and Atchison, Topeka & Santa Fe Railway January 1, 1899.

Complete Report on the Construction of the Los Angeles Aqueduct. Department of Public Service City of Los Angeles, 1916.

Decisions of the California Railroad Commission. 1895, 1899, 1901.

Earthquakes in Kern County 1952. U.S. Geological Society Bulletin No. 171, 1952.

Interstate Commerce Commission. Report No. 3486. S.P.Co. Accident at Allard August 22, 1952.

Report on Feasibility of a Proposed Joint Use Tehachapi Tunnel. State of California, Department of Public Works Division of Highways. January 1947

Index

271

the Tehachapi Loop

CABLE

MARCEL

Tunnel No. 12

Tunnel No. 11

Tunnel No. 10

Tehachapi Creek

WALONG

Tunnel No. 9

BARSTOW

DESERT

ANTELOPE VALLEY

PALMDALE

Rosamond

Lancaster

MOJAVE

TO OWENYO

MOJAVE

TEHACHA

WARREN

CAMERON

ERIC

MONOLITH

SUMMIT

TEHACHAPI

CABLE

Tunnel No. 16

Tunnel No. 15

Tunnel No. 14

Tunnel No. 13

MARCEL

Tunnel No. 12

Tunnel No. 11

Tunnel No. 10

WALONG

Tunnel No. 9

WOODFORD

ROWEN

Tunnel No. 8

Tunnel No. 7

Tun

Caliente Creek

SOUTHERN SAFETY PACIFIC

TEHACHAPI
busiest single track mou